Life After Reform

A CAMPAIGN FINANCE INSTITUTE BOOK

The Campaign Finance Institute is a nonpartisan, nonprofit institute affiliated with the George Washington University that conducts objective research and education, empanels task forces, and makes recommendations for policy change in the field of campaign finance. This project has been supported by generous grants from The Joyce Foundation, The Pew Charitable Trusts, and Smith Richardson Foundation, which are not responsible for the views expressed in this book.

For the impact of developments after this book, such as the constitutional challenges to the Bipartisan Campaign Reform Act, visit CFI's website, www.CampaignFinanceInstitute.org.

Life After Reform

When the Bipartisan Campaign Reform Act Meets Politics

Edited by
Michael J. Malbin

ROWMAN & LITTLEFIELD PUBLISHERS, INC.
Lanham • Boulder • New York • Toronto • Oxford

ROWMAN & LITTLEFIELD PUBLISHERS, INC.

Published in the United States of America
by Rowman & Littlefield Publishers, Inc.
A fully owned subsidary of the Rowman & Littlefield Publishing Group, Inc.
4501 Forbes Boulevard, Suite 200, Lanham, Maryland 20706
www.rowmanlittlefield.com

P.O. Box 317, Oxford OX2 9RU, United Kingdom

British Library Cataloguing in Publication Information Available

Library of Congress Cataloging-in-Publication Data

Life after reform : when the Bipartisan Campaign Reform Act meets politics / edited by Michael J. Malbin.
    p.   cm.— (Campaigning American style)
    Includes bibliographical references and index.
    ISBN 0-7425-2832-4 (cloth : alk. paper)—ISBN 0-7425-2833-2 (pbk. : alk. paper)
    1. Campaign funds—United States.   2. Campaign funds—Law and legislation—United States.   3. United States. Bipartisan Campaign Reform Act of 2002.   I. Malbin, Michael J.   II. Series.
    JK1991.L54   2003
    324.7'8'0973—dc21   2003008290

Printed in the United States of America

∞ ™ The paper used in this publication meets the minimum requirements of American National Standard for Information Sciences—Permanence of Paper for Printed Library Materials, ANSI/NISO Z39.48-1992.

Contents

Figures and Tables

FIGURES

TABLES

I

NEW LAWS AND PROCESSES

1

Thinking about Reform

Michael J. Malbin

The Bipartisan Campaign Reform Act of 2002—or BCRA, pronounced "Bikra" by acronym-crazed Washingtonians and better known outside the Beltway as McCain-Feingold, after the Senators—is the most important federal campaign finance law in decades. Everyone is agreed about that, but not too much else. Whether the law will achieve its intended purposes, what it will mean for the parties and interest groups, and how it will affect elections, remain hotly contested. This is the first serious and dispassionate book about BCRA's aftermath. It presents the research and early conclusions of political scientists brought together by the nonpartisan Campaign Finance Institute to think about how the law is—and is not—likely to change politics. The authors do not share a common political outlook, or even a common perspective about campaign finance reform. What they do share are reputations for being among the country's best scholars of money and politics. As such, some of their common premises put them at odds with three points of view that seem to have gained currency during the long debate over campaign finance reform.

The first is the so-called hydraulic theory, which holds that money, like water, will almost instantly find its way undiluted into the cracks, no matter how the law changes. Under this "theory," laws and regulations make almost no difference to outcomes or processes. The second—sometimes inconsistently expressed alongside the hydraulic theory—is that laws do make some difference, but the differences are unpredictable. The so-called law of unintended consequences means that a legislator can never tell what a new statute might do. The third perspective seems at first blush not to be cynical, but is. It is most commonly expressed by editorial writers, who seem to think that if a law fails to accomplish everything its most ardent supporters had wished, then the law will have "done nothing."

The views in these pages are more complicated, but also more in keeping with the intuitive common sense of things, as well as with the actions of Members of Congress on both sides of the issue. Laws do "make a difference." They alter the costs and benefits of certain paths of action, making some choices more likely and others less so. Some people and organizations will indeed try to find a way around the new rules. But people and organizations are not made of water. Therefore, some will be better positioned than others to shift. A law regulating money in politics will constrain some givers and spenders more than others, some candidates more than others, and some kinds of party activities more than others. Some of the law's consequences may not now be foreseen. Over time, as BCRA's supporters themselves have said, adaptations will lead to new problems that in turn may call for new legislation.

Despite these possibilities, this book's conceit is that careful students of the process can know more than the intellectual cynics acknowledge. In a perhaps foolhardy decision, we chose to go through this exercise, and publish our thoughts, before the law had even a single electoral cycle to work. Some of this book's predictions may be overtaken by events, including a Supreme Court decision on the law's constitutionality. This does not concern us. Of course, we could have waited for the Court before we began writing this volume. Had we done so, the book would not have appeared until most of the 2004 election cycle was over. There is no perfect time to write. The value of doing so early is to force us to work through a process, without hindsight, for thinking about the potential effects of any campaign finance reform—whether this one or the next.

THE IMMEDIATE BACKGROUND

Some of my good friends will endorse the next sentence. Debates over campaign finance law do *not* make for scintillating reading. In fact, several of my friends find the whole subject dull. I see their point, but it can become interesting when you see how the rules play a role in shaping who wins, and how they govern.

The immediate story of BCRA began, in earnest, after the 1996 election. President Bill Clinton, the "Comeback Kid" of 1992, had just come back again—this time from a devastating setback in the 1994 midterm elections—to win a 9-percentage-point victory over the Republican nominee, Bob Dole of Kansas. The Clinton reelection campaign began a year earlier, in 1995. The President ran against the new Republican majority in Congress, defining his issue agenda early while Dole was still fighting for his party's nomination. Republican mistakes helped the President gain the edge, but so did an unprecedented advertising campaign, supported by creative interpretations of the law. The President's campaign advisors and lawyers had figured out that they could use political party "soft money," subject neither to contribution limits nor to the usual prohibitions on corporate, labor, or foreign support, to pay for "issue advertising" that featured the President along with his issues, as long as the ads did not use express language to advocate his election.

By Election Day, soft money and issue ads had become the year's major campaign finance issues. This was the election associated with White House overnight visits for major contributors, donations from foreign sources, and money contributed illegally in the name of impoverished Buddhist monks. Nor did this remain only a Democratic story for long, as Republicans imitated the Democrats, raising soft money in large chunks to advertise their candidate too. By year's end, soft money raised by the six major national Democratic and Republican party committees had more than tripled since 1992, from $86 million to $262 million.

Nonparty organizations also were breaking new ground in 1996, led by the newly assertive AFL-CIO. Interest groups and advocacy organizations on right and left were learning from each other, as the number of candidate-specific issue ads mushroomed. Although less money was involved for the nonparty groups than for parties, the amounts were quite substantial, and—unlike contributors of party money—the funding sources could stay hidden, with no public disclosure (Campaign Finance Institute Task Force on Disclosure 2001).

These were stunning developments for people who were interested in the role of money in politics. Before 1996, the dominant agenda for reformers was to extend public funding with spending limits from presidential to congressional elections. After the election, they realized that they would have to work hard just to preserve the twenty-year-old system they had. Soft money and issue ads had

1. all but destroyed spending limits for publicly funded presidential candidates, who could work with the parties to create soft money issue ads, that would not count as spending under the limit;
2. rendered contribution limits meaningless by permitting the candidates to raise soft money for earmarked party accounts that would provide money for non–express advocacy advertising to help the candidates;
3. let corporations and labor unions use their treasury money to pay for candidate-specific advertising, even though the same organizations had long been prohibited from making campaign contributions and independent expenditures from these same treasuries (they could always make them from their political action committees, or PACs); and
4. bypassed the law's disclosure requirements, for all who were content to get a perfectly obvious message across, without express words.

The system thus seemed to be sliding back toward the years before Watergate, relying on unlimited contributions from who-knew-what sources. Unless these elements could be repaired, everything else about campaign finance law would be a subterfuge. It might be more honest just to scrap the whole system, as some deregulators were urging. Reformers, unsurprisingly, chose not to follow this path. Instead, they shifted their focus. The result—after two more election cycles, another near doubling of party soft money (to $495 million in 2000), much substantive legislative refinement, and six years of lobbying—was the Bipartisan Campaign Reform Act of 2002.

FECA, *BUCKLEY,* AND BCRA

The larger background to BCRA began not in 1996, but with the predecessor law of 1974. The Federal Election Campaign Act (FECA) Amendments of 1974 (Public Law 93–443) enacted a fairly comprehensive regulatory system that included

- limits all on contributions to federal candidates and political parties;
- mandatory spending limits for congressional candidates;
- voluntary spending limits for presidential candidates who chose to accept partial public financing in the primary, or full public funding in the general election;
- mandatory limits on self-financing by all federal candidates (a carryover from a 1971 law);
- limits on the amount of money a person could spend independently of a campaign or party to influence an election;
- limits on the amount a party could spend in a coordinated manner with a candidate to help the candidate win; and
- a system of disclosure for all receipts and disbursements intended to influence the outcome of an election.

Like BCRA, the 1974 law was challenged immediately on constitutional grounds. In the 1976 landmark case of *Buckley v. Valeo* (424 U.S. 1), the Court upheld some of the 1974 major provisions, but overturned others. The Court upheld: contribution limits; public funding for presidential election campaigns coupled with voluntary spending limits; and a broad system of disclosure. It overturned: mandatory limits on spending by candidates; limits on funding one's own campaign; and limits on independent spending.

The *Buckley* Court also engaged in an important piece of statutory construction that was to have decisive consequences later. The Court had a problem, not with disclosure per se, but with the law's vague definition of the activity that would trigger disclosure, particularly for independent spenders. FECA had defined a contribution or disbursement as being a transfer of funds "intended to influence the outcome" of a federal election. This formulation had two problems. First, it was so broad that it could easily include a great deal of pure issue speech that should not be regulated by election law. Second, the law's vagueness could potentially chill speakers who were afraid to get close to the line because of the law's penalties. These people deserved clear definitions of what the law did and did not allow. The Court therefore read a "bright line" test into FECA, interpreting it to cover only speech that advocated a candidate's election or defeat with such express words as "vote for," "vote against," or the equivalent. The "express advocacy" test was not in itself a constitutional mandate, but was offered as a statutory interpretation by the Court to avoid unconstitutional over-breadth and vagueness.

For some years after *Buckley,* the country had in place a system with strong disclosure, contribution limits, and public funding combined with spending limits for presidential campaigns. The pieces functioned more or less as intended for several elections, and then started to erode. During the 1980 and 1984 elections, according to Herbert Alexander's quadrennial studies of election financing, virtually all spending on the presidential election fit within FECA's boundaries (Alexander 1983, 111; Alexander and Haggerty 1987, 85). By 1996, in contrast, the old system's restraints had been all but negated. The part of the 1996 campaign that was outside of FECA's limits was almost as large as the part inside (Alexander 1999, 22). Express advocacy—offered by the Court before FECA's first election as a reasonable rough-cut attempt to fit the law within constitutional bounds—became, a few decades later, with soft money and issue ads, the vehicle political entrepreneurs used to bring a functional end to much of FECA.

BCRA's overriding purpose was to restore what had once been in effect under FECA. The new law sought, first, to restore contribution limits (and spending limits for publicly funded presidential campaigns) by prohibiting unlimited soft money for national political parties—placing limits on all contributions to national party committees, and controlling potential "end runs" by restricting contributions to state and local parties for what the law describes as "federal election activities." The law's second important purpose was to bring back disclosure, as well as corporate and labor spending restrictions, to "electioneering" speech by all persons other than candidates and parties. The definition of "electioneering" (see table 1.1) is meant to supplement express advocacy with a broader test that would still satisfy the Court's concerns about vagueness, by including targeted, candidate-specific broadcast advertising that appears within sixty days of a general election or thirty days of a primary.

Additional BCRA provisions increased the contribution limits that had not been adjusted since 1974, and had therefore lost two-thirds of their real value to inflation. The new limits increased the maximum individual contribution to candidates from $1,000 to $2,000 per election, and indexed those limits to adjust for future inflation. Special, variable contribution limits were also introduced for candidates who faced wealthy, self-funded candidates. Finally, the new law contains a series of miscellaneous provisions to improve electronic disclosure and to refine the difficult, but crucial, distinction between coordinated and independent campaign activity. A summary of these provisions is provided in table 1.1. A more detailed summary, with links to the underlying statute and related regulations, is available at the Campaign Finance Institute's web-based "eGuide" at www.CampaignFinanceInstitute.org.

Table 1.1   Summary of the Bipartisan Campaign Reform Act

Political Party Soft Money

National Party Committees

National party soft money is prohibited. The national parties and their affiliates may raise and spend only money subject to federal contribution limits and source restrictions ("hard" money), no matter how the money is spent.

State and Local Parties

State, district, and local party committees funding "federal election activities" must do so with money subject to federal contribution limits. Federal election activities are defined to include:

- voter registration activity within 120 days of the election (whether candidate-specific or generic);
- voter identification, get-out-the-vote (GOTV) activity, or generic campaign activity conducted in connection with federal election (whether candidate-specific or generic);
- communications naming a federal candidate that promote or attack the candidate (as opposed, for example, to sample ballots).

"Federal election activity" does not include: communications naming state candidates with no federal candidates; contributions to state candidates; state/local political conventions; state candidate grassroots materials; state/local party office construction/purchase costs.

Levin Amendment Exception—Voter registration and GOTV may be funded with soft money, limited to $10,000 per source, if such contributions are allowed under state law. Contributors may include corporations and labor unions, if state law permits. Money raised under this exception must meet the following conditions:

- Federal officeholders, candidates, national parties, and their agents may not raise "Levin Amendment" funds.
- The funds cannot be used for federal-candidate-specific or generic advertising.
- All receipts and disbursements must be disclosed.
- Party committees are prohibited from jointly raising these funds.
- A state party committee cannot raise the money for use in other states.
- The funds cannot be transferred between party committees.
- The soft money must be matched by hard money under Federal Election Commission (FEC) allocation rules.

Table 1.1 (*continued*)

Nonparty Electioneering

Definition/Coverage

An "electioneering communication" is a broadcast, cable, or satellite communication that refers to a clearly identified candidate within 60 days of a general election or 30 days of a primary, and that is "targeted." A communication is targeted if it can be received by 50,000 or more persons in the district or state where the election is being held. Subsequent FEC regulation said this provision was limited to paid advertising.

Corporate/Union "Electioneering" Prohibited

Corporations and unions are prohibited from directly or indirectly making or financing electioneering communications, although they may still form a registered political action committee (PAC), funded with voluntary, limited, individual contributions (hard money), for election communication. The corporate restriction extends to nonprofit corporations and to incorporated political committees (other than PACs, parties, and candidates) as defined by section 527 of the tax code. Subsequent FEC regulation exempted nonprofit charities (501(c)(3)s) which are prohibited from political activity under tax law.

Electioneering Disclosure

Entities making electioneering communications (individuals and unincorporated associations) must file a disclosure report within 24 hours, once an aggregate of $10,000 is spent, and thereafter each time an additional $10,000 is spent. Disclosure includes the identity of the spender, all persons sharing control over the communication(s), and all donors giving $1,000 or more.

Federal Office Holders, Candidates, Party Officials, and Agents

Federal Election Activity

Federal officeholders, candidates, national parties, and their agents (as well as entities directly or indirectly established, financed, maintained, or controlled by, or acting on behalf of, federal candidates or officials) may not solicit, receive, direct, transfer, or spend any soft money in connection with a federal election, with a limited exception for nonprofit corporations described below. This includes "Levin Amendment" funds for registration and GOTV.

Table 1.1   (*continued*)

State or Local Election Activity
Any solicitation by federal officials or candidates in connection with a state
or local election (e.g., for state or local candidates or parties) must be
limited to money consistent with federal contribution and source
limitations.

Appearances at State Party Events
Federal officials, candidates, etc., *may* appear at, and be a featured guest or
speaker at, a state party event at which the party raises soft money for its
purposes. Although the law says the candidate may not solicit money at
these events, the FEC said in its subsequent regulations that it would not
police formal speeches or informal conversations at such events. Nothing
in the law prohibits state party officials from soliciting money at an event
at which a federal official speaks.

Fund-Raising for Nonprofits
• Federal officials and candidates may *solicit* funds *without limit* for the
  general treasury of any tax-exempt organization described in section
  501(c) of the tax code, as long as the principal purpose of the
  organization is not to conduct certain specified federal election activities.
  ○ Amounts and sources are limited if the contributions are earmarked
    for registration or GOTV, but not if they are contributions for general
    funds and the organization uses some of its general funds for political
    activity.
• *National Parties* may not contribute to or solicit money for nonprofit
  corporations or political committees as defined by section 527 of the tax
  code.

Contribution Limits

Individuals
• *To a candidate:* Increased from $1,000 per election (primary, general,
  runoff) to $2,000 and indexed for inflation.
• *To a single national party committee:* increased from $20,000 per year to
  $25,000, within the aggregate limits below.
• *To a state or local party committee:* Changed from $5,000 for a state
  party's federal account (with no limit for a nonfederal account) to
  $10,000 for each state, local, or district committee that engages in federal
  activities, within the aggregate limits below.

Table 1.1 (*continued*)

- *To a PAC:* $5,000 (no change). Also no change in the limit of $5,000 per election for a contribution by a PAC to candidate. PAC limits are not indexed.
- *Aggregate Limit:* Increases the maximum an individual can give, in combined contributions, from $25,000 per year ($50,000 for two years), with no sublimits, to $97,500 for two years, with the following sublimits:
  - $37,500 to candidates;
  - $57,500 to all PAC and party committees combined;
    - No more than $37,500 to all PACs combined;
    - The remainder to party committees. (All $57,500 may go to parties if nothing is given to PACs.)
- *Indexing:* Limits on individual contributions to candidates and parties and individual aggregate limits are indexed for inflation, as are the limits on coordinated party support for a candidate.
- *Millionaire Opponent Provision* (Variable Contribution Limit): Increases contribution limits for congressional candidates facing self-financed candidates. These go up on a sliding scale, depending on the amount of self-financing, with qualifying thresholds and maximum contributions differing for the House and Senate. At its highest, the maximum contribution to Senate candidates may be increased sixfold, and the limits on party support for the candidate are removed. Increased contributions triggered by this provision do not count against a donor's aggregate limits.
  - Self-financed candidates are also prohibited, after any given Election Day, from repaying outstanding loans the candidates make to their own campaigns in excess of $250,000.

Coordination
- *Coordinated spending as a contribution:* Any expenditure made by a person other than a candidate or party will count as a contribution if it is coordinated with the candidate or party. Coordination is defined as a payment made in cooperation with, at the request or suggestion of, a candidate, candidate's agent, or campaign, or party. This reiterates previous statute law. Congress also told the FEC to discard its current regulations and write new ones that do not require agreement or formal collaboration to establish coordination. The FEC's subsequent regulations covered all election-related communications disseminated within 120 days of an election if the person making the communication meets any one of a series of conduct standards, including using a common vendor who makes use of material information learned from one client to prepare communications for the other.

Source: Campaign Finance Institute.

UNCERTAINTIES

Before we consider the new law's potential effects, we must first acknowledge two major uncertainties—one constitutional and the other regulatory. First, most of this book was written while the new law's constitutionality was still being reviewed. On the day after the new law was signed, the National Rifle Association and Senator Mitch McConnell (R-Ky.) filed suits to challenge BCRA. Soon involving more than eighty plaintiffs and united under the heading of *McConnell v. Federal Election Commission*, the case went directly to a three-judge U.S. District Court under expedited procedures. Lawyers in the case originally said they hoped for a Supreme Court decision by June 2003, but this timing cannot be assured.

Virtually every one of the law's major provisions is under review. The soft money ban's definition of "federal election activities" is criticized as an overly broad intrusion of federal authority into state election practices, the "electioneering" ban is said to be an intrusion on free speech, and BCRA's new contribution limits are under a two-sided assault. Since we know that some provisions of the law could be declared unconstitutional, or given restrictive interpretations, the authors have been asked to proceed as if all sections will be upheld, but to indicate where they want to draw the reader's attention to vulnerable sections. The editor will write an afterword when the rest of the book is in press—after the decision, or end of the term, whichever comes first.

A second major uncertainty stems from a fact of life applying to all laws as they work out in practice. Few significant laws have self-evident meanings for all of their potential applications. Controversial laws, including BCRA, also contain known ambiguities, because attempting to settle them before final passage would have threatened a tenuous winning coalition. The real law-on-the-ground, therefore, becomes the law as it is interpreted by the agency that enforces it, the courts that have to decide on those interpretations, political actors as they adapt to the law-as-interpreted, and Congress's subsequent reactions. This book comes at the start of this process. The chapters were drafted shortly after the Federal Election Commission (FEC) issued the first regulations mandated by BCRA. Some were controversial, prompting a legal challenge by the law's two main sponsors in the House, Representatives Christopher Shays and Martin Meehan, who claimed that the regulations ran counter to the spirit and in some cases the letter of the law. A few of the regulatory issues are noted in table 1.1. Others come up in relevant places in the chapters that follow. The book does not attempt to keep up with this ongoing story. A reader who wants a more complete summary of the regulatory and constitutional controversies as they develop, in nontechnical language, will find it in the "eGuide" section of the Campaign Finance Institute's website, www.CampaignFinanceInstitute.org, as well as the other links provided there.

FRAMEWORK FOR ANALYSIS

The authors of this volume, having acknowledged to ourselves that the effects of this law are bound to evolve, decided to move forward in spite of these uncertainties. This book is not *about* legal controversies, whether regulatory or constitutional. Whatever a court may decide, the part of the system we write about will stay in flux. In this book, we treat the law not as our *object* of study, but as part of the *context* within which political actors and organizations make their decisions. Our goal is to figure out how these political actors will try to adapt. If sound, our reasoning ought to stand up, even if some specific predictions would shift with a court decision.

Our approach begins with the understanding that laws gain their effect by altering the thoughts and decisions of flesh-and-blood human beings. BCRA (like FECA and other campaign finance laws) works primarily by constraining the decisions and actions of candidates, parties, and donors (or direct spenders). But the people on (and through) whom the law operates have different goals from those who wrote and lobbied for it. Candidates, party leaders, and their consultants or other agents run in elections to win. They will do whatever they can, within the law, to serve that objective. (To be sure, some candidates run in hopelessly lost races, but these tend not to put stress on the system.) Candidates and parties naturally will look for the most efficient ways to serve their own ends, legally, even if that means exploiting a "loophole" in a manner that runs counter to the sponsors' intentions. There is a fundamental and intractable tension between those who write laws *to constrain* people's decisions, and those on whom the law operates, who will seek maximum *freedom* for themselves within the law. The tension is inevitable. The fact that it occurs is not by itself a sign of a law's failure. People adapt, laws shift in their practical consequences, and laws must be revisited. The sponsors of McCain-Feingold and Shays-Meehan would say this is what happened between FECA and BCRA, and that knowledge guided many of their efforts to foresee and forestall loopholes in BCRA.

Figure 1.1 portrays this perspective schematically. In it, the law is seen as but one piece of a larger political context. The major political actors are portrayed, in a stylized way as receivers and givers. The receivers include candidates, parties, and their agents. The givers (or suppliers) include individuals and organizations. They contribute to candidates and parties, or spend their money directly to communicate with the public or their own members. All of these actors are independent agents, pursuing their own goals, but all are also part of a system in which each interacts with and affects the others. Individual candidates want to win their own elections; parties want to maximize the number of their copartisans in office (see Dwyre and Kolodny, chapter 5). These receivers may pursue secondary goals, of course. For example, safe incumbents may become agents of their party by raising extra money to turn over to party committees (see Bedlington and

Figure 1.1   Receivers and Givers: A Decision Chart

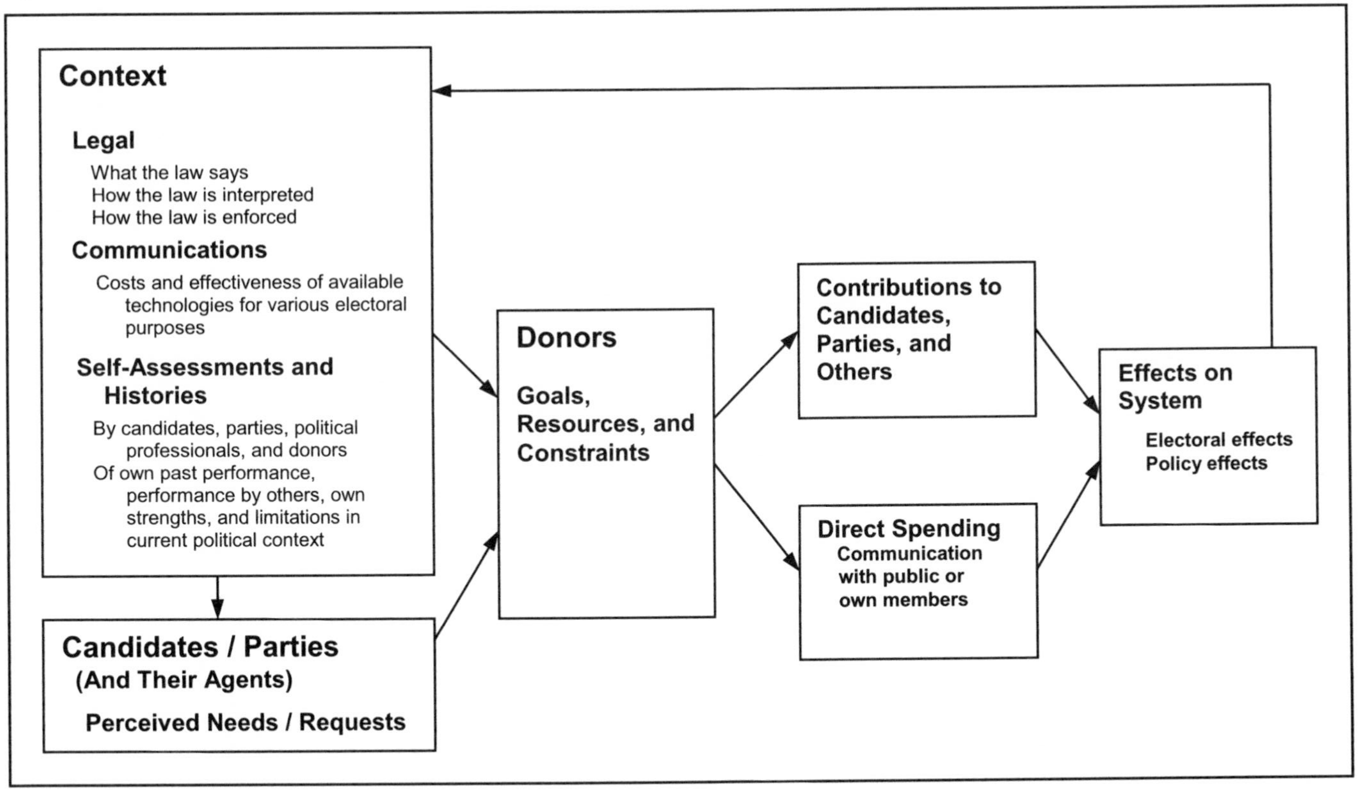

Context

Legal
What the law says
How the law is interpreted
How the law is enforced

Communications
Costs and effectiveness of available technologies for various electoral purposes

Self-Assessments and Histories
By candidates, parties, political professionals, and donors
Of own past performance, performance by others, own strengths, and limitations in current political context

Candidates / Parties
(And Their Agents)

Perceived Needs / Requests

Donors

Goals, Resources, and Constraints

Contributions to Candidates, Parties, and Others

Direct Spending
Communication with public or own members

Effects on System

Electoral effects
Policy effects

Malbin, chapter 7). But this will happen only after the primary goal is safely in hand. Donors have more complex motives. Some are concerned about gaining and maintaining access to incumbents. Others pursue ideological or policy motivations, even if it means taking on some incumbents. (See Boatright et al., chapter 3, which contains a more detailed diagram and argument about organizational donors and direct spenders. For individual donors, see Wilcox et al., chapter 4.)

Whatever the precise motives, receivers and givers operate within the same context, all with their own goals. But much of the driving force in the system comes from the receivers. Most money comes into the system because candidates, parties, and their agents feel that they need it, and ask for it. The context— the law, the cost-effectiveness of varying communications techniques for a particular race, the political economy, the demography and competitiveness of the district, the issue context, and so forth—will help them decide how much to ask for, and in what form. Asking for money does not guarantee it will come, but failing to ask almost always means it will stay home.

The requests for money then get filtered through the donors' own goals, and the donors' own sense of the context. If all a donor wants is to stay on the good side of the person asking for money, we can describe the resulting contribution as money "pulled" into the system. Pulled money is the kind most sensitive to contribution limits—and most likely, therefore, to be affected by a ban on party soft money. In contrast, people or organizations with strong political agendas are more likely to "push" money into the system on the givers' initiative. They are less likely to be deterred by contribution limits, and more likely to look for alternative avenues appropriate to the immediate context.

This is a dynamic system. Political professionals learn from each other, and what they learn creates a new context for the next set of decisions (represented by a feedback loop in the schematic). The system evolves because these professionals will look for the most creative and cost-effective techniques available, within the law, to serve their own goals. In the end, not all of the techniques will work equally well, the professionals will learn, and the system will adjust yet again.

PREVIEW OF THE BOOK

After these inevitable adaptations, the big questions are whether the new law will achieve its intended purposes, and with what side effects. To address these matters, it is important to state the law's goals with some specificity. BCRA was not supposed to produce what even its main sponsors would have considered heaven on Earth. It was not designed to make all contributors equal, enhance the role of small givers, level the playing field between challengers and incumbents, or remove special interests from politics. BCRA's purposes were important enough, but the bill was always presented by its main sponsors quite frankly as a patch job. (See Corrado, chapter 2, for a detailed account of the path to reform.)

General comments about special interests and big donors did fill the debates and editorial pages, but the law aimed principally at two specific kinds of activities. First, it sought to restore the integrity of contribution limits, and to break or at least attenuate the connection between public officials and unlimited donors, by shutting down unlimited contributions to the parties. The second major purpose was to reinforce long-standing prohibitions against the use in elections of money from the treasuries of corporations and labor unions—as opposed to money from their PACs. These primary purposes of the law are addressed most directly in part II of this book, entitled "Givers and Spenders."

Interest Groups

Chapter 3, by Robert G. Boatright, Michael J. Malbin, Mark J. Rozell, Richard M. Skinner, and Clyde Wilcox, examines the likely adaptations to be made by interest groups and advocacy organizations under the new law, using a model that elaborates on the one in this chapter (see figures 1.1 and 3.1). The analysis is based on extensive interviews with a diverse selection of organizational leaders conducted as part of a multielection study covering the elections of 2000 through 2004. Based on those interviews, the chapter concludes that at least some of the soft money that is now being pulled into the system reluctantly, particularly some of the business money, is likely to stay on the sidelines after soft money is banned. Some will be converted to "hard money" through active PAC development programs and through the efforts of party leaders to raise money through new channels. But the party leaders will not be able to ask directly for unlimited contributions, and not all of the money is likely to find its way back. To that extent, BCRA will have partly achieved one of its major purposes. In contrast, the electioneering provisions regulate money that gets into the system because highly motivated players want to make a difference. Most of these players—including peak business associations, labor unions, ideological and issue groups—will look for ways around the electioneering ban, perhaps by shifting to nonbroadcast communications. However, not all organizations will be equally well positioned to adapt. Their capacity to switch will depend on their particular organizational strengths and resources.

Major Donors

One possible source of replacement money for soft money could come from increased contributions from individuals, which could then be bundled by interest groups and forwarded to parties or candidates. BCRA increases the limits on individual contributions to candidates and parties. The limit for contributions to candidates went from $1,000 per election (primary or general) to $2,000. Since this was the first time the limits had been increased since 1974, the change made up for less than half of the erosion, due to inflation, in the value of the original limit. In the future, these limits will be indexed. In chapter 4, Clyde Wilcox and his colleagues report on the results of two extensive surveys: one of major donors to congressional candidates in 1996 and the other of major donors to the presidential candidates in 2000. One question in each survey asked the respondents if they would give more in the future with a higher contribution limit. Only about 15 percent of the congressional donors and 22 percent of the presidential donors said they would give more. The authors consider this to be a baseline minimum estimate, since the answers were given to a survey researcher, and not to a fundraiser during the heat of a campaign. The donors as a whole are much wealthier, more conservative, and more likely to belong to business or professional associations than the general population, and the ones who would increase their giving are even more likely than other contributors to be Republican, conservative, and business or professional association members. Since approximately three-quarters of the soft money donated to the parties in 2002 came from corporations or individual business executives (see chapter 3), it is tempting to look at the individual contributions as replacements for the soft money. From these data, however, it looks as if the major contributors share many commonalities with the soft money donors, but it also looks as if the amounts will not come close to making up for what the soft money ban will eliminate.

National Parties

So, if the soft money ban is likely to achieve part (but not all) of its stated purpose, the next matters to consider are the effects on other parts of the political system. We have already discussed the probable first-level effects on interest groups and advocacy organizations. Part III of the book is about the organizations most directly affected by BCRA: the political parties. Diana Dwyre and Robin Kolodny point out in chapter 5 that the national party organizations surely will have less money in the near future, since soft money made up fully half of the six major national committees' total receipts in 2002. This will favor Republicans in the short term, because the Democrats have depended more on soft money than have the Republicans. The parties will probably make up for some of the lost soft money with better hard money fund-raising, but Dwyre and Kolodny also expect to see substantial adaptations. In BCRA's first weeks, leading Democrats and Republicans were already forming a variety of unofficial quasi-party or friends-of-the-party committees to pick up the slack. Because public and party officials cannot solicit funds for these committees, the committees are not likely to substitute fully for the parties. Nevertheless, they may play a significant role. Similarly, partisan consultants may play a facilitative role for state and local efforts that has them replacing another piece of what the formal parties can no longer do. In the end, the consultants and quasi-party organizations are not likely to replace all of the lost soft money. However, Dwyre and Kolodny argue, less money is not the same thing as less important parties. Much of the soft money in recent years has been used to match the other side's advertising in races that were already competitive. If the parties' efforts are redirected, that will surely mean a changed party system, but not necessarily a weaker one.

State and Local Parties

Raymond J. La Raja has a different perspective on state parties (chapter 6). His data about state party budgets and expenditures show that some are far more ready than others for the political world after BCRA. In general, parties whose state laws have limits comparable to BCRA's are more prepared for living with BCRA's restrictions, particularly if they have not relied too heavily in the past on transfers from the national parties to run their basic operations. La Raja's tables and charts show some clear winners and losers among the states. The law's efforts to restrain federal election activities are also likely to make cooperation between the state and national parties more difficult. Within states, the law is likely to strengthen the hands of governors as party leaders, since national figures will have to keep an arm's length from the state parties.

Members as Givers

The final chapter in the section on parties (chapter 7), by Anne H. Bedlington and myself, is based on research about Members of Congress as contributors. We put the chapter here because of its lessons about what parties are, and how to think about them. The importance of Members' contributions has soared over the past decade, from about $4 million in contributions to other candidates in 1992 to more than $30 million in 2002. Equally dramatic has been the steep increase in Members' contributions to party committees. In 2002, more than 15 percent of the two congressional campaign committees' hard money receipts came from Members of Congress, who transferred their excess funds to the parties for use in close elections. This confirms something we learn from the previous two chapters' discussions of party allies: a party is better thought of as a series of interwoven relationships than as a set of formal committees. The Members help the party because being in the majority is important to them, and the balance of power is precarious. With BCRA's higher contribution limits, we expect the importance of Member transfers to continue to increase for as long as most Members are safe and majority control of the institution remains in doubt.

Congressional Incumbency

The safety of incumbent Members of Congress is the focus of chapter 8, the first of three that shift away from BCRA's impact on organizations to its effects on candidates and campaigns. Interestingly, for all of the controversy over BCRA in Congress, James E. Campbell does not expect it to have much effect on most congressional campaigns. That is because there is such a vast imbalance in hard money between incumbents and challengers in most districts that the race is over before soft money even becomes an issue. In an analysis that is sure to provoke interest, Campbell maintains that the hard money financial imbalance is the single most important cause of the growing importance of incumbency in House elections—and of the consequent decline in competition. Despite some loose rhetoric during the congressional debate to the effect that BCRA would weaken incumbents, Campbell argues that nothing in the law will have any significant effect on incumbency or competition.

Millionaires' Amendment

The Members of Congress probably did not think BCRA was doing anything *major* to competition, but they did think they were having an important effect at least in the subset of races with rich, self-financed candidates. Because of the *Buckley* decision, self-financed candidates face no restrictions on what they may give to their own campaigns. In the name of equality, Members of both chambers pushed for candidates to be able to raise larger contributions, under a higher set of limits, when the candidate has to run against a self-financer. The willingness of incumbents to support competition in this situation is perhaps explained partly by the fact, revealed in Jennifer A. Steen's data in chapter 9, that of the eleven races in the 2000 general election with incumbents running that would have triggered the "Millionaires' Amendment," the incumbent would have been the beneficiary in eight of them. Steen looks carefully at these eleven races, and nine other open seats in which the amendment would have been triggered, to see whether higher contribution limits would have made a significant difference in the contest. In most cases, the answer is no, but the Millionaires' Amendment could have become a factor in three Senate and three House contests. The amendment might also have made a difference for potential candidates as they decided whether to run. The potential effect on the strategic decisions of potential candidates in the long run may prove to be the most important effect of this set of provisions.

Presidential Elections

While congressional elections may be stagnant, in Campbell's phrase, presidential elections are anything but. As Anthony Corrado and John C. Green note in chapter 10, the rush of primaries toward the early part of the primary calendar has made obsolete the presidential primary finance system that Congress fashioned three decades ago. George W. Bush's successful decision to reject public funding during the 2000 presidential primaries undoubtedly will lead others to consider the same option in future years. By increasing contribution limits, restraining parties, failing to increase public funding formulas, and failing to increase the spending limits for publicly funded candidates, BCRA will increase the incentives for primary candidates not to participate in the system. Based on a painstaking analysis of past contributions, Corrado and Green are able to show which past candidates, and what kinds of likely future candidates, would find it advisable financially to say no to public funds. The result, they say, is likely to be a system with two tiers of candidates: establishment candidates and self-financed millionaires will opt out of the system and spend without limit, while insurgent and populist candidates will have to rely on a relatively more stingy system of public funding.

CONCLUSION

BCRA's potential effect on the presidential race, not anticipated during the congressional debates, should lead us to pause as we make our predictions—to pause, but not to stop. As the system gets used to BCRA—as campaign finance reform meets politics—some unanticipated issues undoubtedly will arise, along with adaptations. Change and adaptation are inevitable. That does *not* mean it is futile to change laws. Adaptation is not the same as nullification. Whether a particular law is beneficial or harmful is a long debate. At the start of this book, it is enough to say that its authors intend to point out which changes under BCRA will be consequential. If we succeed in identifying their general shape, then we will also have succeeded in making a larger point: in a policy arena noted for taking policy makers down unexpected paths, we will have shown at least the broad contours of change to be foreseeable. That alone would disprove those cynics who portray lawmaking either as meaningless or as a leap into the unknown.

2

The Legislative Odyssey of BCRA

Anthony Corrado

The passage of the Bipartisan Campaign Reform Act in March of 2002 signaled the beginning of a new stage in the regulation of political finance. It also signaled the end of a long and arduous congressional debate on campaign finance reform.

The immediate debate that produced the new statute began in the aftermath of the 1996 election, and initiated a legislative struggle that was carried out during three successive Congresses until a version of the original bill was finally passed five years later. The roots of this debate, however, extend even farther, reaching back almost two decades to the time when Congress first sought to change the regulatory structure created by the campaign finance reforms of the 1970s. Viewed from this perspective, the Bipartisan Campaign Reform Act (BCRA) represents the end of a legislative process that started in the mid-1980s and continued with little interruption for more than fifteen years.

As might be expected from such a protracted period of legislative deliberation, the path followed on the way to reform was rarely straight or typical; indeed, it often proved to be highly unusual, even precedent setting. Instead of reflecting textbook models of the legislative process, campaign finance exemplified the type of "unorthodox lawmaking" that has become increasingly prevalent in Congress (Sinclair 1997; Dwyre and Farrar-Myers 2001). Bills rarely reached the floor of the House or Senate through the traditional committee referral process. On reaching the floor, proposals often became the subject of extraordinary procedural maneuvering that turned the process into a sophisticated parliamentary chess game rather than a serious discussion of policy issues. When one chamber did manage to pass a bill, it often failed to succeed in the other, or fell victim to a conference committee or the stroke of a president's veto pen.

By tracing the path Congress took in producing BCRA, including a brief overview of some of the many false starts, wrong turns, and dead ends encountered along the way, this chapter offers an understanding of how the new law was achieved. It presents an overview of the diverse policy views that characterize the reform debate and the difficulty of resolving the many substantive concerns that legislators hope to address through campaign finance legislation. It also provides insights into the divisive issues and parliamentary obstacles that any future campaign finance proposal will be forced to overcome.

THE POLITICS OF REFORM

BCRA grew out of a bill introduced in the Senate after the 1996 election by Senators John McCain, an Arizona Republican, and Russell Feingold, a Wisconsin Democrat. A companion bill was introduced in the House under the sponsorship of Representatives Christopher Shays, a Connecticut Republican, and Martin Meehan, a Massachusetts Democrat. As compared to the 1974 Federal Election Campaign Act (FECA) and its amendments of 1976 and 1979, which were the last major pieces of campaign finance legislation to be adopted by Congress prior to 2002, the McCain-Feingold proposal was not especially ambitious. The bill's principal purpose was to restore the regulatory framework established by FECA. Its major provisions sought to address the issues raised by the growth of party soft money and issue advocacy advertising, two innovations that emerged after FECA was implemented which significantly undermined the efficacy of the law. The bill did not call for a fundamental change in the financial activities of candidates or attempt to expand FECA by adding such comprehensive reforms as public financing for congressional elections or free broadcast time for candidates. Even so, the proposal spurred a divisive debate and was defeated a number of times before it was finally approved.

Passing a new law was difficult because campaign finance reform is a particularly contentious issue. Members of Congress hold diverse opinions with respect to regulation, which makes coalition building especially problematic. At the root of these differences are strongly held ideological views on the principles that should govern political finance. Some Members, especially conservative Republicans, believe that campaign finance is a form of political speech that deserves the fullest possible protection from government restrictions. Others, especially liberal Democrats, recognize the First Amendment implications of regulation, but place greater emphasis on the principle of equality and believe that a central purpose of campaign finance laws is to reduce the influence of large donors and thereby enhance the equity of the political finance system. Liberals also support public financing of elections as a means of leveling the playing field in elections, while many Republicans regard election funding as an unjustified or inappropriate use of taxpayer dollars.

The goals to be achieved by a campaign finance system are also a matter of dispute. All Members generally agree that a principal purpose of regulation is to safeguard the political process from the potentially corruptive effects of private campaign contributions, but views differ as to what constitutes corruption and how this concern can best be addressed. Advocates of reform also seek to achieve a number of other objectives. These include claims that the law should ensure full and robust political debate, reduce campaign spending, promote equality in the political system, enhance political competition, provide for an informed electorate, and encourage citizen participation in the electoral process. A legislator's stance is often determined by the goal(s) he or she considers to be most important. Moreover, these goals often conflict. For example, a reduction in campaign costs may reduce the ability of candidates to communicate with the electorate and thus diminish the amount of political debate that takes place in elections. An informed electorate or improved citizen participation may require a greater freedom to raise and spend money, which can undermine the goal of greater equality in the political process. Legislators are therefore often forced to make choices among competing objectives or priorities. This inevitably leads to different opinions with respect to proposed reforms.

Members of Congress also define the "problems" of the campaign finance system differently, and accordingly express diverse preferences as to the best solutions. There are those who support the basic regulatory approach established by FECA, but believe that further regulation is needed to address new forms of financial activity that have become commonplace in response to the law. Others regard the experience under FECA as an example of the futility of recent regulatory efforts, and advocate a less restrictive regime largely based on public disclosure rules alone. Some claim that the problem is high campaign costs. In their opinion, there is too much money in federal elections, and rising campaign expenditures are increasing the deleterious influences of money in the political process and pricing out many potential candidates. These Members tend to support some form of public subsidy and expenditure limits to reduce campaign costs. Others hold a contrary view, arguing that not enough is spent on political activity, and that greater resources are needed to help challengers overcome the advantages enjoyed by incumbents. Another perspective is more narrowly focused on the influence of "special interest" money and the role of unregulated sources of funding in the electoral process. Those who espouse these concerns tend to support greater restrictions on political action committees (PACs), a prohibition on party soft money financing, and greater regulation of interest group activities, including issue advocacy communications. Members also disagree on the role parties should play in political finance. Some are advocates of political parties and believe that campaign finance rules should promote party organizations, since parties have a stake in improving the competitiveness of their candidates and encouraging citizen participation. Those opposed to this view are more cautious, noting that parties can serve as vehicles for circumventing campaign finance limits and do little to promote citizen engagement, since they focus most of their resources on a relatively small number of targeted races. These Members therefore support stricter regulation of party committees.

Partisan interests further complicate the debate. Democrats and Republicans have experienced varying patterns of financial support under FECA. As a result, certain reform proposals have a disproportionate effect on one party as compared to the other. For example, the Republican Party has always enjoyed greater success than the Democratic Party in soliciting contributions subject to federal limits (hard money). Consequently, in recent elections, the Democrats have been more dependent on unregulated contributions (soft money) in the financing of their election-related activities. Similarly, the political activities of labor unions are overwhelmingly conducted in favor of Democrats, so any new restrictions on union political activity are generally viewed as a disadvantage for Democrats. Such differences often lead to deep partisan divisions in the reform debate and make the need to balance the competing interests of the two parties a key concern in the crafting of legislation, especially during times of divided government. Legislators also have to be aware of the differences in campaign funding that characterize House and Senate races. The greater financial demands of a Senate race can lead to divisions between the two chambers on the best approach to regulation, even when the two chambers are controlled by the same party.

The separate interests of incumbents and nonincumbents constitute another dividing line. Current officeholders are usually well aware of their sources of campaign funding and can assess the potential influence of a proposed reform on their own reelection efforts. More importantly, incumbents usually show little interest in reforms that will change a system that has been integral to their success and perhaps make it easier for prospective opponents to mount a challenge against them. This desire to secure their positions in Congress, however, must be balanced against constituency pressures or pressures from organized groups that are actively involved in election contests. This combination of personal political considerations often leads incumbents to prefer the status quo to less predictable changes in the law.

This array of considerations and attitudes creates crosscurrents of opinion that make it difficult to construct an effective coalition in support of new legislation. This task is particularly challenging because campaign finance reform often fails to conform to the usual practices used to build coalitions in Congress. Typically, party leaders or sponsors of a particular bill can work to build support in Congress by shaping a proposal to meet the specific preferences of individual Members. This objective can be achieved by adding provisions to appease a Member or bloc of Members, as in the case of a transportation bill, defense appropriation, or educational funding bill, where a pet project or an additional programmatic component can be incorporated into a proposal to secure additional votes. Another common tactic is for sponsors to trade their own support on other legislative proposals to gain votes from party leaders or Members with an interest in those proposals. But such "pork-barrel politics" or "legislative logrolling" rarely works with campaign finance legislation. Indeed, the coalitions supporting a reform package are often so fragile, due to the competing interests that need to be balanced, that the addition of a new provision can lead to less support rather than more. A package of reforms cannot be built by simply combining the ideas of different Members, because many ideas are so polarizing that they serve to fracture working coalitions.

Moreover, any debate on reform is necessarily constrained by constitutional imperatives. The Supreme Court has ruled that campaign finance is an essential element of political speech and is therefore subject to the protections afforded by the First Amendment. Most importantly, in the 1976 landmark decision in *Buckley v. Valeo* (424 U.S. 1), the Court set forth regulatory parameters that have governed government action ever since. Specifically, the *Buckley* decision and its progeny have held that Congress is justified in establishing contribution limits and other restrictions only for a compelling reason, and the only reasons the courts have upheld so far have been reducing corruption or the appearance of corruption in the political process. Other possible rationales, such as stemming rising campaign costs or equalizing the relative ability of individuals and groups to influence election outcomes, do not constitute a state interest that justifies burdens on free speech. To avoid concerns about vagueness, the courts have further interpreted FECA to limit its coverage to activities that expressly advocate the election or defeat of federal candidates. Courts have also consistently held that certain areas of political finance, such as monies spent independently by individuals or political groups, are forms of political speech that may not be restricted. Other limitations, such as expenditure ceilings or limits on a candidate's use of personal funds, are constitutionally permissible only when voluntarily accepted as a condition for receiving some form of public subsidy and only insofar as this incentive is not considered to be so compelling as to make it in effect compulsory. This linking of expenditures ceilings to public funding, as well as the need to distinguish express advocacy from issue advocacy, are two aspects of this constitutional framework that have proven to be particularly important in the recent legislative debates on campaign finance reform.

Finally, all of these political considerations must be filtered through a system of parliamentary rules and procedures that make it possible for determined minorities to impede legislative progress. In this regard, the Senate filibuster has proven to be especially important. In practice, a simple majority is not enough to pass a campaign finance bill. Advocates of reform often need to secure sixty votes in the Senate, and must be cognizant of the possibility of a presidential veto that would raise the bar even higher. During the past two decades, such a broad consensus has been uncommon. That a new law was eventually achieved, given this context, is more a testament to the determination and tenacity of the legislation's sponsors than to the success of the legislative process.

All of these crosscurrents have been evident in Congress's long-standing deadlock over campaign finance reform. For more than a decade, from the mid-1980s through mid-1990s, reformers tried to pass bills to reduce the importance of political action committees, limit campaign spending, and provide some form of partial public financing to candidates. The bills failed repeatedly, sometimes after appearing to be close to final passage (see table 2.1). Then came the election of 1996.

THE McCAIN-FEINGOLD DEBATE

The financing of the 1996 elections produced a watershed in the reform debate, as new financial practices and a national controversy over the sources of campaign funding led to a redefinition of the central issues facing policy makers. Advocates of reform shifted their attention away from PACs and rising campaign costs to focus on party soft money and candidate-specific issue advertising. The role of unregulated monies in the 1996 election created a political environment more favorable to reform. It also brought new approaches to resolving the problems that proved just as fractious as earlier ones.

Many of the financial patterns in the 1996 election by this time were familiar: rising candidate expenditures, increasing PAC contributions, a widening resource gap between incumbents and challengers, and a growing number of self-financed candidates. What distinguished this election was a substantial increase in the amounts of soft money raised by party committees and its use as a means of financing federal-election-related campaign activities. The national party committees raised a total of $262 million of soft money in 1996, more than three times the $86 million received in 1992 (Federal Election Commission 2001). The Democrats increased their soft money resources from $36 million in 1992 to $124 million in 1996, while the Republican funds rose from about $50 million to $138 million (Federal Election Commission 2001). The greatest growth occurred among the House and Senate campaign committees, which are supposed to be primarily concerned with the election of federal candidates. The Democrats' two congressional campaign committees increased their soft money fund-raising from less than $5 million in 1992 to more than $26 million four years later, and their Republican counterparts increased their soft monies from $15 million to almost $48 million (Federal Election Commission 2001).

This explosive growth of soft money was spurred by a number of factors. Parties began to emphasize the solicitation of contributions of $100,000 or more from corporations, labor unions, and wealthy individuals, which allowed them to amass large sums with great efficiency. In 1991, the Federal Election Commission (FEC) adopted regulations that set clear formulas for the expenditure of combinations of hard and soft money for use in financing party-building activities, including overhead and administrative costs, as well as voter registration and turnout programs. These rules, in effect, sanctioned the use of soft money in connection with federal elections, and parties responded by spending tens of mil-

Table 2.1   A Decade of Stalemate: Major Campaign Finance Bills and Their Fates, 1985–1996

Congress	Party in Majority	Major Bill (Lead Sponsors)	Major Provisions	Fate of the Bill(s)
99th (1985–86)	Sen.: R HR: D Pres: Reagan	S. 1806 (Boren)	Restricts PACs.	Considered in Senate; no vote on passage.
100th (1987–88)	Sen.: D HR: D Pres.: Reagan	S. 2 (Boren-Byrd)	Public funds; spending limits, PAC limits.	Senate filibuster; multiple cloture votes failed.
101st (1989–90)	Sen.: D HR: D Pres.: Bush	S. 137 (Boren) H.R. 5400 (Swift)	Spending limits; postage and broadcast advertising discounts; PAC limits.	Passed both chambers. Conference never met.
102nd (1991–92)	Sen.: D HR: D Pres.: Bush	S. 3 (Mitchell-Boren) H.R. 3750 (Gejdensen)	For both: Spending limits. For Sen.: Postal/TV vouchers. For HR: Public matching funds.	Passed. Presidential veto sustained.
103rd (1993–94)	Sen.: D HR: D Pres.: Clinton	S. 3 (Boren) H.R. 3 (Gejdensen)	Similar to previous.	Passed both chambers. End-of-session Senate filibuster prevented appointment of conferees.
104th (1995–96)	Sen.: R HR: R Pres.: Clinton	S. 1219 (McCain-Feingold) H.R. 2566 (Shays-Meehan-Smith, D leaders supported) H.R. 3820 (Thomas, R leaders supported)	S.: Similar to previous. H.R. 2566: Similar to S. 1219. H.R. 3820: Index individual contribution limits; lower PAC limits; remove limits when facing self-financed candidates; ban Leadership PAC's; state majority of money in-district.	Senate Filibuster. Cloture not successful. House defeated both approaches.

lions of dollars on efforts designed to turn out party supporters, especially where a heightened turnout could affect the outcome of the presidential race or key Senate and House contests.

The most important factor in 1996, however, was the advent of candidate-specific issue advocacy advertisements. Because a number of federal courts had ruled that communications that did not include terms of express advocacy—such as "vote for," "elect," or "defeat"—were not subject to the restrictions of FECA, party committees and other political groups began to craft broadcast advertisements that featured specific federal candidates but did not include the words that triggered federal regulation (Corrado 1997; Potter 1997). In advance of the presidential nomination contest, the Democratic National Committee transferred millions of dollars to state party committees and spent more than $40 million, most of it in soft money, to pay for ads designed to promote President Clinton's bid for reelection. In the summer of 1996, the Republican National Committee adopted a similar tactic, spending a reported $20 million on ads in support of its prospective presidential nominee, Robert Dole (Corrado 1997). None of these expenditures were counted against the presidential candidate spending limits.

In addition to undermining the restrictions of the presidential public funding system, the rise of issue advocacy electioneering drove the demand for soft money, since most of the costs of these advertisements could be paid for with unregulated funds. Furthermore, the parties' new approach to campaigning encouraged other political groups to follow suit, which led to a virtual explosion of such ads. The most notable campaign was conducted by labor unions, which spent an estimated $35 million on mobilization activities during the election, including $20 million on issue advertisements that were primarily targeted against freshmen Republicans (Kosterlitz 1996; Carney 1996). Business groups and tax-exempt organizations also began to finance issue ads, including a coalition of business associations organized by the U.S. Chamber of Commerce that spent $7 million to broadcast ads in thirty-three congressional districts (Salant 1996; Carney 1996).

Suddenly, the federal campaign finance system seemed to be awash in undisclosed money from sources that were supposed to be banned by FECA. This development led to allegations that emerged late in the presidential campaign that the Democrats had engaged in questionable fund-raising practices in raising soft money, including "selling access to the White House" by granting large donors privileged meetings with President Clinton, accepting illegal contributions from foreign sources, and using government offices to solicit contributions in violation of federal law. The allegations ignited a national controversy.

By early 1997 formal investigations of party fund-raising had been launched by Senate and House investigating committees, the Federal Election Commission, and the Department of Justice. These probes revealed a wide range of financial abuses and eventually led to an admission by the Democratic National

Committee that it had received at least $3 million in illegal gifts or contributions from questionable sources; these donations were later returned to the donors. The documents produced by these inquiries also showed that the Democrats had used the White House for "sleepovers" in the Lincoln Bedroom for political supporters and had held more than one hundred "coffee klatches" for the President and Democratic supporters who donated a total of more than $26 million (Rosenbaum 1997). Other abuses included Vice President Al Gore's use of his office to make fund-raising telephone calls and his attendance at an event at a Buddhist monastery where funds were solicited, both apparently in violation of federal law. Republican actions were also called into question (Carr and Koszczuk 1998). These included transfers made from party coffers to tax-exempt organizations and the role of a private corporation in soliciting contributions for organizations that engaged in issue advocacy electioneering (Carr and Koszczuk 1998).

The Reinvigorated Debate

In the view of most advocates of campaign finance reform, the abuses associated with the unprecedented financial activities of 1996 signaled the collapse of the regulatory regime created by FECA, since the innovative use of soft money and issue advocacy had eviscerated the law's contribution and spending limits. The controversy reinvigorated the reform debate in Congress, and legislators responded with an outpouring of proposals for reform, which ranged from complete elimination of FECA restrictions, save for disclosure, to public funding of congressional campaigns. The bill that became the focal point of congressional deliberation was sponsored by Senators McCain and Feingold (S. 25), with a companion bill sponsored in the House by Representatives Shays and Meehan (H.R. 493).

McCain and Feingold originally submitted a bill similar to a measure that they had proposed in the previous Congress; it included spending limits and reduced broadcast and postal rates. That bill had succumbed to a filibuster in the 104th Congress after only a brief debate. With Republicans in control of the Senate and House, the legislators decided to modify their proposal in an effort to garner Republican votes. They eliminated the subsidies and spending caps to focus on the issues of soft money and issue advocacy (Doherty 1997c). They also revised some provisions in part based on a package of reforms, prepared by a group of campaign finance experts, that was designed to promote bipartisan support and was endorsed by the League of Women Voters (Ornstein et al. 1997).

The twin pillars of the McCain-Feingold bill were a ban on soft money and a new conception of express advocacy communications. These provisions were considered essential in order to reduce the potentially corruptive influence of large, unregulated contributions in federal elections. The Senators' plan eliminated soft money by prohibiting federal officeholders, candidates, national party committees, or their agents from soliciting, spending, directing, or transferring monies that were not subject to federal contribution limits. The bill also prohibited state and local party committees from spending soft money on "federal election activities," which were defined to include voter registration drives conducted in the last 120 days of an election; voter identification, get-out-the-vote drives, and generic party activities conducted in connection with an election in which a federal candidate was on the ballot; and communications that refer to a clearly identified federal candidate with the intent of influencing that candidate's election (Cantor 1997).

With respect to issue advocacy, S. 25 called for a new "bright line" test that moved beyond the "magic words" test used by most federal courts to determine whether a public communication constituted express advocacy and thus had to be financed with monies governed by federal contribution limits. Instead of the narrow magic words doctrine, McCain and Feingold adopted criteria that had been supported by the Federal Election Commission and had their basis in a federal court decision that offered an expansive interpretation of express advocacy (*FEC v. Furgatch*, 807 F2d 857 [9th Cir 1987]). Under these proposed criteria, a communication would be considered express advocacy if (a) it used words or phrases that in context would have no other reasonable meaning than election advocacy; (b) it was broadcast on television or radio and referred to a federal candidate in the affected state within sixty days of an election; or (3) it expressed "unambiguous" advocacy when viewed as a whole given "limited reference to external events" (Cantor 1997). The central purpose of this provision was to expand the scope of federal regulation to include what some advocates of reform were calling "sham" issue ads—ads featuring specific federal candidates that were designed to influence election outcomes—and ensure that the financing of such ads would be federally regulated.

The Democrats rallied around the McCain-Feingold plan, and President Clinton called for its passage, but most Republicans supported alternatives. Senator Mitch McConnell of Kentucky argued that McCain-Feingold's restrictions on issue communications and on the ability of party organizations to raise and spend nonfederal funds violated the freedom of speech and rights of association guaranteed by the First Amendment. Republicans also noted that one reason the law was being circumvented was that federal contribution limits had not been increased since 1974 and were too low. They therefore supported higher contribution limits, as well as an increase in the ceiling imposed on an individual's aggregate annual federal donations.

In addition, most Republicans contended that a reform bill, to be meaningful, had to address unregulated labor union spending. To this end, Senate Majority Leader Trent Lott supported a plan (S. 9), known as the "paycheck protection act," that would require written, prior authorizations from union members and nonmembers for the use of union dues or other payments for political purposes. Similarly, the bill required authorization from employees or stockholders for any use of dues or payments that were a condition of employment for political purposes. Since most corporations had no such dues, the bill principally affected labor unions. Those who were not union members, but worked in union shops, already had the option of requesting a rebate of the portion of dues used for political purposes as a result of the Supreme Court's 1988 decision in *Communications Workers of America v. Beck* (487 U.S. 735). McCain-Feingold proposed to codify this decision. For most Republicans, however, this provision did not go far enough, since it would allow labor unions to continue to spend millions of dollars on mobilization activities largely targeted against Republicans. In their view, all monies used for political activities should be voluntarily contributed; unauthorized use of union dues violated this principle.

Senate

These contrasting partisan views created a deadlock in the Senate, since the Democrats, who were united in their support of McCain-Feingold, were adamantly opposed to any further restrictions on labor unions. Many also were against increasing contribution limits, since they believed higher limits would be of greater benefit to Republicans. Accordingly, the legislation's sponsors were given little room to craft a compromise, and were forced to deem any effort to include additional labor restrictions or higher limits as "poison pills" designed to defeat the bill, since they would cause a loss of Democratic support.

In October of 1997, in the midst of extensive press coverage of video clips that had been discovered of Clinton's White House coffees, Senator Lott brought the McCain-Feingold bill to the floor. But he relied on his power as majority leader to construct a procedure that presented the paycheck protection bill as an amendment to S. 25 (Doherty 1997b). Lott opposed S. 25, claiming that it restricted free speech and favored Democrats by failing to constrain unions. He therefore presented his amendment in order to force a Democratic filibuster. The Democrats did filibuster, but the Republicans failed to invoke cloture on a vote of fifty-two to forty-eight, with three Republicans joining the forty-five Democrats. The Republicans, in turn, filibustered on consideration of the bill, and the McCain-Feingold supporters failed to invoke cloture, falling eight votes short, as only seven Republicans joined the forty-five Democrats (Doherty 1997a). After two failed cloture votes on Lott's proposal and three on consideration of the bill, the Senate moved to other business.

Searching for Cloture

The Senate sponsors and Senate Minority Leader Tom Daschle refused to accept defeat and threatened to tie up other legislation unless an up-or-down vote on the McCain-Feingold bill was permitted. In February of 1998, a vote was scheduled, and the sponsors presented a version of their bill that contained a substantial modification.

In an effort to garner the additional votes needed to break a filibuster, Senators Olympia Snowe of Maine and Jim Jeffords of Vermont, two of the Republicans who voted with McCain in October, had worked to develop a compromise that they hoped would appeal to moderate Republicans by alleviating some of their concerns about the First Amendment implications of the bill and the role of labor unions in federal elections. Their proposal offered a narrower test for express advocacy communications, designed to affect only certain broadcast communications that reached a certain threshold of spending. It also would permit such advertising, but require corporations or labor unions engaging in the defined "electioneering communications" to finance these messages with PAC funds or other monies disclosed and regulated under federal law. Specifically, the proposal, which was presented as an amendment to McCain-Feingold and was crafted with constitutional imperatives in mind, defined "electioneering communications" according to specific criteria: (1) a message broadcast on television or radio; (2) featuring a clearly identified federal candidate; (3) aired within sixty days of a general election or within thirty days of a primary election; and (4) targeted to the electorate that would vote on that candidate. Any expenditure on such electioneering communications in excess of $10,000 per calendar year would have to be disclosed. These communications would have to be paid for with monies raised in accordance with federal contribution limits (Carney 1998).

This change, however, made little difference in the voting. When McCain-Feingold was brought up on the floor (as an amendment to Lott's paycheck protection bill, now S. 1663), McConnell again initiated a filibuster and the Senate again failed to invoke cloture. The vote was fifty-one to forty-eight against limiting debate (Democrat Tom Harkin was absent). The Snowe-Jeffords compromise had produced no additional Republican support (Doherty 1998). The vote demonstrated the solidity of the positions on both sides, and indicated that the McCain-Feingold bill would not become law until it could muster the sixty votes needed to break a filibuster.

House

With legislation stalled in the Senate, the House was reduced essentially to a symbolic effort to pass reform. The House debate in 1998 was noteworthy, however, for the divisions it revealed. From the outset, the leading reform plan was the bill sponsored by Shays and Meehan. The Republican leadership, especially House Speaker Newt Gingrich, opposed the bill and prevented it from coming to the House floor. This action forced Shays-Meehan supporters, led by a conservative group of Democrats known as "Blue Dogs," to undertake a rarely used procedural device, a formal discharge petition, to force the bill to the floor. The petition required 218 votes to be successful, and once it surpassed 200 signatures, including twelve Republicans, the Speaker agreed to schedule a debate (Katz 1998b).

The debate revolved around two alternatives, a bill (H.R. 2183) crafted by a bipartisan group of House freshman, led by Republican Asa Hutchinson of Arkansas and Democrat Tom Allen of Maine, and the Shays-Meehan proposal. The freshmen bill also focused on soft money and issue advocacy, but offered a more moderate approach to reform. The bill banned soft money at the national level, but permitted soft money at the state level, only banning the transfer of soft money from one state party to another. It also called for a doubling of individual contribution limits, including the aggregate limit for individuals, and removed the coordinated spending limits imposed on party committees. With respect to issue advocacy, the bill only required disclosure of the amounts spent on ads that feature federal candidates and only for groups that spent more than $25,000 on an ad or more than $100,000 in total.

The Republican leaders established a complicated legislative procedure for consideration of the bills, which forced the Shays-Meehan bill to compete with ten substitute amendments and pitted it directly against the freshmen bill. In the end, the freshmen bill, now positioned as a vote against Shays-Meehan, garnered 147 votes, with 61 Members voting "present." This cleared the way for passage of Shays-Meehan, which was passed on a vote of 252 to 179 in early August, with 61 Republicans voting for the bill and only 15 Democrats against it (Katz 1998a). In September, McCain again tried to obtain a Senate vote, but still lacked the eight votes needed to break a filibuster.

106th Congress (1999–2000)

During the 106th Congress, the sponsors continued to press for the McCain-Feingold bill, but although majorities in both houses once again supported this reform, no progress was made. The 1998 elections produced little partisan change in Congress and there were no further developments to alter the political environment on Capitol Hill. Consequently, the House supporters again had to rely on a discharge petition to get a vote and then navigate their way through a complex series of procedural obstacles. The procedures included an atypical "queen-of-the-hill" process in which votes were taken on three different plans, with the one receiving the greatest number of votes constituting the base bill (Dwyre and Farrar-Myers 2001, 88–89). In September of 1999, the House adopted the Shays-Meehan bill (H.R. 417) by a vote of 252 to 177, which represented the same number of "yes" votes as in the previous Congress (Martinez and Doherty 1999).

In the Senate, events proved to be even more interesting, as Senators McCain and Feingold attempted a new strategy in an effort to make some progress. McCain offered a pared-down version of the bill that included the provisions on soft money and the codification of *Beck*, but omitted the issue advocacy provisions. The idea was to reduce opposition based on First Amendment arguments and force a straight vote on the issue of soft money reform (Martinez and Doherty 1999). But even this more modest proposal was rejected, failing to defeat a Republican filibuster on a vote of fifty-three to forty-seven. McCain also tried offering the bill passed by the House, which was also filibustered, and fell eight votes short on the cloture vote (Doherty 1999). For the fifth time in six years, reform fell victim to a filibuster, with virtually no change in the voting alignments.

The Route to Reform: 107th Congress (2001–2002)

After the 2000 elections, the congressional logjam began to show signs of breaking. McCain's surprisingly strong bid for the Republican presidential nomination in his race against George Bush was accepted by many political observers as a sign that campaign finance reform was an issue of concern to voters, and McCain kept up his call for reform throughout the general election period, campaigning on behalf of dozens of congressional candidates who pledged to support reform if elected. The need for reform was also highlighted yet again by the rising amounts of soft money and issue advocacy advertising, which by 2000 had become staples of both parties' campaign strategies. The amount of soft money nearly doubled the sum received four years earlier, reaching $495 million or about 40 percent of the national parties' aggregate revenue (Federal Election Commission 2001). Issue advocacy advertising was also predominant, with tens of millions of dollars spent on ads featuring candidates in the final months of the election in targeted races (Holman and McLoughlin 2001; Magleby 2002b).

More importantly, the election produced a turnover in the Senate that improved the prospects for reform. The Democrats picked up four seats in the Senate elections, and when Senator Jeffords shifted his affiliation from Republican to independent, the Democrats became the majority party. The turnover also added an anticipated three or four votes in support of McCain-Feingold, leaving reformers only two votes short of the sixty needed to break a filibuster (Doyle 2000). Before the end of the election year, McCain was claiming that he had gathered the sixty votes needed to invoke cloture (Doyle and Bolen 2000).

These changes in the political environment altered the dynamics of the congressional debate. With a successful filibuster less likely, Members of Congress had to focus on the substantive issues, since for the first time in more than a decade they would face meaningful votes that might produce new legislation. The congressional sponsors also faced new challenges. First, they would have to shepherd their bills through each house without allowing any amendments that would serve as "poison pills" and undermine the fragile coalition they had built during the past two Congresses. Second, they would need to produce a bill that President George W. Bush would be willing to accept. If this second challenge was not met, the sponsors faced the possibility of a veto, which would serve to increase their "magic number" from the sixty votes needed for cloture to the sixty-seven votes needed for an override. All knew that no version of McCain-Feingold was likely to attract such support.

The effects of this new legislative context became evident in March of 2001, when the McCain-Feingold bill (S. 27) was placed before the Senate. Instead of a scripted debate with a predetermined outcome, the Senate engaged in a free-wheeling, substantive debate that extended over the course of two weeks. Senators offered numerous amendments, which were often changed on the Senate floor, and held almost daily votes on major issues. Many of the issues raised in the debate had been heard before, and the supporters of McCain-Feingold had to vote down a number of amendments that offered versions of paycheck protection (which the President supported and to which the Democrats objected), as well as other provisions that might cause Republican defections, including a proposal by Democrat Paul Wellstone that would have allowed the states to provide public funding for federal elections.

Much of the debate, however, concerned issues that had not been previously discussed as part of this bill, including the need to provide some compensation to candidates facing millionaires who were spending their own money in a bid for office, the need for better guarantees that candidates *and party committees* would receive the lowest unit rate on broadcast advertisements, and the need for better rules defining the concept of coordination with respect to campaign contributions and expenditures. These issues all led to new provisions in the underlying bill. The Senate adopted a "Millionaires' Amendment" that would ease contribution limits for donors supporting candidates who faced self-financed opponents, with the limit on individual contributions increasing on the basis of a complicated formula that included the amount of personal money a self-financed candidate spent. The body also adopted, by a wide margin, a provision sponsored by Democrat Robert Torricelli that would guarantee lowest unit rates and prime-time broadcast slots to federal candidates and extend this guarantee to political parties (Taylor and Cochran 2001). An amendment sponsored by McCain that directed the Federal Election Commission to draft new regulations on coordination also passed easily (Taylor, Willis, and Cochran 2001).

The most important changes, however, concerned the restrictions on issue advocacy and the hard money contribution limits. The McCain-Feingold bill's issue advocacy provisions, as established by the Snowe-Jeffords proposal, were drafted to focus on corporate and labor broadcast electioneering, since such a provision was considered to be constitutionally defensible. The approach did not encompass all tax-exempt advocacy organizations, and thus left a potential loophole in the law. Democrat Paul Wellstone proposed an amendment to address this concern, which narrowly passed on a vote of fifty-one to forty-six. The amendment was adopted with the support of Senator McConnell, who thought its addition would weaken the proposal by making it more susceptible to constitutional challenge (Taylor, Willis, and Cochran 2001).

Republicans continued to push for higher contribution limits. Many supported a cap on soft money contributions as an alternative to an outright ban on this form of funding. This issue threatened to divide the McCain-Feingold coalition. Some liberal Democrats continued to oppose a substantial increase in the limits (Bolen 2001b). Other Members were concerned about the effects of a soft money ban, which would cost the parties a half-billion dollars in revenue, and considered higher limits a means of helping to compensate for this loss of party resources (Bolen and Doyle 2001). An indication of the support for higher limits was provided by a vote on an amendment offered by Republican Chuck Hagel that proposed a tripling of all hard money contribution limits, and was defeated by a margin of only five votes (Taylor, Willis, and Cochran 2001).

As the debate evolved, higher contribution limits emerged as central to passing McCain-Feingold. The congressional sponsors were able to negotiate a compromise, in part because Common Cause and other public interest advocates moved away from their traditional opposition to higher limits, agreeing to accept some increase if it were essential to the bill's passage (Taylor and Cochran 2001). The compromise increased the individual contribution limit from $1,000 to $2,000, and raised the aggregate limit on annual contributions to $37,500. It also increased the amount an individual could contribute under federal law to a national party committee from $20,000 to $25,000. This amendment passed overwhelmingly, with only sixteen Democrats opposed (Taylor, Willis, and Cochran 2001).

Another significant change sought to reduce the effects of a soft money ban by permitting state and local party committees to raise soft money in amounts of no more than $10,000, if allowed by state law, solely to finance voter registration and get-out-the-vote programs. This amendment, which was sponsored by Democrat Carl Levin, was designed to address concerns, especially as expressed in the House by members of the Congressional Black Caucus and Hispanic Caucus, that a ban on soft money would reduce the funding of voter registration and turnout efforts (Cochran 2001b; Clymer 2001).

The version of McCain-Feingold that resulted from the Senate debate constituted a more extensive package of reforms than that contemplated in the original proposal, but it was easily adopted on a vote of fifty-nine to forty-one, with twelve Republicans voting for the bill and only three Democrats opposed. The House sponsors now had to follow suit and pass a bill that would avoid the need for a conference committee, which might serve as a roadblock to reform, as it had in some past years. Shays and Meehan acted accordingly, replacing their bill with a modified version of the Senate bill (H.R. 2356), which included the Torricelli, Wellstone, and Levin amendments, but did not call for an increase in the $1,000 contribution limit for House candidates.

Progress in the House was delayed by procedural obstacles. When the rule for debate was presented by the Republican leadership in July, Shays and Meehan considered it unfair, since it would require separate votes on each of the provisions they wanted to add to their bill to make it conform to the Senate version (Cochran 2001a). Consequently, Shays-Meehan supporters voted against the rule, which prevented the bill from reaching the floor, and began a discharge petition to bring a new rule before the House. By late January 2002, the discharge petition had gathered the requisite 218 Members, including 20 Republicans.

The House debate took place over three days in early February of 2002, in a political environment that gave further impetus to reform. By this time, the bankruptcy of the Enron Corporation and other corporate scandals were matters of national attention, and raised alarming questions about the role political contributions played in policy decisions favorable to Enron and other corporations (*USA Today* 2002). Many Members wanted to respond to the public clamor over Enron's collapse, and saw campaign finance reform as a vehicle to fulfill this end.

Nevertheless, Shays and Meehan still had to maneuver their proposal through a complex legislative procedure. In one of the more bizarre twists in this extraordinary saga, the Republican leadership offered two alternatives—a straight soft money ban without issue advocacy provisions and the version of Shays-Meehan passed in the previous Congress—in an attempt to siphon votes away from the new Shays-Meehan bill (Bolen and Ognanovich 2002). These tactics failed, and the debate then focused on the amending process.

Two major substantive changes were adopted in the course of the House debate. First, the House, responding to intense lobbying on the part of the National Association of Broadcasters, stripped the Torricelli amendment from the bill, with 327 Members voting for this change (Bolen and Ognanovich 2002; Moller 2002). Second, the House decided to increase the individual contribution limit to $2,000 per election for House candidates. This change was sponsored by Republican Zack Wamp of Tennessee, one of the leaders of the group of moderate Republicans supporting the bill. The issue proved to be one of the most closely fought issues in the entire debate, and passed by a slim seven-vote margin, largely due to the support of 201 Republicans, who were joined by only 17 Democrats. With the issue of hard money limits finally decided, the House approved the revised Shays-Meehan plan on a 240-to-189 vote, with 41 Republicans voting for the plan and only 13 Democrats against.

With slightly different versions of the bill adopted by the House and Senate, the sponsors had to bring the bill back to the Senate and have that body approve the House version. Otherwise a conference committee would be necessary, which would in all likelihood produce a bill unacceptable to some McCain-Feingold supporters, since Senator McConnell would be included on the committee and House appointments would be made by the conservative Republican leadership. Senate Majority Leader Daschle worked with McCain and Feingold to develop a procedure that would allow the House bill to come to the floor without any further amendments. Senate Minority Leader Trent Lott and Senator McConnell pressed for additional changes, but after two weeks of procedural maneuvering and informal debate, Daschle filed a cloture motion to end debate on a consent agreement to move the bill to the floor. The motion to end debate received sixty-eight votes, and soon thereafter, on March 20, the Senate approved the House version of the bill by a margin of sixty to forty (Doyle 2002b). After years of debate and numerous failed attempts, Congress passed the Bipartisan Campaign Reform Act (BCRA), the first major piece of campaign finance reform legislation to emerge from Congress since 1992.

Prior to the final Senate vote, opponents of McCain-Feingold held out some hope that President Bush would veto the bill, just as his father had, in 1992, vetoed the last major campaign finance reform bill approved by Congress. This hope was premised on the fact that the proposal did not reflect all of the President's views. In particular, Bush had called for a ban on corporate and labor soft money contributions, but believed individuals should be allowed to contribute soft money to parties. Bush also supported greater restrictions on labor and had publicly called for paycheck protection regulations (Bolen 2001a). But in the midst of a public controversy over corporate scandals and allegations that the Bush administration had given preferential treatment to major corporate donors, the President did not want to position himself as an opponent of reform. Even before the House vote, the White House was sending signals that the President could not be counted on to veto the bill. On March 27, he quietly signed the bill without the type of public signing ceremony that usually accompanies the passage of major legislation. In a one-page statement released that day, the President acknowledged that "the American electorate will benefit from these measures to strengthen our democracy," but noted that "the bill does have flaws. Certain provisions present serious constitutional concerns" (Doyle 2002a).

CONCLUSION

The adoption of BCRA did not bring a temporary end to the campaign finance debate. Even before the law went into effect, supporters and opponents had begun to reenact their arguments in the courts and in administrative proceedings at the Federal Election Commission. Some advocates of reform quickly began to espouse the need for additional changes not considered in the act, such as free broadcast time for candidates or revisions in the presidential public funding system, the inadequacies of which had stimulated the major innovations BCRA was designed to address. Others awaited the outcome of the judicial and administrative decisions, or the initial responses to the law by political operatives, in hopes of using these developments as an opportunity to restart the debate.

Whatever the outcome of the pending actions related to BCRA, it is unlikely that they will lead to a new consensus on the issues associated with political finance. As demonstrated by the experience of BCRA, the campaign finance debate is characterized by complex policy perspectives that are not open to easy reconciliation. At the core of this debate are sincerely held philosophical views that serve to divide policy alternatives. Some legislators, like Senators McCain and Feingold, believe that large contributions corrupt the political process and that the First Amendment permits a broad scope of federal regulation to safeguard the political system from the undue influence of political donations. Others share the basic outlook expressed by Senator McConnell, who considers First Amendment protections to be paramount and regards unrestricted free speech and robust political debate as essential elements of a healthy democracy. Many opponents also place great emphasis on the importance of upholding the principle of federalism and the rights of association that obtain to political parties under the Constitution. These kinds of differences leave little room for compromise. In addition, these policy views are reinforced by partisan influences and practical considerations that stem from the distinctive patterns of campaign funding that characterize Democrats and Republicans, incumbents and challengers, parties and nonparty organizations. These differences have their origins in the various determinants of the behavior of political donors, which are unlikely to be altered so radically by BCRA as to produce wholly new patterns in resource distribution. Republicans will continue to raise more hard money than Democrats. Incumbents will continue to outspend challengers. Parties and nonparty groups will continue to display varying approaches in their electioneering efforts. Consequently, many of the diverse policy preferences revealed in past debates are likely to endure.

This diversity means, as a practical matter, finding consensus will continue to be difficult, but *not* impossible. As BCRA's passage suggests, Congress is capable of acting. Amidst all of the political maneuvering, Congress eventually engaged in a richly textured and highly substantive debate on the issues. Legislators broke new ground on express advocacy, electioneering, contribution limits, state party finance, and making resources available to those facing self-financed opponents. Finding new ways to overcome obstacles has always been a necessity on the path to reform.

NOTE

The author wishes to acknowledge the support of The Pew Charitable Trusts, which funded some of the research on which this article is based. The author also thanks Heitor Gouvêa and Sarah Barclay for their assistance on background research. The opinions expressed herein are solely those of the author and do not necessarily reflect the views of The Pew Charitable Trusts.

II

GIVERS AND SPENDERS

3

BCRA's Impact on Interest Groups and Advocacy Organizations

Robert G. Boatright, Michael J. Malbin, Mark J. Rozell, Richard M. Skinner, and Clyde Wilcox

Much of the rhetoric during debates over the Bipartisan Campaign Reform Act (BCRA) was about curbing the role of "special interest" contributors to the parties, and restraining "electioneering" ads paid for by corporations and labor unions. Despite the sweeping character of the public statements about interest groups, we know that any change in the law will affect different organizations in different ways. In this chapter, we begin to sketch out some of the effects we expect to see, as interest groups and advocacy organizations begin adapting to the new law by shifting their tactics as well as their structural forms.

The material is drawn from research that spans several elections before and after BCRA. As part of this project we have selected a sample of twenty-seven different electorally engaged interest groups and advocacy organizations, designed to represent a diversity of ideological viewpoints, resources, and strategies. We conducted a series of forty-six interviews with representatives from these groups during the 2000 and 2002 election cycles to establish a pre-BCRA baseline and to begin assessing how they adapt their political activities to changing circumstances. Subsequent interviews will focus on learning, adaptation to BCRA, and electoral activities during the 2004 cycle. The interviews have led us to develop a conceptual framework, which we present in the first part of the chapter and apply in the second. The second half of the chapter follows the order of the new law's main titles by discussing soft money contributors before discussing organizations that communicate directly with their members or with the public.

BROAD BRUSH STROKES

BCRA has two major sections affecting interest groups and advocacy organizations. Title I bans unlimited (soft money) contributions to political parties. Title II requires disclosure for all electioneering communications (above a minimum threshold) and prohibits direct or indirect corporate and labor funding for these communications. The two sections will have a major impact on the role and relative power of interest groups, but will affect groups differently according to the groups' goals and resources. To help sort out the effects, we have found it useful to distinguish money that is being "pulled" into the system from money that is being "pushed." Money is pulled into the system when it is drawn out of more-or-less reluctant givers, in response to requests from receivers or their agents, because the givers see the contributions as a price of gaining access to the receivers. Money that is pushed into the system comes from people who give or spend out of a more direct set of political motivations.

With these push and pull distinctions in mind, and assuming the law survives constitutional challenge largely intact—we would expect BCRA's two major titles to have the following broad effects on interest groups.

Title I—Soft Money Ban

Because the law bans soft money contributions to parties, we expect the law to reduce the political money that comes into the system directly or indirectly from some of the organizations that were giving large soft money contributions. This will be particularly true for those—primarily corporations and trade associations—whose money was reluctantly being pulled into the system by party leaders. Some of these organizations will try to energize their political action committees (PACs) and individual hard money contributions, but part of the money may stay on the sidelines. How much will depend on the extent to which party leaders find alternative ways to persuade reluctant givers to continue participating, which we discuss later. We expect to see some of this money recaptured, but not all of it. In contrast, we expect that organizations pushing their money into the system—those playing because they are eager to play—will continue to find ways to participate.

Title II—Electioneering

BCRA prohibits direct or indirect funding by labor unions or corporations (including nonprofit social welfare corporations) for electioneering advertising—that is, communications on radio or television naming a candidate, appearing within sixty days of a general election or thirty days of a primary, and targeted to the named candidate's electorate. While the constitutionality of these provisions is being challenged as this book goes to press, it is important to note what

the law does *not* cover. Communications not meeting *all* of the definitional criteria are not electioneering and therefore not affected at all—not even with a disclosure requirement. This includes nonbroadcast communications delivered
through other media (such as mail, telephone, or the Internet), communications
that do not name a candidate (even if they do promote a candidate's issues or
use a candidate's theme language), or communications that occur before the six-
ty- or thirty-day time window. Not covered, for example, would be a multi-
phased campaign run by a corporation, labor union, or advocacy organization
that begins with television before the time window and then segues into a campaign with TV ads that promote a candidate's issue themes without naming the
candidate, running at the same time as hard-hitting, candidate-specific direct
mail, telephone, and Internet advertising or voter mobilization campaigns. Most
active, self-motivated organizations (organizations whose money is pushed
rather than pulled) are likely to gravitate toward these other forms of communication if they are able to do so. In fact, we have seen in our previous interviews
that many were doing so even before BCRA (Malbin et al. 2002).

These predictions seem straightforward, but they also are abstract. Indeed,
some of our research questions are all but telegraphed by the way these predictions are phrased. What kinds of organizations fit into the "push" and "pull"
categories? What are their political goals or motivations? Given two groups with
similar goals, what kinds of resources help differentiate one group's strategic
decisions from another's? How does a change in the law work to affect these
decisions? How can we separate the effects of a new law from the effects brought
about by changes in other aspects of the broader political context?

CONCEPTUAL FRAMEWORK

Based on interviews over two pre-BCRA election cycles, we have formulated a
schematic flowchart to help us think about these questions (see figure 3.1). Without dwelling excessively on the model's fine points, we think of an organization's
electoral behavior as involving (1) a series of decisions (see the middle of the
figure) (2) to deploy the organization's resources (column on the left) (3) within
organizational constraints, (4) to achieve the organization's electoral goals, (5)
within a specific context—of which the legal context is only one of many relevant
parts.

This is a dynamic model to portray the structure of organizational decisions
over several election cycles. In certain respects, it resembles more static models
other scholars have used. Consider electoral goals, for example. When political
action committees (PACs) were going through a major growth spurt during the
1970s and 1980s, they were often described as pursuing some blend of two distinct kinds of goals: *gaining access* to incumbents, versus *affecting who is elected*.
Access-oriented groups—including most corporations and trade associations—

Figure 3.1 Election Cycle Flow Chart

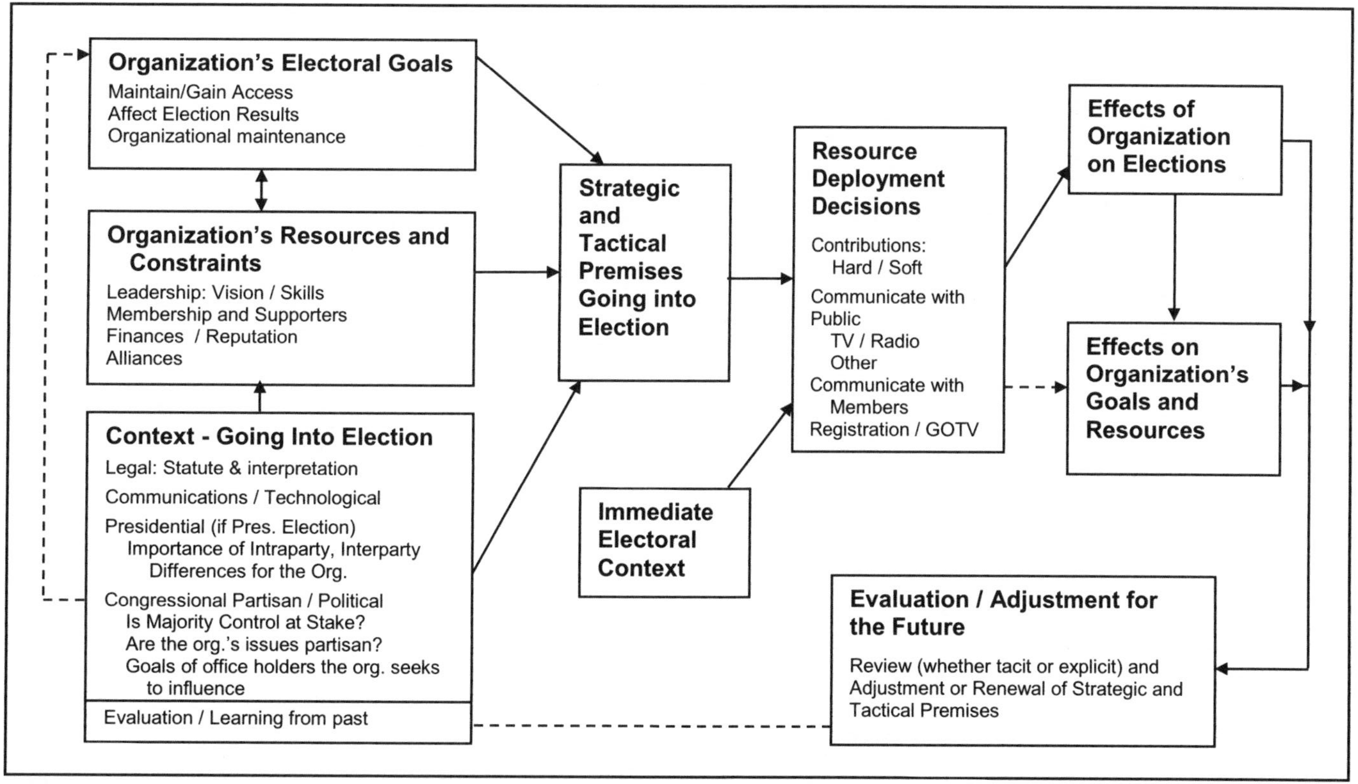

Organization's Electoral Goals

Maintain/Gain Access
Affect Election Results
Organizational maintenance

Organization's Resources and Constraints

Leadership: Vision / Skills
Membership and Supporters
Finances / Reputation
Alliances

Context - Going Into Election

Legal: Statute & interpretation
Communications / Technological
Presidential (if Pres. Election)
Importance of Intraparty, Interparty
Differences for the Org.
Congressional Partisan / Political
Is Majority Control at Stake?
Are the org.'s issues partisan?
Goals of office holders the org. seeks
to influence

Evaluation / Learning from past

Strategic and Tactical Premises Going into Election

Immediate Electoral Context

Resource Deployment Decisions

Contributions: Hard / Soft
Communicate with
Public
TV / Radio
Other
Communicate with
Members
Registration / GOTV

Effects of Organization on Elections

Effects on Organization's Goals and Resources

Evaluation / Adjustment for the Future

Review (whether tacit or explicit) and
Adjustment or Renewal of Strategic and
Tactical Premises

sought the ear of people in office by giving most of their contributions to safe incumbents in both political parties (Handler and Mulkern 1992). Others—ideological groups, labor unions, issue groups, and a few business organizations—sought to influence the composition of Congress by recruiting candidates to run for office, providing help to candidates in primaries, supporting some challengers, and targeting their assistance to close elections (Eismeier and Pollock 1988; Wilcox 1989a). These goal orientations—corresponding roughly to our earlier distinction between money pulled and pushed into the system—were said to produce fairly stable election strategies from one election to the next.

The distinction between access and electoral goals continues to be useful, with important caveats, but there are serious problems with the assumptions about stability. The earlier PAC studies were conducted within a political, legal, and technological context that persisted for some time: unchallenged Democratic control of the House of Representatives, no change in campaign finance law for twenty-five years, little soft money, few candidate-specific "issue ads," network dominance of television, weak grassroots targeting tools, and no Internet. In contrast, we are writing when the key contextual elements—legal, technological, political, and institutional—are in flux. This puts us in a better position to see interactions among items on the left-hand side of our diagram—electoral goals, resources and constraints, and context—as all of them change.

We have long known, for example, that changes in the law, or interpretations of the law, open or close avenues of activity in ways that play to the advantages and resources of some organizations over others. We will address the subject at length in the rest of this chapter. Before we do so, however, we need to stress the importance of the other contextual features in figure 3.1.

Some of the contextual changes that drive organizational strategies have little to do with politics in the first instance. For example, the economics and technology of television changed politics profoundly during the fifty years following the first broadcast political advertising. As expensive as it might be, television has been considered a relatively cost-effective way to reach large numbers of voters. In recent years, however, there has been a growing disillusionment with the medium among political professionals. Although television is still useful, several of our interviewees thought its efficiency had been cut by the increasing cost of airtime, the decreasing cost of other communications media (including the Internet) and new television technologies (cable, and the remote control's mute button). All these considerations had been moving advocacy organizations away from broadcast issue ads before BCRA.

A more overtly political portion of the contextual section of our diagram is what we describe as the congressional partisan/political context, which has undergone several important changes in recent years. The parties have become much more polarized since the 1980s (Fleisher and Bond 2000; Jacobson 2000a). As the parties' positions diverge, majority control of the chamber becomes more important to those who care about major policy issues. The narrowness of the majority's control in each chamber also makes each competitive House or Senate race more important than it would be if the chamber were decisively in one or the other party's control.

Finally, the Members of Congress whom the groups want to influence, especially the leaders, have been changing their signals about what *they* expect in a more partisan and hotly contested environment. This point is particularly important for groups whose money is being pulled into the systems by Members' requests. Party leaders have become more heavily and directly involved in making fund-raising pleas to potential donors. Of course, fund-raising by the leaders is nothing new, but soft money has made them far more heavily involved, raising much more money than they did in the early years of the Federal Election Campaign Act (FECA).

There is no question that at least some givers respond to the signals they get from receivers. Consider the following: In 1980—the last year before Representative Tony Coelho became chair of the Democratic Congressional Campaign Committee and began aggressively raising business money for the Democratic Party—corporate PAC giving was pro-Republican (65 percent) and took risks (31 percent to challengers). By 1994, the last of forty-two consecutive years of Democratic control of the House, corporate PAC giving was bipartisan (52 percent Republican) and strongly proincumbent (only 8 percent to challengers). By 2000, after two elections of hard work by GOP leaders, who were now in the majority, corporate PACs became pro-Republican again (67 percent Republican in 2000), but did not revert to supporting challengers (5 percent to challengers in 2000). That is, business became more partisan without shedding the risk-averse features typical of organizations aiming for access. In terms of our diagram, organizations shifted their strategic behavior at least in part because of shifts in the perspectives, and power, of the people whom they were seeking to influence.

ORGANIZATIONAL LEARNING

The last element in the contextual section of figure 3.1 refers to organizational learning. Unlike campaign committees, interest groups and advocacy organizations have important business to conduct after Election Day. They never get everything they want out of a single election. Even if they do very well, they function in a competitive environment in which potential opponents are working to improve their own positions for the next round. Cyert and March (1963) suggest that organizations learn from experience and have a sort of memory. Learning therefore is an essential part of their election cycle, and groups can save themselves the trouble of developing new tactics by adopting successful strategies pioneered by other groups (Kollman 1998).

Our interviews uncovered many examples of competitive imitation as well as cooperative sharing. These examples include the adoption by peak business organizations of the voter mobilization and contact strategies pioneered by the AFL-CIO; ProNET, an umbrella organization of liberal interest groups; the movement of interest group leaders from the Christian Coalition to the National Rifle Association and from the Human Rights Campaign to the Sierra Club; and the assistance of the Sierra Club in the development of the NAACP National Voter Fund's efforts. These examples focused our attention on the fact that most successful organizations periodically evaluate what they are doing. After each election, most of the organizations explicitly or implicitly review their own and others' performance to see how they might improve in the next round, within the next cycle's new political context. Last year's evaluation becomes part of the context for next year. Thus, change is built into the system. Organizations survive because they manage to adapt.

With these elements of the framework in place, we return now to our original broad categories—soft money and electioneering—to analyze how different types of groups behaved before BCRA, and are likely to adapt afterward. In the next section, we consider what kinds of groups engaged in each major activity before BCRA, and how each might shift its money or attention afterwards.

CONTRIBUTIONS, HARD AND SOFT

Pre-BCRA

Soft money contributions through 2002 were primarily the province of industry-related groups and individuals. According to The Center for Responsive Politics' data, approximately 75 percent of the $349,966,791 in 2002 soft money donations to the parties through November 25 was from groups, corporations, or individuals affiliated with business sectors (excluding lawyers and lobbyists), while 8.1 percent was from labor unions and 3.9 percent was from ideological or issue-oriented groups. While it is impossible to assess the rationale for donations from many of the individuals in the business sector—some may have donated to further business aims, while others may have drawn on their personal wealth to make contributions unrelated to their business interests—it is evident that, of the various kinds of groups in our study, the soft money ban will have the greatest effects on industry-specific business organizations. Few issue groups rely on soft money donations: among the more prominent issue groups, only the National Rifle Association, which gave $678,400 to the Republican Party, and EMILY's List, which gave $103,000 to the Democratic Party, were major soft money donors in 2002. Peak business organizations often represent corporations that donate large amounts of soft money, but peak associations themselves gave only a total of $439,000 in 2002.

The major types of soft money donors share some goals and resources, while differing in others. In the case of corporations and industry-specific business groups, the importance of access to lawmakers raises the possibility that these donations would not be made absent requests by parties or politicians. It is difficult to tell how much of the soft money these groups have contributed has been for purposes of access; in 2002, 27.9 percent of the business groups donating more than $100,000 to the parties gave no more than 75 percent of their money to one party—a clear sign of access giving and a baseline estimate of the percentage of groups that may decrease their giving or political spending. In the case of labor, on the other hand, bipartisan access is less important. Unions give almost exclusively (98 percent of contributions in 2002) to Democrats, which poses access problems in a Republican Congress. Only one of the unions that gave more than $100,000 to the parties also gave 25 percent or more of its soft money to the Republican Party. Unions, however, spend far more money on mobilizing and communicating with their own members than they do on soft money contributions. The differences in whether money is being pushed or pulled from these groups, then, suggests different likely responses to the soft money ban.

One important unknown is whether soft money givers will convert their effort to hard money—which is called hard money partly because the money is hard to raise. Based on their 1998–2002 performances, not all business groups are equally well poised to make this transition. For example, AT&T increased its soft money giving from just over $1 million in 1998, to $3.8 million in 2000, before easing back down to $2.0 million in 2002. In contrast, the AT&T's PAC has given markedly less in hard money contributions to federal candidates, dropping from $772,000 in 1998, to $480,000 in 2000, and $345,000 in 2002. In other words, AT&T went from a ratio of 44 percent hard money to soft money in 1998, to 11 percent in 2000, and 15 percent in 2002.

Like AT&T, the Microsoft Corporation's soft money contributions soared over the last three pre-BCRA elections, from $775,000 in 1998, to $2.3 million in 2000, and $2.2 million in 2002. Microsoft's hard money PAC contributions also jumped between 1998 and 2000, from $212,000 to $821,000, before easing off to $709,000 in 2002, when PAC contributions represented about one-quarter of Microsoft's hard and soft money contributions.

The National Association of Realtors also increased its soft money giving, from $185,000 in 1998, to $506,000 in 2000, and $482,000 in 2002. It did so in direct response to Congress's consideration of legislation allowing banks to serve as real estate brokers. However, in contrast with both of the corporations just cited, the National Association of Realtors gives much more hard money than soft—$3.4 million in 2002. The association, which for decades has run one of the country's largest PACs, therefore is better prepared for a politics without soft money than many of the other major business contributors of recent years.

Understanding the importance of being ready for the abolition of soft money, the Business-Industry Political Action Committee (BIPAC), a peak organization that does not give soft money itself but has many members that do, counseled its members throughout the 2002 election season to start working to build up their PACs. BIPAC's PAC Council has vigorously promoted a new graduate program in PAC management developed by the Graduate School of Political Management at

George Washington University, and one major BIPAC initiative in 2002 was to provide advice to corporate leaders about how to solicit PAC contributions from their firms' employees (Tennille 2002). The growth of employee stock ownership plans has also greatly expanded the number of "solicitable" employees, expanding the potential audience for corporate political advocacy and facilitating the turn from soft money to hard money (Weisman 2002). An example of this transition is the Siebel Systems PAC. While Siebel gave $215,000 in soft money to the parties in 2002 (down from $850,000 in 2000), the company's PAC raised over $2 million from employees in its first few weeks of existence, almost instantly becoming the second largest corporate PAC in the country (VandeHei 2002).

Labor unions have also been major soft money donors. While most unions continue to operate large PACs, they may have less capacity than corporations to increase their hard money giving. The country's first PACs were labor committees formed during the 1930s. Indeed, in a remarkable irony, the business PAC explosion of the 1970s and 1980s was enabled by labor's insistence that provision be made for these organizations in the 1971 FECA (Epstein 1980). Despite this history, the AFL-CIO seems to be on a different path now. The AFL-CIO's soft money contributions declined in 2002, from over $700,000 in 1998 and 2000, to only $230,000 in 2002. Total soft money giving by all labor unions held steady from 2000 to 2002 at approximately $30 million. While business organizations spoke frequently of PAC building, however, labor PAC contributions have held steady over the past three elections at approximately $50 million. Instead of focusing on contributions, labor seems to have diverted party soft money toward member education and mobilization purposes, to be described later.

These varying approaches to soft money donations start from different goals and resources. Many industry-specific groups are less interested in bringing about partisan change, so for them the evolution in soft money donations has been instigated by politicians, political trends, and pending legislation, not by the groups themselves. In the case of labor and peak business organizations, the goal is to affect elections; soft money has constantly been measured against alternative uses for the same money. These differing goals will likely produce different directions for soft money in future elections under BCRA.

Post-BCRA

Many of the large soft money donors with whom we spoke professed that they would not miss soft money and would be able to channel the money they had previously given to the parties into more efficient activities. Among unions, the pool of funds available for political purposes can be turned toward mobilization efforts. Unions may have a harder time than businesses in raising hard money, but they also have a track record of effectively using their treasury money elsewhere. Business soft money donors can try to convert from soft money donations to hard money donations. The BIPAC program is one instance of an effort to speed this conversion, but the immediate capacities of different organizations will vary with their past efforts at mobilizing employees to participate. (According to Federal Election Commission [FEC] data, only about 1,500 of the country's millions of business corporations have active PACs at all.) Outside of the business community, there are several examples of groups that can shift to hard money. For instance, the Association of Trial Lawyers of America, another major soft money donor, has tripled the size of its PAC since 1998 from $2 million to $6 million, and many observers have predicted that its PAC can easily continue to grow, because its members have enough disposable income to allow them to give. Some other groups may welcome the freedom from being pressured to give money they did not really want to give. However, we are also hearing stories of groups being pressed to give more hard money to incumbent Members, who then will turn excess over to the national party committees (see chapter 5).

Potential Indirect Effects

Several leaders of issue-oriented groups have told us in interviews that they expect to benefit from the redirection of contributions that had formerly gone to the parties. Organizations that solicit and collect (or "bundle") contributions from individuals are potential beneficiaries: Stephen Moore of the Club for Growth has spoken frequently about the club's potential new role as a standard bearer for people who can no longer donate to the Republican Party or who have grown frustrated with the spending priorities of the party's campaign committees. Currently existing liberal groups might also be expected to benefit from such a spillover effect, especially because of the greater reliance of the Democratic Party on soft money. However, leaders of some groups were skeptical that currently existing groups automatically would benefit. For example, Gloria Totten of the Progressive Majority said in a 2002 interview: "We expect some donors will see the value of a progressive organization like ours that brings more hard money into the process. But it won't be easy. There's sure to be a proliferation of '527' organizations [organizations registered as "political" under Section 527 of the Internal Revenue Code whose activities may be structured to avoid some campaign finance law regulations], and that's going to muddy the waters and be confusing to donors."

It should be noted that the soft money about which these leaders speak comes primarily from individuals, not corporations. That is, they are speaking about *motivated* givers. Business executives may have the wherewithal to give, but may not have the motivation to do so unless congressional party leaders ask them.

ELECTIONEERING

Pre-BCRA

Television advertising expenditures by nonparty organizations have increased since 1996, but the scope of this undisclosed activity is hard to measure over time. Perhaps the best estimates for 2000 were done by the Brennan Center for Justice, based on data initially provided by Kenneth Goldstein of the University of Wisconsin. Goldstein's material, in turn, was derived from data collected by the Campaign Media Analysis Group (CMAG) on all advertising in the country's seventy-five largest media markets. According to the Brennan Center, nonparty groups bought approximately $50 million of airtime in 2000 for electioneering advertising (Holman and McLoughlin 2001). (Comparable data for 2002 are not yet available.) The estimate is surely low, for reasons the authors acknowledge: for example, it only includes an estimate for purchasing airtime, with no production costs. However, the method is consistent across advertising categories, permitting us to conclude that nonparty groups spent about one-fourth as much on election-related advertising in 2000 as did the political parties.

Whatever the precise cost, this is a significant amount of money. Unlike the sources and amounts of candidate and party spending, the sources and amounts of this money did not have to be disclosed before BCRA. In addition, the new law's sponsors and opponents alike predicted that a ban on party soft money could increase the importance of nonparty groups. Sponsors offered this as a reason to regulate electioneering. Opponents said they expected the electioneering provisions to be found unconstitutional and argued, therefore, that the likely shift of soft money to electioneering was a reason not to ban soft money. Since both sides assumed some form of displacement, it behooves us to consider what kinds of groups engaged in the activities defined as electioneering by the new law and to consider how they might act when the law's provisions take effect.

The key question is what kinds of nonparty organizations in the past have chosen to pay for television and radio advertising, and why. Provided that one can afford the medium, and can afford politically to be identified with a message that is strong enough to cut through the clutter of other advertisements, broadcast advertising can be a cost-effective tool for groups that want to appeal to a diffuse audience broader than their own memberships or mailing lists. For groups that did find such advertising useful, the extent to which the new law restricts their political behavior will depend on how easily they can divert their resources away from television toward other forms of persuasion.

Resources and Constraints

The decision to use broadcast advertising depends on resources more broadly defined than just money, such as the size of a group's membership, the value of its reputation, or the appeal of its message. These factors are related and can fluctuate over time. For example, the 750,000-member Sierra Club estimates that it spent $2 million on television in 2002 (CMAG estimated the cost of its airtime purchases at $1.2 million, making the group the fifth-biggest nonparty buyer of election-related airtime in 2002). The Sierra Club's reputation and size—not too big or too small—helps explain its use of TV. It is large enough to do some membership mobilization, but small enough that its political impact would be limited if it communicated solely with its members. Therefore, when it was able to raise money from large contributions to its "527" committee, it decided to use its "brand name" to increase the saliency of environmental issues for nonmembers in targeted election races. The Brady Campaign to Prevent Gun Violence is a good example of fluctuating resources: the organization purchased television time in thirteen states during 2000, when shootings in public schools raised the public's concern over the issue, but scaled back its advertising in 2002, when gun issues were lower on the public agenda, to only one state (Maryland, where sniper attacks occurred).

For some groups, the ebbs and flows of resources are reinforced by internal considerations. Planned Parenthood, for instance, received a large grant from Jane Fonda's Pro-Choice Vote in 2000. The grant paid for a substantial portion of a $7.2-million advertising campaign against Republican presidential nominee George W. Bush (Wisconsin Advertising Project 2001). The decision to run these advertisements was unusual for Planned Parenthood because it is a service organization, with a federated structure, whose clinical operations rely on a bipartisan core of health care delivery personnel. That is, its organizational needs made the perception of partisanship, caused by the advertising campaign's singling out of a Republican candidate, riskier internally than the same operations would be for its normal ally, the National Abortion and Reproductive Rights Action League. In 2002—partly because it did not have a large outside grant and partly because it wanted to strengthen the organization's credibility—Planned Parenthood's television campaign was limited to a $660,000 campaign aimed primarily at raising issues and promoting Planned Parenthood without mentioning candidates. Several other issue groups in our interviews, including the National Rifle Association and Human Rights Campaign, also gave us reasons related to their resources, broadly defined, for their decision to avoid television and focus on more narrowly targeted media, on member contacts, or on providing political training to members.

The Move toward Targeted Personal Communication

Many groups with larger memberships have spoken of moving away from television for at least the past two election cycles. This development indicates that many groups with diverging ideological views can nonetheless effectively learn from each other. The National Associated for the Advancement of Colored People (NAACP) was cited by several organizations in this regard. In August 2000, the NAACP formed two new committees, the NAACP National Voter Fund (NVF), a 501(c)(4) social welfare organization, and Americans for Equality, a political committee as defined by section 527 of the tax code. The NVF reportedly raised most of its funds in 2000 from a single anonymous source. Some of the money was used to air two controversial commercials based on the murder of James Byrd in Texas (Campaign Finance Institute Task Force on Disclosure 2001). The bulk of the NVF's efforts, however, went into a direct contact program that served as a blueprint for other groups seeking to mobilize voters outside of their membership. The NVF identified 3.8 million infrequent voters in African-American areas of forty congressional districts, and made as many as nineteen contacts—by mail, telephone, or in person—with each potential voter. The campaign cost more than $11 million and drew upon forty thousand volunteers. The program required a major influx of new money to get off the ground, but its characteristics—reaching out to a targeted subgroup of nonvoters—made broadcast advertising inefficient after an initial flurry.

The NAACP's example tells us that a decision not to broadcast one's message may depend on a group's ability to single out and reach its targeted audience. For other groups with large membership bases, the ease of targeting one's own members can be another reason for moving away from TV. For example, the thirteen-million-member AFL-CIO spent $35 million on television advertising in 1996 but has spent a declining amount on television since then. In 2000, the labor federation spent only $10 million of its $40-million budget on television, concentrating instead on phone calls, mailings, and an estimated sixty thousand door-to-door contacts. In 2002, although the AFL-CIO still spent the second-largest amount on television of any group (an estimated $3.5 million), it pulled all of its television advertisements by October 7. According to political director Steven Rosenthal, the AFL-CIO advertises primarily in areas where there are few union members; in more heavily unionized areas, labor has concentrated on ensuring that union members are registered to vote, on dispatching union members to campaign door-to-door, or on increasing electioneering communication between shop stewards and workers. This development is perhaps most vividly illustrated in Nevada's Third District, where in 2002 union members conducted door-to-door visits with an estimated ten thousand union members, recording data on handheld personal organizers for analysis and follow-ups (Hitt and Hamburger 2002). The AFL-CIO's postelection surveys demonstrate the program's success, Rosenthal says: labor union members' share of the voting electorate has gone from 19 percent in 1992 and only 14 percent in 1994 to 23 percent in 1998 and 26 percent in 2000, while the percentage of union members among registered voters has held steady at 19 percent.

Labor's 1996 and 1998 successes were self-consciously copied by peak business organizations in 2000 and 2002. Organizations such as the U.S. Chamber of Commerce, the National Federation of Independent Businesses, and the Business Roundtable advertised extensively in 1996, 1998, and 2000 but were largely absent from the airwaves in 2002. Instead, general business organizations such as these, as well as industry groups such as the Associated Builders and Contractors, have helped their members walk through the legal issues surrounding political communication with employees and then helped them develop sophisticated websites to communicate with their employees. BIPAC developed a program entitled the "Prosperity Project," in which businesses encourage their employees to register and vote. BIPAC makes voting records and other materials available in a form that can easily be customized to emphasize each business's issues and to appear with the company's logo. BIPAC has also introduced state-level prosperity projects, has worked with individual businesses to customize issue messages to particular industries or regions of the country, and has expanded its use of Spanish-language materials. According to BIPAC's Greg Casey, BIPAC has now recruited several large businesses for the project—including Procter and Gamble, Halliburton, and Exxon-Mobil—and has gone from an audience of two million employees in 2000 to twenty million in 2002. Casey has spent much of his time since arriving at BIPAC in March of 1999 promoting this program, arguing that businesses can register voters for a fraction of the cost per voter that the AFL-CIO and the NAACP have incurred.

"Shell" Groups

Of course, not all organizations have internal members with whom to communicate. This is particularly true for ones we, perhaps unfairly, call "shell" organizations, for want of a better term. In 2000, Citizens for Better Medicare, Americans for Job Security, and American Family Voices attracted substantial attention for their large advertising purchases. None of their donors have been disclosed officially. Of the three, American Family Voices was the smallest, starting with $800,000 from the American Federation of State, County, and Municipal Employees to run negative advertising against George W. Bush at the end of the 2000 Republican National Convention (Campaign Finance Institute Task Force on Disclosure 2001). Americans for Job Security, reportedly funded by the insurance industry, was a bigger spender, purchasing an estimated $2.8 million in advertisements.

Citizens for Better Medicare, reportedly funded by the pharmaceutical industry, spent an estimated $15 million on candidate-specific advertising and $50 million on issue advertising in 2000. This made it the most prolific nonparty advertiser on television in 2000. In 2002, however, Citizens for Better Medicare had reconstituted itself, with a fraction of its 2000 budget, as a civic education group. A new pharmaceutical industry group that appeared in 2002, the United Seniors Association, was the biggest spender on television in the 2002 elections, disbursing an estimated $9 million just to pay for airtime in fifteen different markets (Wisconsin Advertising Project 2002).

These organizations exist primarily for the purpose of advertising. As the Citizens for Better Medicare's example shows, they can come and go without reflecting the persistence of their issues or the fortunes of their sponsors. For that reason, it is not clear—and cannot be clear without disclosure—whether some of these should be thought of as organizations at all, or as labels of convenience for the activities of others.

BCRA Time Window and Early Advertising

Any analysis of past activities to predict the potential impact of BCRA must take note of the new law's time window. The law will only apply to advertisements that appear within sixty days of a federal election or thirty days of a primary. In 2002, even without the compulsion of law, we already began to see many of the organizations in our study running their advertisements earlier than they had in the past—well before BCRA's future time window. Advertisements for the South Dakota Senate race began running in October 2001; the Sierra Club began its advertising campaign against Republican John Thune in that race in April 2002, months before the early June primary and only days after the filing date. Advertisements in Minnesota, likewise, aired well before the primary. The Club for Growth ran advertisements in open-seat primaries in Indiana, Iowa, New Jersey, Maryland, and New York more than a month before each state's primary in 2002; and during the summer it ran an advertisement against Senate Majority Leader Tom Daschle in South Dakota—not to influence Daschle's election (he was not running that year) but to demonstrate to the group's members early that it was committed to playing a role. According to the Sierra Club's Margaret Conway, "With more money in a race, everyone is extending their advertising farther and farther away from Election Day. They're starting earlier than they ever had, and so that drives us earlier and earlier as well."

Post-BCRA

Electioneering has largely been self-motivated, rather than a response to appeals from candidates or the parties. While there have sometimes been questions about candidates and organizations using "winks and nods" to skirt the edges of illegal "coordination," there have been at least as many stories of candidates expressing frustration at supposedly friendly advertisements that take them "off message" or identify them with controversial or polarizing groups. Because their money is pushed into the system, rather than pulled, electioneering groups are often quite different from soft money contributors in their goals, resources, and constraints.

Presumably, if BCRA's electioneering provisions stand, television advertising will be less common, or earlier—or if late will avoid identifying candidates by name. Of course, this still could leave substantial room for television advertising, particularly for groups that use it to set an early agenda or to promote their own identities. Nevertheless, television advertising is only one of a range of options open to an issue group. The audiences for all traditional mass communications vehicles are shrinking, but TV and radio are the only media regulated by BCRA. Even before BCRA, groups of all types (other than shell groups) were increasing their use of media other than television. Because these groups push money into the system, rather than having it pulled from them reluctantly, we expect them to continue to spend after BCRA. Spurred in part by research showing the efficacy of personal contact for voter mobilization (Gerber and Green 2000), by the small number of competitive races, and by the close partisan balance in Congress, labor unions and peak business associations in particular have already been turning toward direct voter contact. Issue groups also have much experience with direct mail, and several groups reported to us in 2000 and 2002 that they had been diverting more of their resources toward the Internet, prerecorded phone messages, and other techniques. This trend would likely continue without BCRA, but BCRA will solidify this direction.

CONCLUSION

To conclude this analysis, we turn the argument on its side, so to speak. So far, we have ordered the discussion according to the kinds of electoral activities in which an organization might engage. We shall now recapitulate the discussion by type of organization. The types are by no means hard-and-fast, but they are nonetheless useful to our discussion (see table 3.1).

In our view, BCRA's strongest impact may be on those corporations and trade associations that gave soft money largely for access. Major business associations will try to motivate them to participate, as will Republican congressional leaders, but these businesses have resisted similar entreaties in the past. We assume that some will resist again, while others will increase their hard money contributions. The impact of the electioneering provisions will be more mixed and uncertain. Peak business organizations and labor unions that were moving away from television anyway should be prepared for the landscape they will confront under BCRA. However, some organizations clearly continue to think late television advertising was politically useful in 2002. These groups will have to rethink their tactics. Most ideological organizations probably will be motivated to remain active, within the law, but their ability to shift communications methods may depend on the characteristics of their membership and donor bases. Finally, shell groups that spent corporate or labor funds on electioneering will have to change. If they shift to an earlier phase of the cycle, this will have the fully intended effect of shielding candidates from anonymous, last-minute attack ads on television or radio. But if the donors who underwrite the shell groups continue to find it in their interest to pay for late advertising, the same attack ads could migrate to telephone, direct mail, or the Internet.

The conclusions in this chapter so far have been based on straightforward readings of BCRA. We must, therefore, add two significant caveats. The first has to do with a potential Supreme Court decision. BCRA's electioneering restrictions extend to nonprofit issue advocacy corporations. If the Court strikes this down, while keeping the rest of BCRA's original issue ad provisions for unions and businesses, the ruling would allow nonprofit organizations to use individual contributions to pay for unlimited electioneering advertising. This would help a few politically significant ideological organizations that have good individual fund-raising capabilities, particularly if their membership characteristics make it hard for them to shift toward grassroots mobilization campaigns. However, if

Table 3.1 Group Activities Before and After BCRA by Type of Group

	Group Type					
	Business/Industry	*Business/Peak*	*Labor*	*Issue/Ideological/ Membership*	*Issue/Ideological/ Nonmembership*	*Shell Groups*
Examples in Our Study	National Association of Realtors, Associated Builders and Contractors, Association of Trial Lawyers of America	Business-Industry PAC, U.S. Chamber of Commerce	AFL-CIO, National Education Association, SEIU	Sierra Club, League of Conservation Voters, National Rifle Association, Brady Campaign	Club for Growth, Progressive Majority PAC, EMILY's List	United Seniors Association, Americans for Job Security, American Family Voices
Money/Activity Pushed versus Pulled	Pulled (primarily)	Pushed (primarily, but mixed)	Pushed	Pushed	Pushed	Pushed (pass-through)
Pre-BCRA Activities	PAC contributions, soft money	PAC contributions, grassroots work; TV largely absent in 2002	Grassroots work, PAC contributions, soft money, TV and other advertising	TV, radio, and other advertising; endorsements; some grassroots	Bundled contributions; some TV and soft money; other advertising	TV, mail, telephone, and other advertising
Post-BCRA Prediction	Increase PAC and individual hard money giving. More internal communication to increase willingness to give hard money—that is, to convert from pulled to pushed. Some unmotivated money may stay on the sidelines.	Internal communications and mobilization	Redirect soft money and issue ad money to internal communication mobilization. May be some early ads to frame agenda.	Earlier TV. Shift later TV money to mail, phone, etc. Form more complex organizations, with different pieces conforming to different sections of the tax code.	Continue bundling; increase Internet to facilitate; redirect advertising. Form complex organizations, with pieces conforming to different sections of the tax code.	Decrease in TV ads from undisclosed sources late in campaign. If groups survive, will be because sponsors wish to shift advertising earlier, or into media that do not trigger disclosure.

the Court strikes down the underlying ban on corporate and labor contributions, the effect could be even more significant, depending on the rule of law used for the holding. Under the narrowest possibility, it would return electioneering to the status quo ante BCRA, with the qualification that organizations would have to disclose their donors. (Of course, disclosure by itself would deter some contributions.) Under the broadest possibility, the Court could declare broad First Amendment rights for corporations and labor unions, overturning long-settled law by permitting direct labor and corporate involvement in a broad range of campaign activities. This could, in turn, lead to more basic shifts of political power than anything we have described so far in this chapter.

Beyond the court ruling, we need to be aware that statutes take on meaning as they are enforced. Several of the FEC's regulations for BCRA could well affect the scope allowed to advocacy organizations. For example, the FEC has said that it would exclude from the definition of "electioneering" any communication by a nonprofit charitable corporation organized under section 501(c)(3) of the tax code. Its rationale was that it did not want to create unnecessary burdens for these organizations, since they are prohibited from political activity anyway under the tax code, and the Internal Revenue Service enforces the probation effectively. But reform organizations that supported BCRA were concerned that a sweeping exemption for 501(c)(3) corporations would encourage activities not yet foreseen (Campaign Finance Institute 2002a). As a second example: the statute explicitly permits federal officials and candidates to help raise money for the general treasuries of nonprofit 501(c)(4) social welfare organizations, including many of the advocacy organizations mentioned in this chapter. Combined with the growth of quasi-party organizations created in reaction to BCRA (see chapter 5), this could be a window through which Members of Congress, including party leaders, are able to pull money back into the system that might otherwise have been lost. If so, the effect will probably favor organizations whose agendas mesh with those of the party leaders or other fund-raising superstars.

In short, BCRA has set a dynamic process into motion. We do not subscribe to the "hydraulic" theory, which argues that money, like water, will finds its way back into the system without transformation, no matter what law or regulation Congress might pass (Malbin et al. 2002). Our view is that much of the money will find its way back, but not all of it, and not without change. The organizations that continue to participate will do so on an altered playing field that favors some of them more than others. Moreover, the playing field is still changing, and will continue to do so as the FEC and judges, candidates, party leaders, and new organizations all adapt to the new law and alter its legal meaning in practice. These structural changes, in turn, will be interpreted by group leaders who have to make cost-effective decisions to use their organizations' particular resources in a way that makes the best of changing technologies in a shifting political and issue environment. No one ever said their jobs would be simple.

4

With Limits Raised, Who Will Give More? The Impact of BCRA on Individual Donors

Clyde Wilcox, Alexandra Cooper, Peter Francia, John C. Green, Paul S. Herrnson, Lynda Powell, Jason Reifler, Mark J. Rozell, and Benjamin A. Webster

Although most of the attention in the debate over the Bipartisan Campaign Reform Act of 2002 (BCRA) and its impact has focused on soft money and issue advocacy, the law also increases the limits on donations that individuals can give to candidates and to political parties. This provision was actively debated, and both sides shared an assumption that significant numbers would give more if the limits were raised. Yet neither side had evidence to support this assumption. We will use data from two surveys of contributors to help us understand who will give more when the limits are raised.

Individual contributors are the major financiers of congressional elections and presidential nomination campaigns. In each election cycle since 1978, when the Federal Election Commission began collecting such data, individuals have provided the vast majority of funds that were raised by Republican and Democratic candidates, and have been the major source of funds of parties and political action committees (PACs) as well. Thus, the increased individual contribution limits enacted by BCRA will affect the most important source of funds for federal campaigns. Although individual donors receive much less attention than party or PAC contributions, they are central to understanding how the campaign finance system may change under the new law.

In this chapter we draw on two recent surveys of individual donors to federal

61

campaigns as well as the literature on individual donors (Brown, Powell, and Wilcox 1995; Francia et al. 2003, in press) to investigate the likely effects of the increased contribution limits. Although our findings must be speculative, we find that there is likely to be a modest yet significant increase in giving. This increase is most likely to come from wealthy businessmen who are active in politics, Republican, conservative, and comfortable with the new campaign system. Congressional Republicans and business-oriented presidential candidates in both parties are the most likely to benefit from these expanded donations, at least initially.

Of course, the net impact of the law will depend not only on increased limits on hard money, but on the soft money ban, limits on issue advocacy, and other provisions. The soft money ban may well eliminate a major source of conservative business money in elections (see Boatright et al., chapter 3). Our data suggests that the increase in individual giving will be only a fraction of the amount previously given as soft money. Thus the ultimate impact of BCRA will depend both on how individual donors respond and on how much corporate soft money finds another way into the campaign finance system, among other things.

THE LAW: FECA AND BCRA

In 1974, Congress amended the Federal Election Campaign Act of 1971 (FECA) to produce one of the most sweeping campaign finance reforms in United States history (Corrado 2000). These reforms imposed limits on individual contributions to candidates, PACs, or parties for federal elections. Funds raised under these limits came to be known as "hard money," and the centerpiece of the hard money system was limits on individual donors.

Under FECA, individual donors were limited to giving $1,000 to any specific federal candidate in any specific election; this generally capped contributions to any single congressional candidate at $2,000, including for the primary and general elections (exceptions included special and runoff elections, for which the limits were correspondingly higher). The $1,000 limit also applied to presidential primary campaigns, where the first $250 could be matched by public funds if the candidate decided to accept matching money and abide by other restrictions. If major party presidential nominees accepted the general election public financing, they were prohibited from accepting individual contributions to presidential general election campaigns. If candidates did not accept public funds, or were not eligible (such as minor party candidates), the $1,000 limit applied to general elections as well. In addition, individual donors faced other limits: $20,000 to political party committees in any year ($40,000 per election cycle); $5,000 to a PAC; and a total limit for contributions to all candidates, parties, and PACs, capped at $25,000 per year ($50,000 per election cycle).

These individual contribution limits did not increase between 1974 and 2000, and the double-digit inflation of the 1970s has eroded the value of the original

$1,000 donations to candidates. By 2001, it would have taken $3,834 to purchase the same basket of goods that $1,000 bought in 1974. The $50,000 overall contribution limit was so eroded by inflation that in 2001 it was worth only $13,042 in 1974 dollars. For campaigns that relied on television advertising, such as senatorial and presidential primary races, the effect was even more dramatic, for media costs rose more quickly than the overall cost of living.

Candidates responded to the decreasing value of the maximum contribution by soliciting larger numbers of contributors and by seeking to increase the average size of donations (Green and Bigelow 2002; Herrnson and Patterson 2002). In addition, party leaders spent increasing amounts of time soliciting large soft money contributions from corporations, unions, other interest groups, and wealthy individuals (see Dwyre and Kolodny, chapter 5). Many interest groups ran "issue advocacy" campaigns to increase their impact on elections (Cigler 2002; Magleby 2002b). Taken together, all these changes seriously undermined the campaign finance system created by FECA (Wilcox 2002).

BCRA was a response to these changes, and in large part sought to restore the system created by FECA. Its key elements include a ban on most soft money, some restrictions of issues advocacy by corporations and unions, and, of most relevance here, an increase in the individual hard dollar contribution limits. The maximum contribution to federal candidates was doubled to $2,000 per election, restoring less than one-half the original purchasing power of the 1974 $1,000 donations. In addition, the overall contribution limit for individuals in a two-year election cycle was increased to $57,500 to all parties and PACs, and $37,500 to federal candidates, for a grand total of $95,000. Individual contributions to candidates and parties (but not PACs) are indexed to inflation. The individual contribution limits to candidates are substantially relaxed in the case of candidates running against "millionaires" who self-finance their campaigns (see table 1.1 for the details of BCRA).

The reform community was divided over the increase in the individual hard money limits in BCRA. Many reformers argued that the increased individual contribution limits would allow federal candidates and parties to finance their activities without reliance on very large soft money contributions, and also lessen the incentives for extensive issue advocacy efforts by interest groups. They noted that increasing the contribution limits would restore only part of the effects of inflation on the original contribution limits. And many noted that, without an increase in the limits, the entire package would likely fail.

But others argued that the increased contribution limits would expand the role of the wealthy in national politics. They argued that only the wealthiest donors would increase their contributions, and that some financial constituencies (especially business) would be the most likely to respond to changes in the law. They believed that raising the limits would remove the incentive for candidates and parties to broaden their financial base in an effort to replace the revenues lost by the soft money ban. Both these hopes and fears rest on the assumption that many individual contributors were constrained by the limits and would be willing to give more if the limits were raised.

The 2004 elections will be the first test of this assumption. What is the likely impact of increased limits on the funds raised from individual donors? Although it is certain that many donors will give more in 2004, the literature on campaign contributors suggests such donors will not be a random sample of all contributors, and thus, the impact will not be neutral in political terms, with some kinds of candidates—and the interests and issues they champion—benefiting relative to others.

THE DONOR SURVEYS

The data for this study come primarily from two surveys of individual contributors of at least $200, "significant contributions" that the law requires be disclosed to the Federal Election Commission (FEC). The first study was a mail survey of a national random sample of donors of $200 or more to congressional candidates competing in the 1996 congressional elections, drawn from FEC disclosure records. The initial wave of the survey was mailed in the summer of 1997, with two follow-up mailings. The response rate was 47 percent, excluding undeliverable questionnaires, producing 1,047 usable responses. These respondents were then matched with 1996 FEC contribution records, and this process generated 647 cases with complete survey and financial data. The data were weighted to reflect the likelihood of an individual donor being selected from the FEC records.

The second study was a mail survey of a stratified random sample of donors to the primary campaigns of the major Democratic and Republican presidential candidates in 2000. For most candidates, random samples of donors under and over $200 were drawn from the records of the FEC; the two exceptions were for Steve Forbes (who did not accept public financing and thus did not report his under-$200 donors) and Bush (who also did not report donors under $200, but information was available on his campaign website, www.georgewbush.com, during the campaign). The first wave was mailed in summer of 2001, with two to four follow-up mailings. The response rate was 50 percent, excluding undeliverable questionnaires, producing 2,881 usable responses. These respondents were then matched with 2000 FEC contribution data, and this process generated 2,655 cases with complete survey and financial data; 1,119 were significant donors. The data were weighted to reflect the likelihood of an individual donor being selected and the relative number of donors to each subset of the campaign.

We will focus on the significant congressional and presidential donors. These surveys were conducted four years apart, so it is possible that some of the differences that we observe are the result of changing attitudes over this period. Our data suggest that these two sets of donors are remarkably similar (Francia et al. 1999), but we will note where—and why—important differences occur.[1]

Both surveys asked respondents to predict how their own contributing to federal candidates would change if the individual limits were raised: Would they give more, give the same amount, or give less? This question allows for a baseline estimate of how many donors are likely to increase their giving under BCRA as well as estimates of the financial impact of such an increase. In addition, the surveys ascertained a wide range of information on the respondents' demography, political activities, views and affiliations, motives for giving, and attitudes toward campaign finance reform. This information will allow us to assess the characteristics of donors who predict they would give more. Thus, it is helpful to begin with a brief overview of significant donors to congressional and presidential campaigns.

SIGNIFICANT DONORS: AN OVERVIEW

Table 4.1 provides some basic demographic information on significant donors to federal candidates. As one might imagine (and the literature on campaign contributors documents), significant donors are characterized by very high social status. It is not surprising that donors are wealthy, but it is worth noting just

Table 4.1   Demographic Profile of Congressional and Presidential Donors

	Congressional Survey (1996)	*Presidential Survey (2000)*
Annual Family Income		
Less than $100,000	22%	14%
$100–$249,000	40	42
$250–$500,000	24	21
More than $500,000	14	23
Education		
Less than college degree	19	14
College degree	23	27
Some graduate training	12	12
Postgraduate degree	48	47
Age		
35 years or less	3	2
35–50 years	29	29
50–65	42	41
Over 65 years	27	28
Gender		
Male	77	70

Source: Surveys by authors.

how affluent they are. Almost 80 percent of the congressional donors and an even larger percentage of the presidential donors reported an annual family income of more than $100,000 a year. About one-sixth of congressional donors and more than one-fifth of the presidential donors had income of greater than $500,000 a year. These donors are also well educated, with nearly one-half holding postgraduate degrees, typically JDs or MBAs. Most are employed in business or the professions, such as law or medicine, although a sizable minority works in government, politics, or the nonprofit sector (data not shown).

This high socioeconomic status is associated with other social characteristics. For instance, significant donors tend to be older, with more than one-half of each sample over fifty years of age, and only a tiny portion under 35. These donors are also overwhelmingly male, despite the recent entrance of women into electoral politics (Wilcox, Brown, and Powell 1993). In addition, almost all such donors are white, and they are drawn from the dominant ethnic, cultural, and religious groups (data not shown). Thus, significant donors to federal candidates are elites in sociological terms, and quite unrepresentative of the American population as a whole (Francia et al. 1999).

Interestingly, this basic pattern has changed little since the introduction of individual contribution limits with FECA (Brown, Powell, and Wilcox 1995; Francia et al. 2003, in press; Wilcox et al. 2002). Despite the pressures on candidates and parties to recruit more contributors, donors in 2000 were just as concentrated among affluent white businessmen as they were in 1972. In addition, the "small" donors, those who gave less than $200 to federal campaigns, also tend to partake of elite social status compared to the public at large, with the biggest difference between them and the significant donors being income. It is thus unlikely that BCRA will alter the social profile of significant donors very much, although it might change the relative influence of elements among the significant donors.

One reason for this stability is that significant donors are part of a continuing pool of campaign contributors, many of who give habitually in every election. There is somewhat more variation among presidential donors because of the flux of candidates from year to year. For example, the greater wealth of the 2000 presidential donors compared to the 1996 congressional donors (table 4.1) reflects in part the unprecedented fund-raising among wealthy citizens of George W. Bush; the 1996 presidential donors were less affluent than their congressional counterparts (Francia et al. 1999).

But as table 4.2 reveals, one-half of the 1996 congressional donors reported giving to House or Senate candidates in "most" elections, and only slightly fewer of the 2000 presidential donors gave the same report. Indeed, many congressional donors give to presidential candidates in most elections, and many presidential contributors give to House and Senate candidates in most elections as well. George Bush's record-breaking campaign was not a result of mobilizing many new GOP donors—he had half as many first-time donors as other presi-

Table 4.2   Political Profile of Congressional and Presidential Donors

	Congressional Survey (1996)	Presidential Survey (2000)
Political Activity*		
Give most elections	50%	46%
Work most elections	20	11
Partisanship		
Strong Republican	16	18
Weak/Lean Republican	34	36
Pure Independent	19	16
Weak/Lean Democrat	19	18
Strong Democrat	12	12
Ideology		
Conservative	46	56
Moderate	22	15
Liberal	32	29
Group Membership		
Business association	63	60
Professional association	63	54
Labor union	2	2
Pro-Gun group	23	24
Conservative group	21	18
Pro-Life group	11	10
Environmentalist group	26	26
Pro-Choice group	17	17
Liberal group	10	9

Source: Surveys by the authors.
Note: *For congressional donors, the political activity items refer to House or Senate campaigns; for presidential donors, the items refer to presidential campaigns.

dential candidates. Instead, he mobilized more occasional presidential donors, and convinced those who routinely had given modest amounts to make maximum contributions.

The remaining items in table 4.2 complete a political profile of the significant donors. Republicans greatly outnumber Democrats, especially among congressional donors. There is only a slight GOP edge among strong partisans, but the largest single group is made up of weak Republicans. Significant donors also tend to be conservative in ideology, with a sizable minority of moderates and liberals. In 2000, as in 1996, presidential donors were more conservative than their congressional counterparts.

Despite their elite social status, significant donors do not think alike on all political issues. Republican donors tend to be quite conservative on economic issues, but many are moderate to liberal on social questions. Meanwhile, Democratic donors are more moderate to liberal on economic questions and strongly liberal on social questions.

This combination of social homogeneity and political diversity is reflected in the interest groups to which the donors report belonging (table 4.2). A majority of donors are members of business and professional associations, and union members are very rare. Business group members outnumber union members by a wide margin even among Democratic donors. But membership in ideological groups is more diverse. Significant minorities of both sets of donors belong to prominent conservative and liberal interest groups. Republican donors are more often members of gun owner, conservative, and pro-life groups, while Democrats are more often members of environmental, pro-choice, or liberal groups.

Significant donors also have a mix of motives for contributing to congressional and presidential candidates. Table 4.3 illustrates the three most common types of motivations, listing the percentage of each group reporting a particular motive was "always important" or "very important" to their giving. Most donors claimed to give for purposive reasons, such as the candidate's ideology (better than two-thirds) or partisanship (roughly one-third). Many fewer admitted to a material motivation, but nonetheless one-quarter of the congressional donors reported giving to a candidate who would treat their business fairly or whom they saw as friendly to their industry; the presidential donors named these kinds

Table 4.3   Motivations of Congressional and Presidential Donors

	Congressional Survey (1996)	Presidential Survey (2000)
Purposive Motivations		
Candidate's ideology	69%	75%
Candidate's party	31	35
Material Motivations		
Candidate treats business fairly	23	32
Candidate friendly to industry	25	23
Solidary Motives		
Enjoy social contacts	3	5
Personal recognition	1	2

Source: Surveys by authors.
Note: Percentage of respondents who said these reasons were "always important" or "very important" for contributing. Percentages total more than 100% because respondents were allowed to give more than one reason.

of motives at roughly the same frequency. Far fewer donors reported solidary motives, such as giving because of social contacts or personal recognition. As might be expected, donors tend to give to candidates who can respond to these motivations: purposive motives lead donors to back candidates with a similar perspective; material motives produce support for candidates who can provide tangible benefits; solidary motives generate support for candidates who are part of social and political networks.

In sum, the donor pool is quite homogenous in its social characteristics, but its members differ in their motives and political views. Candidates (especially Democrats) who mingle with donors at fund-raising events may well hear support for social welfare programs, but they are unlikely to meet anyone who has ever actually received these benefits. To paraphrase Schattschneider's famous observation, donors may sing with a strong upper-class accent, but they do not all sing the same song (Schattschneider 1960, 35).

DONOR ATTITUDES TOWARD
CAMPAIGN FINANCE REFORM

Before we turn to the impact of BCRA on donor behavior, it is worth considering donor attitudes toward campaign finance reform, and the provisions of BCRA in particular. Table 4.4 reports an overall evaluation of the campaign finance system, followed by agreement and disagreement with various reform provisions (for ease of presentation, the "no opinion" responses are omitted from the table).

Overall, the significant donors had a negative view of the campaign finance system. About one-third of the congressional donors and nearly one-fifth of the presidential donors claimed that the finance system "is broken and needs to be replaced." Roughly one-half of both groups felt the system "has problems and needs to be changed." Just one-fifth of the congressional donors and almost one-third of the presidential donors claimed it "has some problems but is basically sound." This last figure contains a tiny proportion of the respondents who believed the system "is all right just the way it is and should not be changed."

It is significant that these participants in the campaign finance system had such a negative evaluation. However, it is unclear why presidential donors had a less negative opinion of the system than their congressional counterparts. Perhaps the run-up to the passage of BCRA improved these donors' views of the role of money in politics, or it could be the presidential system is perceived as less problematic. Or this pattern may reflect the greater conservatism of the presidential donors: George Bush's donors make up a major portion of the donor pool, and they were the least likely to think that the campaign finance system was broken. In any event, this small difference persists in the attitudes toward the specific reform proposals.

Table 4.4 Congressional and Presidential Donors' Attitudes toward Campaign Finance Reform

	Congressional Survey (1996)	*Presidential Survey (2000)*
The system:		
Is broken	32%	19%
Has problems	46	50
Is basically sound	22	31
Reform Proposals:		
Ban soft money		
Agree	77	72
Disagree	12	16
Limit candidate spending		
Agree	74	68
Disagree	20	24
Ban PAC contributions		
Agree	53	49
Disagree	33	32
Limit issue advocacy ads		
Agree	n.a.	40
Disagree	n.a.	31
Free media for candidate		
Agree	41	42
Disagree	45	44
Public financing		
Agree	39	34
Disagree	46	52
Raise individual limits		
Agree	37	51
Disagree	42	32
No limits, full disclosure		
Agree	34	42
Disagree	48	40
Raise party limits		
Agree	26	31
Disagree	51	40

Source: Surveys by authors.
Note: n.a. = item not asked.

Consistent with their negative evaluation of the campaign finance system, both sets of donors were supportive of many reform proposals. Three-quarters of both sets of donors supported a ban on soft money, the cornerstone of BCRA. Large majorities also favored limiting candidate spending, a reform that is not part of BCRA and could only be implemented on a voluntary basis.

Roughly one-half of each set of donors agreed with banning PACs, and one-third disagreed. Two-fifths of presidential donors supported limits on issue advocacy, an issue addressed in BCRA. This question was not asked of the congressional donors, but given the similarity of responses on the other reform questions, they may well hold a similarly ambivalent view. Donors were evenly divided on provisions of free media time, and both groups of donors opposed expanding public financing. These public subsidies were supported by large majorities of Democratic donors, but opposed by the larger number of Republican contributors. The final three items in the table relate to contribution limits, including raising individual limits, the object of our concern here. This item produces the largest difference between the two sets of donors: a plurality of the congressional donors opposed raising the limits, while one-half of the presidential donors supported this key provision of BCRA. The strong support among presidential donors was again due to the size of the Bush donor set: 62 percent of Bush's donors favored increasing the limits, compared with only 40 percent of those who gave to other candidates.

Congressional donors also disagreed with the idea of eliminating all contribution limits in return for full financial disclosure, where the presidential donors were evenly divided. Finally, neither group backed raising the contribution limits for parties, although the presidential donors were more supportive.

There are sharp partisan divisions behind these patterns (Francia et al. 2000; Webster et al. 2001). Democrats tend to favor public financing and oppose higher contribution limits, while Republicans oppose public financing and favor fewer restrictions. However, there is something of a consensus for the major provision of BCRA, banning soft money, and some backing for the other key provisions, issue advocacy restrictions and higher individual contribution limits.

INDIVIDUAL DONATIONS UNDER BCRA

In both the 1996 and 2000 surveys, we asked the contributors to predict how their own contributions would be affected if the contribution limits were raised. The responses give us a minimum estimate of donors' response to this provision in BCRA—minimum because the question was asked in the abstract, and not in the context of a campaign and a solicitation from a candidate. Put another way, this measure reveals an underlying preference for making large contributions to candidates.

Among the 1996 congressional donors of $200 or more, 15 percent said they would give more if the limits were raised, 5 percent said that they would give less, and 80 percent indicated that they would give the same amount. Among the 2000 presidential donors, 22 percent said they would give more, 2 percent would give less, and the rest would not change the level of their contributing. Respondents who made at least one $1,000 donation were more likely to report they would give more: 20 percent for the congressional donors and 32 percent for the presidential donors. Other similar evidence put these findings in context. On the one hand, 30 percent of a 1996 sample of the largest donors to federal candidates reported they would give more (Wilcox et al. 2002), and on the other hand, just 4 percent of the small presidential donors in 2000 reported they would give more.

The fact that the overwhelming majority of donors predicted their giving would not change is hardly surprising: most of the reasons for making a donation would be unchanged by increased limits. But why would anyone give less money as a result of an increase in contribution limits?

Donors who indicated that they would give less were much more critical of the campaign finance system, and the most likely to support spending limits, bans on soft money, and public financing. They apparently believed that the campaign finance system is already awash in too much money, and predicted that if the limits were raised they would reduce their involvement in the system. Of course, some of these donors will probably continue to give and may even give more in response to increased solicitation from candidates.

Many of the donors who predicted they would give more did not make a maximum $1,000 contribution to a candidate. Indeed, fully two-thirds of congressional donors who said that they would give more, and one-third of the presidential donors who predicted that they would increase their giving, did not make a maximum contribution in the year that we surveyed them. Since FECA did not constrain their giving, why would they predict that they would give more if the limits were raised, as under BCRA?

These donors are well educated and well integrated into political networks, so it is unlikely that they misunderstood the existing contribution limits. Instead, they may expect that solicitors who once asked them for $200 will ask for $400 in the future, or that a political dinner that they like to attend will increase in price from $500 a plate to $1,000. It is also possible that these well-connected activists anticipate that campaign finance reforms will restrict other sources of funds, thus increasing the pressure on them to give more to their favorite candidates. So, raising the individual limits may well increase giving across the board and not just among the $1,000 donors.

This is an important point that is worth emphasizing. Most of the studies that attempt to predict increased giving as a result of BCRA limit their analysis to donors who made maximum contributions. Our data suggest that this ignores a large number of donors of smaller amounts who expect to give more.

At face value, these figures support the assumption by reformers that some individual donations were indeed constrained by the limits, especially but not exclusively among the largest givers. But these figures also suggest that this pent-up supply of hard money may be smaller than anticipated. Fully exploiting the higher limits under BCRA may require intensive and extensive fund-raising efforts by candidates.

WHO WILL GIVE MORE?

Our survey data can suggest which donors are most likely to respond to such fund-raising efforts under BCRA, and the impact will not be neutral in political terms. Table 4.5 reports on the characteristics of the donors who predicted they would give more under higher limits, presenting the items from tables 4.1 through 4.4 where the predicted increase was significantly larger than for the samples as a whole. For ease of interpretation, the overall predictions for both samples are listed at the top of the table.

Not surprisingly, the wealthiest donors were the most likely to say that they would give more. Donors with incomes of over $500,000 a year were most likely to predict giving more, and donors with the lowest incomes were the least likely to say that they would give more. Neither education nor age was clearly associated with increased giving (hence neither is listed in table 4.5). Men were somewhat more likely than women to say they would give more. In addition, the donors who predicted they would give more had a special political profile. First, the most active donors were the most likely to predict additional giving, including those who claimed to give to candidates or do campaign work in most elections. Strong Republicans and conservatives were also most likely to predict additional giving. Members of business and conservative interest groups also predicted expanding their donations, and among the presidential donors, so did members of gun owner and pro-life groups. In contrast, members of liberal, environmental, or pro-choice groups were *less* likely to predict increased giving compared to the samples a whole.

Donors' motives revealed a sharp difference between the congressional and presidential donors. Among congressional donors, those with material motives were most likely to say that they would give more. These "investors" were more likely to say that they gave to back candidates who would be fair and friendly to their business or industry. Among presidential donors, it was those motivated by ideology who were most likely to predict an increase in their giving. This divergence may reflect the differences between Congress and the White House as political institutions.

Among both congressional and presidential donors, those who thought the campaign finance system was "basically sound" were more likely to predict they would give more. And donors who agreed with raising individual limits were most likely to predict they would take advantage of such a change personally. (Some of the other reform items in table 4.4 showed a similar pattern, but they

Table 4.5   Who Would Give More with Higher Limits?

	Congressional Survey (1996)			Presidential Survey (2000)		
	More	*Same*	*Less*	*More*	*Same*	*Less*
All	15%	80%	4%	22%	73%	2%
Demography						
Income over $500,000	25	73	2	36	64	0
Male	18	78	4	25	73	2
Political Activity*						
Give in most elections	19	79	3	31	68	1
Work in most elections	24	73	3	43	57	0
Partisanship						
Strong Republican	25	72	3	25	74	1
Ideology						
Conservative	19	77	4	25	74	2
Group Membership						
Business association	20	80	4	25	74	1
Conservative group	24	71	4	29	71	0
Gun owner group	—	—	—	27	71	2
Pro-Life group	—	—	—	32	63	5
Liberal group	7	90	3	—	—	—
Environmental group	11	85	5	19	79	2
Pro-Choice group	—	—	—	15	82	3
Motives						
Candidate's partisanship	—	—	—	26	73	1
Treats business fairly	23	73	4	—	—	—
Friendly to industry	21	76	4	—	—	—
Support for Reform						
System basically sound	25	73	1	37	63	1
Raise individual limits	30	68	2	36	84	0

Source: Surveys by authors.

Notes: Dash (—) indicates that difference from sample as a whole not statistically significant.

*For congressional donors, the political activity items refer to House or Senate campaigns; for presidential donors, the items refer to presidential campaigns.

Level of confidence: Plus or minus 3 percentage points.

were highly correlated with increased limits and are excluded for ease of presentation).

Multivariate analysis of these data (not shown) confirm the overall patterns in table 4.5: the donors most likely to give more were wealthy, politically active, Republican, conservative businessmen. This pattern can be illustrated by considering a paired comparison from the 1996 congressional survey. Among wealthy Republicans who were members of business groups and conservative on economic issues, more than 30 percent predicted they would give more. Among wealthy Democrats who were not members of business groups and were liberal on economic issues, only 5 percent predicted they would increase their giving. Clearly the increased limits have partisan and ideological implications.

How Much More Will Donors Give?

Thus, if the donors' predictions of their own behavior hold true, the expanded individual contribution limits are most likely to benefit Republican candidates in the short run. But how much will this increase be? Here our survey questions are not precise—they merely ask whether donors will give more or less, and not how much. Differing assumptions yield different estimates of the magnitude of such gains.

For 1996 congressional donors, the following scenarios provide a sense of the possibilities:

- If all donors who said that they would give more doubled their contributions, and all donors who said that they would give less halved their contributions, the net Republican congressional contributions from the donors we surveyed would increase by 26 percent, while the Democratic net contributions would go up by 13 percent.
- If only those donors who gave $1,000 to a single candidate doubled their contributions, but all who said that they would give less halved their contributions, then the net GOP contributions would go up by 24 percent, and the net Democratic contributions would increase by 10 percent.

The first scenario suggests that congressional fund-raising would have been $49.1 million higher in 1996 if the higher limits had been in place ($35.3 million for Republican and $13.8 million for the Democratic candidates). As one might expect, incumbents of both parties (and especially Republicans) would benefit the most from such increases in giving, for those who say that they will give more direct more of their money to incumbents in Congress than other donors. The real losers in terms of aggregate funds, however, would be Democratic challengers, who would appear to receive the least benefit from the new limits (Wilcox et al. 2002). It may be, however, that some challengers of both parties may find it easier to raise "seed money" for their campaigns under the new $2,000 limits (Campaign Finance Institute 2001). Clearly it would take half as many friends and supporters willing to make maximum contributions to enable a candidate to raise enough money to launch his or her campaign. Our data suggest that incumbents will raise far more money than challengers from those who will increase their giving, but challengers will raise more than they did before, and this may be more important to their campaigns. For the 2000 presidential donors, the analogous scenarios produce much more even results:

- If all donors who said that they would give more doubled their contributions, and all donors who said that they would give less halved their contributions, the net Republican congressional contributions from the donors we surveyed would increase by 26 percent, while the Democratic net contributions would go up by 24 percent.
- If all donors who gave $1,000 to a single candidate doubled their contributions, and all donors who said that they would give less halved their contributions, the net Republican congressional contributions from the donors we surveyed would increase by 20 percent, while the Democratic net contributions would go up by 20 percent.

The cause of this partisan near-parity is the percentage of donors to each candidate who predicted they would give more. As figure 4.1 shows, such percentages were strikingly uniform across the major presidential candidates, with only a modest partisan difference. Only contributors to Gary Bauer and Ralph Nader were distinctive in their low levels of willingness to give more, with the rest of the candidates ranging from 17 percent for McCain to 28 percent for Buchanan.

Some of these differences among the presidential candidates are easier to explain than others. Both Nader and McCain made an issue of the pernicious role of "big money" in politics, so it is perhaps not surprising that Nader's donors are unlikely to give more, and that fewer of McCain's donors would give more than contributors to most other GOP candidates. In contrast, George Bush's campaign emphasized its success among large donors, and not surprisingly fully a quarter of contributors to his campaign say that they will give more.

But the differences among donors to Bauer, Buchanan, and Keyes are more difficult to explain. Bauer's donors were unlikely to say that they would give more, whereas Buchanan's donors were the most likely to predict an increase in their giving. All three candidates ran campaigns that appealed to strong social conservatives, and all raised most of their money in small contributions through direct mail. Bauer stood alone as the only candidate in this trio seeking the presidency for the first time. More than one-third of Bauer's donors were new to presidential contributing, and few of these new donors said that they would give more if the limits were raised. Patrick Buchanan's third presidential bid was mostly funded by repeat contributors—only 6 percent of his donors reported giving for the first time. And Buchanan's donors stand out as the most likely to

Figure 4.1   Donors Who Would Give More, by Candidate

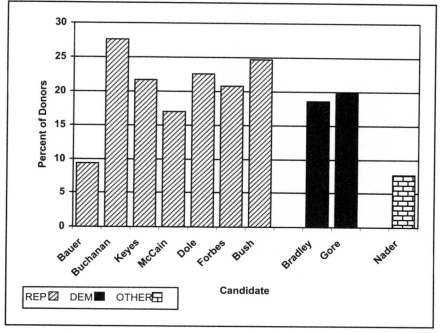

Source: Surveys by the authors.

increase their giving, more than even those who gave to Bush. Yet Buchanan's advantage is illusory, for he had many fewer donors overall.

It is important to remember that in the 2000 presidential race the Republican candidates raised much more money than the Democrats (Green and Bigelow 2002), largely because of Bush's record-setting $81 million dollars in significant individual donations. Democrats Al Gore and Bill Bradley raised just $28 million and $26 million, respectively; John McCain, Bush's main GOP rival, raised $17.6 million.

Under the first scenario above, Bush would enjoy an increase of 30 percent, or some $24.3 million dollars; under the second, more restrictive, scenario, he would gain 24 percent, or $19.4 million. In contrast, Gore's gain under the first scenario would be 24 percent for $6.7 million, and 21 percent under the second scenario for $5.8 million—in both cases just a fraction of Bush's increase. (The analogous figures for Bradley would be 25 percent and $6.5 million, and for the second scenario, 19 percent and $4.9 million).

Of course, presidential primaries are intraparty contests, so the more relevant comparison to Bush is McCain. Under the first scenario, McCain would gain 11 percent for $1.9 million, and under the second, 6 percent for $1 million. The other GOP contenders suffer a similar fate. Thus, the increased contribution limits would appear to favor business-oriented candidates over both reform-minded moderates and social conservatives within the GOP. Among the Democrats, the new rules probably favor moderates, which in the context of the 2000 race would have maintained the financial parity between Gore and Bradley.

However, one must be especially cautious in generalizing from presidential donors in a particular election cycle, since such candidates often mobilize new sets of donors. On the Republican side in 2000 there were many candidates representing a range of issue agendas, and one candidate who raised record sums. But there were only two Democratic candidates, neither of whom spoke to the hearts of the Democratic left. Ralph Nader's Green Party campaign could be thought of as a stand-in for such liberal candidates, but if so, the prospects are even less positive. The partisan implications of increased limits among presidential donors depend on how many of Bush's donors will continue to make maximum contributions to other candidates in future elections.

It is probably safe to say, though, that the increase in the limits provides a strong incentive for candidates who can attract enough money to forgo matching funds (see chapter 10). Bush would have raised far more with the increased limits, but the increase could also have made it more attractive for Bradley and Gore to refuse the match as well. In contrast, the additional funds that would have come to McCain had the limits been higher would have done his campaign little good, since he was up against the overall spending limit.

CONCLUSION

Taken at face value, our findings provide some support for the assumption by reformers that the individual contribution limits in FECA have generated a pent-up supply of hard dollar donations for federal campaigns. However, at least initially, the magnitude of these new funds is likely to be smaller than many reformers anticipated. Our minimum estimates suggest that between one-sixth and one-third of the significant donors to federal candidates are likely to give more. Under reasonable assumptions, this expanded giving is likely to increase overall campaign funds by one-fifth to one-quarter. Some of these gains will come from donors who had reached the maximum donation of $1,000, but additional funds will come from donors below the FECA maximum, due to the dynamics of fundraising under BCRA.

Furthermore, our findings reveal that the donors most likely to respond to the opportunity to give more have a distinctive profile: wealthy businessmen, very active in politics, Republican and conservative, more comfortable than other donors with the current campaign finance system as well as the changes wrought by BCRA. The congressional donors showed a higher level of material motivation and the presidential donors more purposive concerns. Thus, BCRA is unlikely to change the overall social and political character of the pool of significant donors, but it is likely to give business and conservative elements a greater presence in national politics. Thus, the fears of reformers who opposed the increased limits have some substance as well. Of course, the increased limits are only a small part of a complex overall package, and each element of the law may well have different effects. It is likely that the law will remove more soft money from the system than it puts back in increased hard money. The net partisan effects will depend on much more than the increased contributions by individual donors.

It appears likely that Republican congressional candidates will benefit more than their Democratic counterparts from the new individual contribution limits. This effect will surely be felt in general elections. Although our analysis of congressional donors is not fine grained enough to plausibly speculate about congressional primaries, our findings on presidential primary donors are instructive. Business-oriented candidates, such as George W. Bush, are likely to benefit more from the increased limits than more conservative and moderate rivals. In the Democratic contests, centrist candidates such as Al Gore and Bill Bradley will likely gain, but more liberal candidates will probably not.

Yet it is important to bear in mind that our findings are only predictions made by donors on how they would respond to increased limits in the abstract. There is a substantial industry of professional fund-raisers who study ways to part potential donors from their money, and they will doubtlessly adapt to the increased limits with new sets of appeals. Although many Democratic and liberal donors say that they will give less if the limits are raised, they may respond differently to a solicitor who shows them a new growing Republican advantage in congressional hard money or the potential gains of centrist Democrats, and urges them to give to avoid a policy "disaster." Thus, in the longer term, the effects of BCRA may be minimized at a higher level of individual giving. If so, BCRA may well substantially restore the role of individual donations envisioned in FECA.

If the increased limits provide as little additional monies as our survey suggests (especially for Democrats), then candidates may be forced to expand the donor pool. If candidates and parties use this opportunity to broaden the pool as well—to appeal beyond the narrow base of wealthy businessmen—then the donor pool might become a bit more representative. This would surely be a benefit to the reform as well.

NOTES

The authors would like to thank Anthony Corrado for sharing his data. The data collection for the congressional survey was made possible by grants from the Joyce Foundation, the Dirkson Foundation, and various university grants.

1. The figures presented here for the 1996 congressional donors differ slightly from those reported in Francia et al. (1999) due to a different weighting. The substantive conclusions are the same.

III

POLITICAL PARTIES

5

National Political Parties After BCRA

Diana Dwyre and Robin Kolodny

No organizations were affected more directly by BCRA than the two major parties' national, Senate, and House campaign committees. To help us think about the potential long-term effects of BCRA on the national parties, we discuss the parties in terms of their goals, resources, and the political environments in which they must operate. The parties' goals—to win majorities in the two houses of Congress and control of the presidency—will not change. Nor, for the near term, will the highly competitive political environment. What BCRA will change are the means by which parties acquire and spend resources.

The national party committees must change how they raise and spend money in order to continue winning elections to control government. The national parties are the only party committees inclined to focus exclusively on winning elections for *federal* office. Indeed, the national parties break down the responsibility by office, so that each type of federal candidate has a party committee devoted to its electoral interests. The Republican National Committee (RNC) and the Democratic National Committee (DNC) are concerned primarily with the party's campaign for the presidency. The National Republican Senatorial Committee (NRSC) and the Democratic Senatorial Campaign Committee (DSCC) work to elect their partisans to the U.S. Senate, and the National Republican Congressional Committee (NRCC) and the Democratic Congressional Campaign Committee (DCCC) support their parties' candidates for the U.S. House of Representatives.

Since the late 1980s, the national parties have adapted to a variety of changes in the campaign environment, and continue to follow strategies to maximize the number of seats won in Congress and to take the presidency. For congressional elections, the national parties invest their resources in the most competitive races to maximize their chances of holding on to the seats they already control and to win more seats. The close margin of control in both the House and the Senate in recent years has motivated both major parties to raise and spend extremely large sums of money and target those resources efficiently. During the 2002 elections, fewer than forty House seats (Walter 2002, 10) and only fifteen of the thirty-four contested Senate seats (Duffy 2002, 4) were thought to be competitive. To win the White House, the parties concentrate their resources on those few states that are both competitive and rich in electoral votes. In the 2000 election, the presidential candidates and their parties directed most of their energies and resources to only about seventeen states in the last few months of the election.

If the parties' electoral goals and short-term environment are settled, their resources are not. From the 1970s to the mid-1990s, the national parties relied on hard money to support their electoral efforts. After the mid-1990s, parties began to use soft money (which they had collected for "building fund" expenses and nonfederal elections since the early 1980s) to fund issue advocacy campaigns, which greatly increased the size of the parties' monetary presence in campaigns. BCRA restricts the ability of the national party committees to assist their candidates by prohibiting them from raising and spending soft money—the unlimited and largely unregulated contributions to the parties that came from wealthy individuals and otherwise prohibited sources such as corporations and labor unions. At the same time, the new law attempts to encourage hard money fund-raising and certain campaign activities over others, such as grassroots-voter mobilization rather than media campaigns. Thus the important question to ask is how BCRA will change the way that the national parties pursue these goals within this political environment.

WHAT HAS CHANGED?—RESOURCES

The most significant change for national parties is that they will no longer be permitted to raise or spend any soft money (and thus cannot use it for issue advocacy ads or operating expenses). The national party committees have raised tremendous amounts of soft money in recent years. Figure 5.1 shows the dramatic increase in national party soft money receipts since the early 1990s (when soft money receipts were first reported to the Federal Election Commission). The increase in soft money receipts for the 2002 midterm election compared to the 1998 midterm election is particularly significant, because the national party committees typically raise more during presidential election cycles than for the off-year elections. Soft money fund-raising was almost on par with the 2000 presidential election, a clear adjustment in anticipation of BCRA. We doubt the national party committees will be able to replace all of this soft money with hard money in the near future, though others may disagree. Yet, over time, the com-

Figure 5.1 **National Party Committees' Soft Money Receipts, through 20 Days after the General Election**

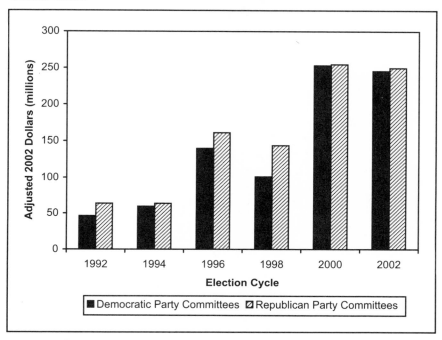

Source: FEC, "Party Fundraising Reaches $1.1 Billion in 2002 Election Cycle." Press Release, 18 December 2002.
Note: Does not include monies transferred among the listed committees.

mittees may find ways to raise large sums in hard money by expanding their donor base and altering the nature of their fund-raising appeals, much as they did throughout the 1980s (Kolodny and Dwyre 1998).

Indeed, the new law does increase the hard money contribution an individual may give to a national party committee, from $20,000 to all national party committees per year ($40,000 per two-year election cycle) to $25,000 per election cycle per party committee, with an aggregate total of $57,500 per cycle to all national party committees and PACs. (These limits, for the first time, were also indexed for inflation.) The amount individuals may give to candidates also increased, from $1,000 per election to $2,000 per election, also indexed for inflation. Yet the amount that a multicandidate PAC may contribute to a national party committee remains the same, at $15,000 per year, and PAC contributions are not indexed to inflation, so their value will continue to erode over time. Further, the law sets a new aggregate limit for individual contributions, from $25,000 per calendar year to $95,000 in a two-year election cycle (and indexes it to inflation). Interestingly, this $95,000 limit is quite structured: no more than

$37,500 can be given directly to candidates and no more than $37,500 can be donated to nonparty and state party political committees. Therefore, anyone wishing to donate the maximum allowed by law will have to give the national party committees between $20,000 and the limit of $57,500 (see table 1.1).

We expect that the national party committees will raise more hard money from large contributors, as BCRA encourages. We also expect that the GOP national party committees will raise more than their Democratic counterparts at first, with their more developed direct-mail fund-raising operation and Republican control of the White House and Congress. Indeed, national party hard money receipts for both parties were significantly up from the midterm election in 1998, as figure 5.2 shows. Republican national party committees raised over $100 million more in 2002 than they had in 1998, and the Democrats increased their take by over $50 million (Federal Election Commission 2002c).

It is important, however, not to define the interests and role of the "national parties" strictly in terms of existing committees. If the parties are understood in terms of functions that serve the needs of office holders and candidates (Monroe 2001), some of the functions may be picked up by new organizations that will be structured to meet the new law's restrictions on parties. In July 2002 the FEC

Figure 5.2   National Party Committees' Hard Money Receipts, through 20 Days after the General Election

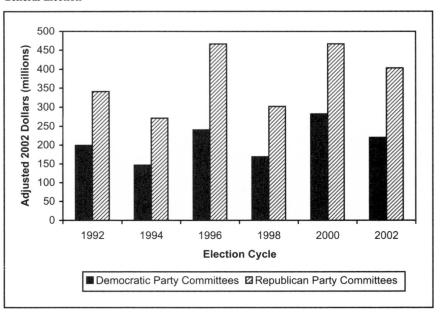

Source: FEC, "Party Fundraising Reaches $1.1 Billion in 2002 Election Cycle." Press Release, 18 December 2002.
Note: Does not include monies transferred among the listed committees.

issued some of the rules to implement BCRA, including one that allowed for the creation of independent nonprofit partisan organizations that have an implied connection to a national party organization. While some of these groups may have had relationships with the national parties *before* the 2002 election, they may escape from the soft money ban *after* the election, as long as federal officials, candidates, national party officials, and their agents do not directly or indirectly solicit money for these groups or direct money toward them (Campaign Finance Institute 2002b). Indeed, operatives close to both parties were busy in the final weeks before Election Day 2002 establishing such nonparty partisan organizations. These friends-of-the-party groups, or what reformers have come to call "shadow" groups (Keller 2002a), are likely to share the national parties' goals, and to spend money in ways that pursue those goals. For example, these new partisan groups can use their soft money to pay for issue advocacy ads, just as the parties had done before passage of BCRA.

Most of these new quasi-party groups were established under section 527 of the tax code, which allows them to spend all of their money on overt political activities but requires them to disclose their contributions and expenditures to the Internal Revenue Service (IRS), including supplying the names and addresses of their contributors. The 527 groups established in the final weeks before the election include the Democratic Senate Majority Political Action Committee, headed by a one-time DCCC political director and former aide to Al Gore, and the Leadership Forum, run by former Representative Bill Paxon (R-N.Y.) who chaired the NRCC from 1993 to 1996, and by a former chief of staff to House Majority Leader Tom DeLay (Keller 2002b).

Before Election Day 2002 the Leadership Forum received $1 million in soft money from the NRCC. The Leadership Forum later returned the check, after reform groups including Common Cause and the Center for Responsive Politics filed an FEC complaint. Ironically, since it was a soft money contribution, the NRCC cannot spend the returned $1 million now that BCRA bans party soft money spending. Since these quasi-party groups are new and exist only in reaction to the new law, they are operating very much in the dark, without much guidance from the law, the FEC, or the IRS. We are likely to see more uncertain actions from them in the future.

Another new nonprofit group, the National Committee for a Responsible Senate, with the initials NCRS—note the similarity to the initials of GOP's Senate campaign committee, the NRSC—was founded by three Republican lawyers who work for one of Washington's most prominent firms, Patton Boggs (Keller 2002b). The NCRS filed as a 501(c)(6) committee, the same designation used by most trade associations. For the IRS to accept this designation, the organization may not be devoted primarily to influencing elections, and the members must have a common business purpose. While 501(c)(6) committees cannot spend a substantial portion of their funds on overt electoral activities, they are not required to disclose any of their donors. Ironically, the NCRS may secretly raise soft money in unlimited amounts, while before passage of BCRA the NRSC was required to report soft money contributions.

Some groups have formed as 501(c)(4) committees, the designation used by social welfare groups. 501(c)(4) committees also may not be devoted primarily to election activity. And like 501(c)(6) committees, 501(c)(4) groups can conduct voter education and issue advertising campaigns that could have an impact on elections. As long as their activities do not include candidate-specific broadcast advertising, these organizations do not have to disclose their donors. One of the new 501(c)(4) committees is the American Majority Fund, directed by Harold Ickes, President Clinton's former top political aide; John Podesta, former Chief of Staff to Clinton; and former Clinton State Department Policy Planning Director Morton Halperin (Weissman 2003). Another is Progress for America, a 501(c)(4) established by Tony Feather, the former political director of Bush-Cheney 2000 (Weissman 2003).

Although these new quasi-party groups cannot be run by the parties, or by House or Senate Members, and cannot coordinate their activities with the national party committees, BCRA allows elected officials to appear at fundraisers as long as they do not directly ask for soft money donations (Stone 2002, 2543–44). It is possible that these new party-allied groups could collect some of the soft money that the parties must now forgo.

The national parties are preparing for the new law in the states as well. For instance, the DNC hired a consultant in 2001 to help with state party development in preparation for the limited soft money fund-raising that the state and local parties will be permitted to do under BCRA. (See the discussion of the "Levin Amendment," described in table 1.1 and discussed below.) A new organization, the Democratic State Party Organization, was created to train and advise state parties on the limited voter registration and get-out-the-vote (GOTV) activities that may be funded with this soft money (Stone 2002).

Reformers say there is a danger that recent FEC regulations will encourage these new quasi-party groups to engage in activities that violate BCRA. House sponsors of BCRA, Representatives Christopher Shays, R-Conn., and Martin Meehan, D-Mass., are suing the FEC in federal court to overturn these permissive soft money rules for quasi-party groups. Senate sponsor John McCain, R-Ariz., also plans to introduce legislation to overhaul the FEC, and reform groups such as Common Cause, Democracy 21, and the Center for Responsive Politics are challenging the new quasi-party groups on legal grounds. The final outcome of the FEC regulations will determine whether these new partisan groups will be the conduits for partisan soft money in the future.

A number of well-established partisan groups are trying to direct soft money their way as well. For instance, the Republican Governors Association and the New Democratic Network (a group of influential, centrist congressional Democrats) both held briefings before the 2002 election for their big donors and fundraisers. They explained that they may raise soft money under BCRA, and encouraged those who gave soft money to the parties in the past to give to them instead. The competition for soft money could get fierce. A former national chairperson of the Democratic National Committee predicts that there "certainly will be [groups] formed just because people think there's gold in them thar hills" (Stone 2002). Thus, as many congressional opponents of BCRA predicted, the amount of soft money in the campaign finance system may not go down significantly, and it certainly will be much more difficult to trace. Instead it might be raised and spent by new and existing groups that are not connected to the national parties. One prominent Washington political attorney, Ben Ginsberg of Patton Boggs, predicts that there will be "a complete transfer of soft money, from the national committees to outside entities" (Stone 2002). We expect, however, that these groups will be less successful at soft money fund-raising than the national parties had been, in large part because the nonparty groups do not represent a direct link to policy makers.

HOW WILL BCRA CHANGE
NATIONAL PARTY ACTIVITIES?

While the national party committees will continue to pursue the same goal of winning federal elections, their activities in pursuit of this goal must change with the new law. One of the primary purposes of BCRA is to stop the national party organizations from raising soft money and spending it on unlimited issue advocacy campaigns. Hence, the main monetary activities of the six national party committees in the last four election cycles (1996, 1998, 2000, and 2002) must cease.

Soft money had allowed the parties to direct huge sums of money to targeted districts and states. Working together with the state parties, the national parties were able to spend significant sums of mixed hard and soft money in these races.[1] Most of it was spent to produce and air issue advocacy advertising (ads that could be paid for in part with soft money because they did not expressly advocate the election or defeat of a federal candidate). Prior to 1996, when the parties figured out how to fully take advantage of the soft money–issue advocacy "loophole," parties generally made only hard money coordinated expenditures and direct contributions to candidates for federal office. With contributions limited to $5,000 per election and coordinated expenditures limited to a modest amount linked to inflation (in recent cycles, the total coordinated expenditure that national and state parties could make together through agency agreements was about $60,000), unlimited issue advocacy efforts were very attractive to the national parties. Indeed, with the average competitive congressional race costing over $1 million, coordinated expenditures equaled at most only about 6 percent of what a candidate spent on his or her own. On the other hand, the parties concentrated their issue advocacy spending in only a handful of races and boasted that they spent just about as much as candidates did.

David B. Magleby studied competitive congressional races in 2000 and found that the major parties spent around $16 million dollars each on TV and radio ads alone in five Senate and twelve House elections (Magleby 2001). Soft money was also spent on party voter registration, voter identification, and GOTV efforts, as well as on overhead costs such as salaries, travel, postage, phone, and capital expenditures. Using soft money to help pay for overhead costs allowed the national parties to reserve scarce hard money for other activities, such as making direct contributions to candidates, or for mixing with soft money to run issue advocacy ads. This soft money spending dramatically increased the amount spent in the most competitive districts and states and is mainly responsible for the belief among candidates, pundits, and contributors that the parties are "relevant" after a long period of not having much impact in the electoral arena.

Our view, however, is that the focus on party soft money issue ads—the multi-million-dollar gorilla, if you will—has taken attention away from what the parties traditionally have done to assist candidates in federal elections and obscured the effectiveness of the various techniques they employ. Clearly, the amount of money spent on party issue ads has been impressive in the aggregate and in particular races. Often lost in the discussion is the fact that these issue ads have been used in only a few highly competitive races, and indeed the number of competitive races continues to decline (see table 8.1). The trends are similar for Senate and presidential elections, with competition confined to only a few states. So, although soft money gave the parties a great infusion of cash, the spending of it appeared in only a small number of states and House districts.

National Party Activities—It's All Hard Money Now

Now, all national party activity must be paid for with hard money, as it had been prior to 1980. For example, national parties may still run issue advocacy ads, but they must use hard money to pay for them. The new law also requires state and local parties to use only hard money to pay for "federal election activities." Yet, since many Democrats objected to a complete soft money prohibition for voter registration and GOTV efforts, the bill's sponsors agreed to the Levin Amendment to BCRA. The Levin Amendment allows state and local parties to raise soft money in limited ($10,000) chunks (as long as state law permits) and spend it in restricted ways on grassroots voter mobilization. But state and local parties may not coordinate their soft money raising or spending with the national parties or federal candidates. (See chapter 6, in which Raymond J. La Raja discusses how Levin Amendment soft money is likely to work on the state and local levels and what impact it might have on federal elections.)

National party electoral activities include direct contributions to candidates, media advertising, direct mail, voter registration, voter identification and GOTV efforts, and polling. We expect that the parties will continue to engage in all of these activities, but that they will have fewer funds available to do some of them because of the loss of soft money. However, if there continue to be so few competitive federal electoral venues, the national parties will still be able to direct extensive resources to targeted races. Below, we discuss recent patterns in party hard money spending and speculate about what might occur in the future.

The new law also requires national party committees to choose how they intend to spend hard money for the support of each of their nominees. Prior to the passage of BCRA, parties were allowed to help candidates with hard money in three ways. Parties could make (1) direct contributions to candidates' campaigns, (2) coordinated expenditures on candidates' behalf and in consultation with them, and (3) independent expenditures, hard money funds spent to promote the election or defeat of a candidate without the favored candidate's knowledge or consent. Originally, FECA allowed parties to make only contributions and coordinated expenditures. Parties won the right to spend independently in a 1996 Supreme Court case, *Colorado Republican Federal Campaign Committee v. Federal Election Commission* (known as *Colorado I*). At issue was whether parties could indeed spend "independently" of their nominees. The court believed that they could, at least before nomination.[2] BCRA aims to *fix* the Supreme Court's decision by requiring that *all* of a party's committees choose to make either coordinated expenditures on behalf of a candidate (which are limited but indexed to inflation) *or* independent expenditures (which are unlimited but cannot be coordinated with a candidate). BCRA's congressional sponsors wanted to limit party spending, and one way to do this was to dispense with the fiction that a party could spend in coordination with a candidate and at the same time independently of that candidate.

BCRA requires political party committees to choose between coordinated and independent expenditures on or after the day a political party nominates a candidate. The FEC's new regulations, adopted on December 5, 2002, codify BCRA's call for recognizing one party "group" among all national and state political party committees. This means that the actions of any one organization in the spending of coordinated or independent expenditures binds all of the other party's committees to pursue only that type of spending, but only after a nomination has been made. At hearings on the regulations, many observers commented on the implications of a "rogue" committee making a spending decision that would bind all the rest, regardless of its wisdom. Making all party committees one party group should certainly have the effect of increasing communication between the various levels of the party to prevent such unforeseen events from occurring. Thus, the distance put between national and state party committees by the requirements of the Levin Amendment may be compensated for by the party group mechanism in the FEC regulations (Federal Election Commission 2002a). However, La Raja (chapter 6) argues that the "pull" of the Levin Amendment will keep party organizations apart despite any "push" from deciding on spending strategies.

The date of nomination, which triggers enforcement of the binding choice between coordinated and independent spending, raises a number of interesting questions. In many states the date for congressional nominations is quite close to Election Day, and in presidential elections the nominees are often known long before they are officially nominated at the national convention. Previously, the FEC allowed parties to make coordinated expenditures on behalf of the "eventual nominee" in congressional races and made special provisions for coordinated expenditures to cover certain administrative and overhead expenses for presidential candidates in the "bridge" period between the time when they hit their spending limit in the primary season and the moment they receive their general election public funds (for the Dole primary campaign in 1996, for example; see Corrado 2002, 84). Under BCRA, total coordinated spending will remain capped for the entire cycle, and when the total limit is reached, that type of spending must cease regardless of the date. In the regulations adopted December 5, 2002, the FEC stated that no additional coordinated spending will be allowed for run-off elections. Once the limit is reached, no more coordinated spending may occur.

Preprimary party spending was often thought of as taboo in the past, particularly for House and Senate races. Yet BCRA may encourage an increase in party spending prior to primaries, for it appears that parties will be able to make both coordinated and independent expenditures during this period (or to spend independently through the nomination and in a coordinated matter thereafter). This will have the practical effect of increasing the overall hard money amount a party spends to help get a federal candidate elected, contrary to the intent of BCRA's sponsors to limit national party spending in federal elections. Party spending limits such as those for contributions and coordinated expenditures seem to force parties to spread their resources around to more candidates, which might enhance competition in races that do not start off as close contests. Yet the new rules continue to allow the national parties to spend potentially unlimited amounts with large hard money independent expenditures, a move they have been reluctant to make in the past but one that is more attractive without the option of soft-money-based issue advocacy ads. Thus the parties are likely to continue to direct resources to very few states and House districts and therefore do little to make more races competitive.

It is difficult to know precisely how the national parties will behave now that soft money is banned, but looking at how coordinated and independent expenditures have been spent in the past in congressional elections gives us some indications of the patterns and strategies the parties have followed. Table 5.1 gives an overall accounting of coordinated and independent expenditures in the 2000 House elections. We chose to analyze House races because the DCCC was the only one of the four congressional campaign committees to engage in indepen-

Table 5.1 Congressional Campaign Committees' Hard Money Spending in 38 House Races with DCCC Independent Expenditures, 2000 Elections

Republican Coordinated Spending		*Democratic Coordinated Spending*		*Democratic Independent Expenditures*	
Total	$2,533,268	Total	$1,778,323	Total	$1,878,442
Average Expenditure	66,665	Average Expenditure	46,798	Average Expenditure	49,433
Media	1,877,351	Media	914,450	Phone	
Direct Mail	655,917	Polling	291,355	GOTV	1,878,442
		Direct Mail	293,380		
		Research	256,612		
		Overhead	9,156		
		Fund-Raising	13,370		

Source: Compiled from FEC data.

dent expenditures in the 2000 cycle. First, we looked only at the thirty-eight races for which the DCCC designed independent expenditure campaigns. Next, we compared how the DCCC and NRCC spent their coordinated money and how the DCCC used its independent expenditure money in those races.

This analysis shows that the end of soft money does not necessarily mean the end of significant party spending, as many pundits have predicted. What is most striking is that the NRCC came close to spending the maximum allowable coordinated expenditure in each of these thirty-eight races (92.9 percent of the legal limit on average). The DCCC, by contrast, spent on average less than $47,000 in coordinated expenditures in each of the thirty-eight races (about 66.5 percent of the legal limit). This implies that Republicans directed more hard money to competitive races than Democrats did. However, the DCCC spent an additional $49,432 per race on average in independent expenditures. Every penny of the nearly $1.9 million the DCCC spent in independent expenditures in 2000 went to GOTV telephone banks. The DCCC ended up spending an average of $96,231 in hard money in each race (coordinated plus independent expenditures) compared to $66,665 (coordinated expenditures only) for the NRCC. This is an interesting point to ponder, since most observers have assumed that most increases in hard money spending by the Democrats went to provide adequate matches to soft money for issue ad spending in the various states. Here, we see that Democrats managed to get more hard dollars directly to races where they felt the money would matter. Also, we know anecdotally that the Democrats' major media spending was through issue ads on television, while the Republicans preferred more of a balance between TV and direct mail. Interestingly, Republicans still paid for candidate media efforts with their hard dollars at about twice the rate of Democrats for the same type of expenditure (coordinated).

Several important points emerge from the preceding discussion. First, the detailed accounting above shows that parties have begun and can learn to maximize the amount of hard money spent in the most competitive congressional elections. Second, party operatives and political consultants we interviewed in 2002 agreed that, despite the attractiveness of soft money spending, parties need to spend about $2 of issue ad money to get the same impact that $1 of hard money spending would provide (Johanson 2002). Words such as "vote for" or "vote against" are very important for an inattentive public. Candidates themselves can more easily convey an appeal for votes without using such words of express advocacy, since it is their names on the ballot. Indeed, the Brennan Center for Justice found that, in 2000, only 10 percent of candidate ads used express advocacy terms, and just 2 percent of party or group ads did so (Holman and McLoughlin 2001). But a party telling voters that Senator Smith loves seniors doesn't motivate them to vote for Senator Smith as much as telling them to "vote for" Senator Smith *because* she loves seniors. BCRA forces parties to spend only hard money, and thus they can freely use these and other express advocacy terms. Therefore, we submit that parties can spend less hard money as effectively as they spent the greater soft/hard money mix previously allowed. Finally, the nature of the spending is noteworthy. Since BCRA's largest effect on parties will be in ending the use of soft money to purchase issue ads, we may find that the already significant allocation of coordinated expenditure's hard dollars to media may shift to a total allocation of hard dollars to media. The national committees may assume that state parties spending Levin Amendment soft money will pick up the task of spending on direct mail and phone banks.

We have no data for independent expenditures by parties for the presidency, because this type of spending had been expressly prohibited by the FEC under FECA. In a move not required by BCRA, the FEC decided to repeal its prohibition on national committees making independent expenditures in presidential campaigns (Federal Election Commission 2002a). Given the provisions discussed above, the FEC decided that national committees could choose to make independent expenditures for presidential campaigns, postnomination, provided they could meet the new rules establishing their "independence" from the candidate. Since BCRA creates an absolute choice for party committees in congressional elections, the FEC thought the choice ought to apply consistently to all federal candidates.

Previously, the FEC had prohibited the making of independent expenditures by the national committees during the general election on the premise that independence between the national committee and the party's nominee was impossible. So, while the national committees spent hard and soft money on issue advertising in 1996 and 2000, they never had the option to make the exclusively hard money independent expenditures. If the national committees can realize hard dollar fund-raising success, they may indeed engage in independent expenditure campaigns. Since the presidential candidates are restricted to spending public funds (if they choose to participate in the public funding system), the parties may be in a better position to spend concentrated amounts in swing states. However, the parties will have to follow the very stringent guidelines for avoiding "coordination" to maintain independence from their candidates.

Party Grassroots Activities and Consultants as Coordinators

The new law attempts to encourage party-sponsored voter mobilization activities, but it casts the state and local parties as the central players for these activities. The Levin Amendment allows state and local parties to spend some soft money (mixed with hard money) on some federal election activities (voter registration, voter identification, GOTV, and generic party activities). However, the national parties are not permitted to work with the state and local parties to raise or spend soft money for Levin Amendment exempt activities. The Levin activity money must be raised and spent by a state, district, or local party committee in a state that permits soft money. There can be no reference to a clearly identified candidate for federal office, and the activity may *not* be conducted through broadcasting, cable, or satellite communication, limiting the utility of these funds.

The availability of soft money on the state and local levels may encourage more of this grassroots party-building activity, as BCRA's sponsors intended. Although party committees will not be able to engage in collaborative fund-raising or intercommittee transfers, collaborative spending of Levin Amendment funds on the subnational level is allowed (Bauer 2002, 32). Moreover, we see no prohibition of a number of state and local committees choosing to hire the same direct mail consultant or telemarketing consulting firm to conduct electoral activities. Clearly, though, the soft money fund-raising ban would prevent parties or their agents from using common strategies or vendors to raise funds.

The national parties already use only a handful of select consultants for media, direct mail, telemarketing, and polling; most of them are former party employees (Kolodny and Dulio 2003). In recent elections, issue advertising paid for with national party hard and soft money was highly coordinated with state parties where there were closely contested congressional races, to take advantage of more favorable soft money spending rules at the state level. The national parties transferred hard and soft money to the state parties, who in turn hired one of just a few media consultants who were crafting virtually all of that party's issue ads for congressional races (Dwyre and Kolodny 2002). Moreover, the outside consultants with whom the parties work are keenly aware of which states and districts are competitive.

Indeed, lurking behind the analysis of hard money spending above is the revelation that less than 10 percent of this spending happened at the party headquarters. More than 90 percent was spent on political consultants who provide these services to the campaigns. This points to a significant set of relationships between party organizations and private "vendors" or political consultants. These partisan consultants may become more important players in the new campaign finance regime, for they may be able to conduct some campaign activities in support of the national parties' goals. For instance, party-allied consultants may help coordinate state and local parties to raise or spend Levin soft money in the states and districts with the most competitive races or the richest Electoral College return potential. These consultants may be able to introduce large soft money contributors in the states to national policy makers after the election. In this way, a fairly small group of party-allied consultants, many of whom worked at the national party committees at one time, or were Members of Congress, or recently held political advisory positions for governmental officials, may become party surrogates in the new campaign finance regime.

BCRA does not appear to prohibit these consultants—since they are not officers of the party (and only the parties' agents when under contract to them)—from coordinating the raising or spending of Levin Amendment soft money on the state and local levels. Thus BCRA might enhance the role of consultants with close ties to the national parties. In fact, the national parties may choose to have fewer employees, whose activities are severely restricted by the new law, and instead rely on the services of consultants. Further, the national parties could suggest to state and local party organizations that they hire competent consultants to assist their Levin money operations, getting the party out of the way of giving illegal direction to their party affiliates. Consultants, in turn, can assist groups friendly to the parties' interests (such as labor unions for the Democrats and chambers of commerce for the Republicans) in identifying which races might benefit from their independent spending and to help them parlay their efforts into better access to the national policy makers later on. Although the FEC has issued regulations clarifying what will and will not be considered a "coordinated communication," the same regulations also make clear that information that would constitute such coordination must be specific and not generally known. In addition, the FEC's test for coordination has three parts, all three of which must be met for coordination to be found. Those bringing charges against parties and consultants for violating BCRA must have a great deal of detailed knowledge to make the charges stick.

In testimony before the FEC in October 2002, attorneys for both parties urged the FEC not to interpret BCRA's restrictions on the use of "common vendors" and "former employees" too stringently because of the parties' reliance on these consultants. NRCC attorney Don McGahn testified that "[l]ike the Democratic Party, we also have people wandering in and out of our structure" (Federal Election Commission 2002d, 78). He noted that the concern for a consultant is,

> If I work for the party committee, does that mean I can't work for campaigns anymore? What if some outside group wants me to do some ads in the off-year? . . . [U]ltimately there's a handful of people on either side of the aisle who do this kind of work, whether it's polling or media or list development or even fund-raising. And,

frankly, we'll run out of people on the bench very quickly if we get too complicated with who can work for whom and who can't work for whom. (Federal Election Commission 2002d, 78–79)

The Commissioners seemed to agree. They also agreed that political consultants are required to make the electoral process work. They therefore did not believe BCRA intended for them to monitor their consultants' alliances to such a point that consultants might not be able to conduct their business. Therefore, the activities of consultants are not likely to be closely scrutinized by the FEC. Hence, we believe that, over the next several election cycles, partisan political consultants will try a variety of arrangements to maximize the parties' influence in campaigns while minimizing the exposure of the parties to legal accusations under BCRA.

CONCLUSION

Campaign finance reforms are famous for producing some of the most contrary unintended consequences. BCRA is likely to be no different. We do know that the new law will change dramatically how the national parties operate. The ban on national party soft money raising and spending means that the national parties will spend far less to help their candidates get elected, at least in the short run.

The new law also may transform the relationship between the national and state parties. The national parties had developed rather shallow financial relationships with the state parties, to which they transferred soft money. However, the new law could discourage cooperation between parties at different levels. If state and local parties raise and spend Levin Amendment soft money, the national parties (and their federal candidates) are not permitted to work with them on activities related to these monies. On the other hand, with the new requirement that *all* party committees must make either coordinated or independent expenditures for a particular candidate, the national, state, and local party committees may work together more closely and meaningfully to pursue the best spending strategies, at least for the targeted federal candidates. Moreover, since the state and local parties are the only party organizations permitted to use Levin Amendment soft money on federal election voter mobilization activities, we might see more involvement by the state parties in congressional and presidential elections. We may see, as one of the unintended consequences of the law, real communication between various state parties and local party organizations about new strategies adopted to comply with the new law. While state delegates to the national conventions and members of the Democratic and Republican national committees have long seemed to have little or no practical function, the need for fast innovation post-BCRA may prompt regional midterm party meetings to share ideas.

Nonparty groups with a partisan tilt, such as the New Democratic Network and the newly established quasi-party groups, are likely to become quite active in federal elections as well. These groups are competing for the soft money that used to go to the national party committees, and if they are successful at raising large amounts they will do more issue advertising, direct mail, phone banking and other campaign activities. Of course, there will be some soft money donors who were willing to give to the parties, because of the access to top policy makers that the parties could deliver, but who are not willing to give to nonparty groups. Under the old campaign finance regime, there were reports that some corporate donors felt they were subjected to a party "shakedown" for soft money, and they will be relieved that the parties will no longer hold such sway over them. It is unlikely that *all* of the soft money that used to go to the national parties will shift to these nonparty groups and to the state and local parties. Yet there will certainly be more campaign activity from them as they are able to redirect *some* soft money their way.

Finally, we expect that consultants, who have for years worked closely with the national parties, could become important brokers of campaign activities that the national parties once orchestrated. BCRA severely limits what the officers and agents of the national parties may do, particularly for activities involving Levin Amendment soft money. Most of the consultants who now work on presidential and congressional races once worked for one or more of the national party committees, and they have continued to work closely with the national parties. The parties already hire private consultants to carry out the vast majority of their electoral tasks. Various firms have established extensive informal relationships with each other (such as between pollsters and media consultants or between pollsters and telemarketing/GOTV firms) and between themselves and various party officials and officeholders.

BCRA will change significantly the way federal campaigns are financed by shifting soft money away from the national party committees to the state and local parties, PACs, and nonprofit organizations. However, the national parties will be able to spend unlimited amounts of hard money on their candidates through independent expenditures. As they have done in the past, the national parties will recast themselves to test the limits of the new rules in order to pursue their goal of controlling the federal government, and, as before, they will find ways to direct quite a lot of money and effort to targeted districts and states.

Ultimately, the concern about BCRA and political parties rests on the assumption that political parties are now very strong, and soft money was the fuel that got them that way. We reject this assumption. The tightening of competition for control of the government forced the parties to become much more strategic about how they used their resources. Before the strategic environment changed in the 1994 election cycle, parties and interest groups did not commit great sums of money to election campaigns. Once the House Republicans proved that the national electoral environment was indeed competitive, the parties became more selective about targeting resources to the most competitive seats that could change party control of governmental institutions. This led to the parties' search for more resources—hence, soft money. Once deployed, soft money issue advocacy campaigns greatly escalated the cost of the increasingly small number of competitive races. Even party operatives in recent election cycles admit that, because of the universal escalation in cost and the activity of more actors (i.e., parties and interest groups), soft money only made a difference in the campaigns of two or three House Members and maybe one Senator each election. Therefore, we do not see that soft money has made the parties more relevant in the electoral arena.

We are not arguing that BCRA will create broader competition because of the absence of soft money. However, we do propose that parties may actually fare better under BCRA because they will be forced to focus on their traditional roles in candidate recruitment and electoral coalition building, and they will begin to exercise influence in primary campaigns. The focus on party money in recent years has obscured the important point that political parties are much more than their bank accounts.

NOTES

1. The Federal Election Commission required political parties to spend both hard and soft money on issue advocacy advertising. Thus, soft money could only be spent this way if hard money was available to match it. The FEC required a mix of 65 percent soft money with 35 percent hard money, although state laws could be far more restrictive or permissive in the mix; therefore state parties often spent the money for issue ads if circumstances warranted.

2. This confusion is understandable, since *Colorado I* was interpreted to allow parties to make both coordinated and independent expenditures in the same year, in essence allowing the party to "forget" about its earlier coordination with the candidate.

6

State Political Parties After BCRA

Raymond J. La Raja

Reformers crafted a new campaign finance system in Washington, D.C., but its provisions will reshape political activities in state and local elections for years to come. Outside of Washington, the political committees most likely to feel the force of the new law will be the political parties in the states, which engage in elections for every level of office. Under the Bipartisan Campaign Reform Act (BCRA), these party committees must reevaluate how they engage in federal elections and revise campaign strategies that previously tied them closely to national party operations. The next several election cycles should be a ripe period for campaign experimentation, as state and local party organizations adapt to new federal laws that were intended primarily for national committees.

The primary goal of BCRA is to eliminate the use of nonfederal funds (soft money) in federal elections. Even casual observers of elections might recognize the difficulty of achieving this goal by perusing a lengthy election ballot that includes candidates for county clerk all the way up to President of the United States. Since American voters often elect local, state, and federal candidates simultaneously, any regulations imposed at one level of government are bound to affect the electoral context for campaigns at any level of office. For example, laws that shape campaign spending for the top of the ticket could have an indirect effect on which voters are mobilized, thereby affecting ballots cast for lower levels of office.

The impact of BCRA is especially far-reaching at the state and local levels, because its provisions are aimed primarily at political parties, which uniquely run campaigns designed to boost candidates across the ballot. Though the new federal law is intended to prevent soft money from influencing federal elections, the constraints it imposes on political parties to achieve this goal will affect orga-

nizational resources, relationships, and strategies beyond the national party committees.

While disagreement exists among political scientists as to whether BCRA
harms or helps state and local parties, few doubt that these organizations will feel
the effects of the federal reforms. Most scholars would agree that three developments are likely. First, there will be greater experimentation as party operatives
search for the best methods of raising money and campaigning under the new
laws. Parties in larger states and where campaign finance laws differ significantly
from BCRA probably will do the most experimenting. Over several election
cycles, other parties will imitate the apparent successes of these early innovators.

A second likely development is the decentralization of party decision making,
reversing a trend toward party integration and centralization during the past two
decades. Now that the national committees no longer control soft money, they
will wield less clout with state and local parties than in the past. More significant
in this regard are provisions in BCRA that ban or severely limit federal candidates and national party personnel from participating in activities involving soft
money. Together, these new rules compartmentalize party affairs more distinctly
than in recent decades, with national committees focusing more exclusively on
federal contests, while state and local units dedicate themselves to local elections.

Finally, BCRA encourages shifts in power among partisan elites. Governors
who raise significant amounts of soft money for the state party and for local
candidates, both within and outside the state, probably will have increased
influence in party circles. Other political actors with increased influence under
BCRA will include interest groups and political consultants that excel in mobilizing crucial voters for federal and state elections. With diminished cash and
restraints on their campaign activity, parties in the states will rely more heavily
than before on organizations outside the formal party structure.

In the following sections, I elaborate on these themes, making predictions
about how state and local parties will respond to the new laws.

CAMPAIGNING IN THE STATES AFTER BCRA

Prior to BCRA, there were two significant trends in party financing that motivated the drafting of provisions in the reform bill. First, the national parties were
raising nonfederal funds at an accelerating pace. Between 1992 and 2002, the six
national committees increased their soft money fund-raising from roughly $86
million to almost $500 million (Federal Election Commission 2002c, 2001). Both
major parties ratcheted up hard money fund-raising simultaneously, and the
proportion of national party funds from soft money jumped from 22 percent to
44 percent during this same period.

The second, parallel trend was that national parties transferred increasing
amounts of nonfederal money to state parties to use in campaigns, because of a

series of regulatory decisions that favored spending in the states. Congress amended FECA in 1979 to attenuate the chilling effect of the 1974 provisions on party activity in the states. Based on these amendments, the Federal Election Commission (FEC) issued regulations identifying campaign activities that were exempt from hard money spending limits for state and local parties (11 CFR 100.8). Generally speaking, these exemptions on expenditures were for party-building activities designed to stimulate volunteer grassroots work, and boost turnout through voter identification, registration, and get out the vote (GOTV). At about the same time, however, the FEC was issuing a series of advisory opinions permitting *all* parties to raise and spend nonfederal money for some generic party activities, based on the argument put forth by party officials that much party-based work assisted federal *and* nonfederal candidates and therefore should be paid for with both federal and nonfederal funds (Corrado 1997, 187; Federal Election Commission 1978). Finally, in 1990 the FEC issued reporting and allocation regulations that permitted higher ratios of soft money spending by state parties, thereby encouraging national committees to transfer money to the states (Corrado 1997, 209).

Perhaps, when it issued these opinions, the FEC did not anticipate the degree to which nonfederal funds would be used for targeted activities that benefited federal candidates. The fact that soft money was routed to states with competitive federal contests implied that nonfederal funds were being used to help federal candidates. For example, political parties in the fifteen states where the 2000 presidential election was decided by 5 or fewer percentage points received 70 percent of soft money transfers from the Democratic National Committee (DNC) and the Republican National Committee (RNC) (Federal Election Commission 2001).

Reform activists accused the national parties of "laundering" soft money through state committees to pay for campaign ads. Party operatives argued that these funds were used generically to identify and mobilize voters, and that the issue ads did not violate the law, since they did not expressly advocate for the victory or defeat of a federal candidate in an election. Data on party spending suggests that the national committees, through their transfers of hard and soft money to state parties, helped fund issue ads that supported federal candidates (Krasno and Goldstein 2002). In the 2000 elections, state parties spent approximately $149 million in soft money on issue ads; at the same time, they spent about $42 million on voter mobilization programs and $100 million on maintaining the party headquarters (La Raja and Jarvis-Shean 2001). While voter mobilization and overhead expenditures seemed like legitimate uses of soft money under FECA, the payments for issue ads did not, since many looked so much like campaign commercials tailored for federal candidates (Krasno and Goldstein 2002). The debates over reform focused on the increasing use of issue ads, since these appeared to evade party contribution limits to federal candidates and fuel an arms race for soft money between the two major parties (Mann 2002b).

To prevent nonfederal funds from influencing elections, BCRA adopted a policy of banning nonfederal fund-raising by the national parties. Reformers anticipated that national committees would rely on other organizations, particularly their state affiliates, to raise nonfederal funds that might be used in federal elections. They therefore included provisions to prohibit the national party committees and their "agents" from soliciting money for, or engaging in, any coordinated fund-raising activity with state and local party committees. The national parties were also not allowed to participate in decision making about how state and local parties spent nonfederal money. Concern lingered, however, about how nonfederal funds could be used by state and local parties in ways that helped federal candidates, even if the national committees renounced all ties to soft money activity. After all, state and local parties have an incentive to elect federal candidates too.

For reasons of federalism, the federal laws cannot simply ban soft money fund-raising by the state and local parties. State laws govern how parties may raise money for state and local elections. Nevertheless, the drafters of BCRA were concerned that state and local parties could circumvent the ban on national party soft money by raising soft money on their own (without having it transferred from national parties) and then spending it (or some of it) to influence federal elections. The new law tries to address this issue by regulating "federal election activity," which may be funded by a state party only with money raised under federal rules. These federal election activities include voter registration (120 days prior to an election in which a federal candidate appears on the ballot), voter identification, GOTV, and public communications that promote, attack, support, or oppose a federal candidate. State parties must use federal funds to pay for most federal election activities. However, state and local parties may set up Levin Amendment committees for some registration and GOTV activities. Soft money contributions of up to $10,000 per party committee are permitted, to the extent that they are permitted under state law. A number of other restrictions on raising and spending this money are also included in the new law. (For a summary of the Levin Amendment, see table 1.1.)

The drafters of BCRA hoped to avoid challenging state laws by drawing a bright line between federal and state election activity. By designating certain activities as "federal" the law creates a residual category of "nonfederal" activities. Within this residual category, state and local parties may spend soft money without restrictions under federal law (so long as state laws permit). One problem, however, is that the activities defined as federal also happen to coincide with party activities (such as registration and GOTV) that may help state and local candidates. A chief complaint of party officials in several states is that BCRA "federalizes" campaign finance laws by compelling parties to spend "hard money" (federal funds) even for activities that may influence only state elections

(Bowler 2002, 27). But drafters of BCRA believed it was necessary to draw a sharp distinction between federal and state election activity to prevent parties at all levels from using soft money (nonfederal) to influence federal elections.

CONSEQUENCES OF BRCA IN THE STATES

BCRA's various soft money provisions should affect each party organization differently, depending on a variety of features unique to a state. Aside from the effect of regulations at the federal level, factors such as state campaign finance laws, partisan competition, and local political culture contribute in some way to the vigor of party organizations. Some parties have been quite active in recent years, while others have been barely noticeable. BCRA now alters how state and local parties acquire campaign resources and influences their relationships with other political organizations, particularly the national party committees. Given the fluid and weblike character of party structures, new committees may emerge that are better suited to the reformed regulatory framework. However, predicting how parties will respond to the new law is not easy, particularly when many other aspects of the electoral environment influence political activity. With this caveat, I draw on the general frameworks of organizational theorists to speculate about how parties might adapt to BCRA in the coming elections.

Experimentation and Learning

One group of theorists posits an "organizational learning" model for understanding organizational change. They claim that organizations are goal oriented, but that they grope toward goals through trial and error (Cyert and March 1963). Far from being omniscient, rational actors, organizations rarely know what technologies or strategies will help them achieve their goals. Instead, they rely on ad hoc approaches to locate strategies that achieve what they perceive as success. In a changing and uncertain environment, organizations will seek out a variety of techniques, not really knowing which ones will get them to their goals. In the end, they choose to retain those strategies that appear to work, discarding those that do not. Applied to the changes in the electoral environment created by BCRA, this theory suggests that political strategies will vary considerably among political organizations, with many notable failures. Successes, however, will be imitated by other political organizations.

As we saw in the previous chapter (see Dwyre and Kolodny, chapter 5), partisans at the national level are already probing new arrangements with committees outside the official party structure. State and local parties will experiment as well. BCRA alters the legal context for raising and spending money in states, even though it applies to federal elections. For example, parties may no longer rely on federal candidates or the national committees to solicit nonfederal funds for them, even though candidates may appear at local fund-raisers. More critically, BCRA carves out an area of "federal election activity" that requires the use of federal funds (or Levin funds). Since federal election activity may overlap with traditional party efforts to help local candidates, parties in the states will need to design strategies to separate federal and state campaigns, and develop capacities to raise funds under Levin Amendment rules.

The boldest experimentation should take place in states where BCRA generates the most uncertainty about what political parties may do with nonfederal funds. These are likely to be states where the state campaign finance laws appear fundamentally different from BCRA. Here, the gap between federal and state law poses administrative and financial challenges for state and local parties. From an administrative perspective, parties in the states must learn to reconcile and comply with two different sets of laws. Many state parties already hire teams of experienced lawyers and accountants to help with these matters. They adapted to the pre-BCRA campaign finance regime, called the Federal Election Campaign Act (FECA), and now they will have to do the same for BCRA. This adaptation, however, will take time, as political operatives experiment with new accounting methods and committee structures to address the legal requirements of BCRA.

A full analysis of state campaign finance laws is beyond the scope of this chapter, but an inspection of laws on contributions to political parties gives some clues about which state parties will need to adjust to BCRA. Table 6.1 categorizes the states according to the strictness of laws on contributions relative to the rules under BCRA. These categories range from states with no limits on contributions to those with limits that are comparable to BCRA's. In between are states that allow unlimited contributions from some groups or allow the size of contributions to exceed that under BCRA. The state parties that will have little problem adjusting to the requirements of BCRA are those in the far right column, with state laws comparable to BCRA. It is no coincidence that seven of these nine states (Alaska, Connecticut, Kentucky, Oklahoma, Maine, Massachusetts, and Rhode Island) joined twelve others to file a court motion in support of BCRA, or that the plaintiffs include the Republican and Democratic parties of California, where the laws are less restrictive than BCRA (Tucker 2002). Parties in the states in the right-hand column will not be forced to change campaign bookkeeping very much, if at all. The parties in other states will need to maintain at least three separate accounts to meet the requirements of federal and state laws: a nonfederal account, a federal account, and a new Levin fund account (described below).

WINNING AND LOSING STATE
PARTIES UNDER BCRA

Changing campaign rules is never a neutral act. New rules play to the strengths of some organizations while exposing the vulnerabilities of others. One would

Table 6.1 State Laws on Party Fund-Raising

No Source or Size Limits	Source Limits but Unlimited from Individuals and/or PACS	Source and Size Limits but Less Restrictive than BCRA	Source and Size Limits Comparable to BCRA
Arkansas	Alabama	California	Alaska
Florida	Arizona	Colorado	Connecticut
Georgia	Indiana	Delaware	Kentucky
Idaho	Iowa	Hawaii	Maine
Illinois	Michigan	Kansas	Massachusetts
Missouri	Minnesota	Louisiana	Oklahoma
Nebraska	Mississippi	Maryland	Rhode Island
Nevada	Montana	New Jersey	West Virginia
New Mexico	New Hampshire	New York	Wisconsin
Utah	North Carolina	Ohio	
Virginia	North Dakota	South Carolina	
	Oregon	Vermont	
	Pennsylvania		
	South Dakota		
	Tennessee		
	Texas		
	Washington		
	Wyoming		

think that the decentralizing effects of BCRA would favor the existing large state party organizations, which will soak up the nonfederal funds that the national committees can no longer receive, but this is not necessarily so. The new law creates challenges for all parties, even for those in large states.

In the near term, state parties that already raise a lot of money without national party help should fare well. According to data from the Center for Public Integrity, the major state parties raised $477 million in nonfederal funds during the 2000 election cycle (Dunbar et al. 2002). National parties provided just over half of these receipts through transfers (see figure 6.1). The balance of funds was divided roughly evenly among individual, interest group, and other party contributors. Some state committees, however, relied more on the national parties than others. The immediate "losers" in the BCRA era will likely be parties that receive significant transfers yet raise few funds on their own. In contrast, the "winners" will likely be those parties that raise money without relying too much on the national committees for funds.

Figure 6.2a illustrates losers and winners for the Democratic party and figure 6.2b for the Republican pary. All the parties shown in these figures have higher-than-average party receipts per eligible voter. However, the parties on the left side of each chart rely most heavily on national committee transfers, while the parties on the right side rely the least on national committee transfers.

Figure 6.1   Sources of State Party Nonfederal Funds

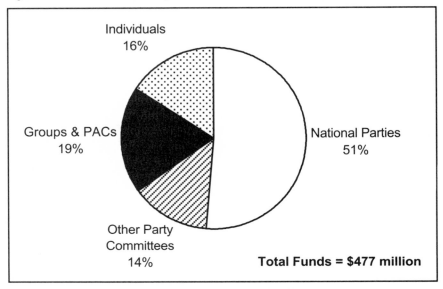

Source: State Secrets, a joint project by the Center for Public Integrity, Center for Responsive Politics, and National Institute on Money in State Politics.

For example, the North Dakota Democrats raised approximately $2.40 per person of voting age in the state (see figure 6.2a). This amount is almost four times the 63¢ fund-raising average for major parties. Significantly, the North Dakota Democrats received relatively little of this money—only 40¢ per person of voting age—through national party transfers. The same pattern is true for Democratic parties in Alabama, Georgia, South Dakota, and New Jersey. In stark contrast to the North Dakota Democrats, however, the Oregon Democrats raised only one-quarter of their own funds, even though they reported receipts greater than $2 per eligible voter. Similarly, other Democratic parties on the left side of the chart—Pennsylvania, Ohio, Wisconsin, and New York—appear to rely heavily on the national committees for funds.

This reliance on national party funds by parties on the left side of the chart is clearly based on the importance of these states in presidential contests. National committees concentrated soft money transfers here precisely because they are critical states for Electoral College votes. In the future, Democratic strategists concerned with presidential campaigns will need to find ways of bolstering these parties if they hope to run widespread GOTV campaigns that could win the states in 2004 and beyond. Only New York predictably favors Democrats in presidential elections. The alternative is for the national party to rely on nonparty organizations to mobilize voters. In the short term, at least, we are likely to see both

Figure 6.2 Losers and Winners Post-BCRA, Fund-Raising Capacity

a. Democratic State Parties

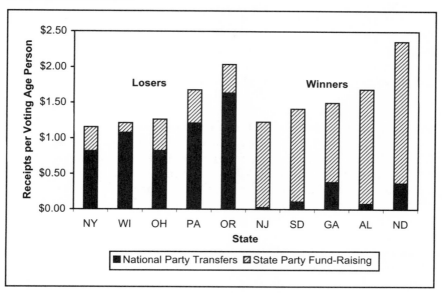

b. Republican State Parties

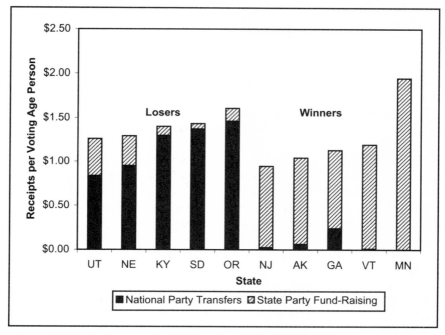

Source: State Secrets, a joint project by the Center for Public Integrity, Center for Responsive Politics, and National Institute on Money in State Politics.

strategies pursued. An early indication of state party success in managing the transition will be the degree to which these parties boost party fund-raising in the coming cycle. If nonfederal funds flow to state organizations, it indicates that political contributors believe the state party has the capacity to manage broad-based mobilization campaigns successfully without the supervision of the national committees. Parties that already raise significant amounts of money on their own have demonstrated they have this administrative capacity.

Among Republican organizations, winners and losers appear more heterogeneous in terms of population and geographic location. Like their Democratic counterparts, the New Jersey and Georgia organizations appear to be doing well independently. Winners also include Vermont, Alaska, and Minnesota parties, which do not rely heavily on the national organization for funds. In contrast, organizations that may struggle post-BCRA include Utah, South Dakota, Nebraska, Kentucky, and Oregon. In the first two states, the Republicans have solid majorities in both chambers of the legislature, so the risk of having a weakly funded party organization appears minimal here. Nebraska has a nonpartisan legislature, which may be one reason parties find it difficult to raise money. The biggest problem for Republicans could be in states where they need to remain competitive, like Oregon, where the State Senate seats are split evenly between the two parties. A similar challenge exists in Kentucky, where each party controls one chamber of the legislature. In competitive states like these, Republicans have a strong incentive to organize, but their task could be made difficult by state campaign finance laws with low limits for contributions to political parties. In Kentucky the limits are only $5,000 per cycle for contributors, while in Oregon the limits have been struck down by a court decision.

The above analysis of party fund-raising must be considered in the context of how state organizations previously invested money they received from the national party committees. To the degree that "losers" listed in figures 6.2a and 6.2b spent transfers on issue ads rather than building the party infrastructure, the immediate impact of BCRA should not affect organizational activity geared toward state and local races. Yet some state parties also used transfers to defray basic organizational expenses and to expand voter mobilizations campaigns. In *these* states, BCRA creates a subset of winners and losers. Specifically, state parties that invested a lot in voter contacts risk being punished heavily by BCRA if they relied too heavily on the national committee funds, or if they typically raise money in increments greater than the Levin Amendment allows. The winners, in contrast, are those parties that spend a lot on voter contacts yet are accustomed, because of state laws, to raising funds under constraints similar to those of BCRA.

Table 6.2 suggests which parties are losers and winners in this scenario by looking at the top ten spenders on voter contacts in 2000 and calculating how much they rely on money that exceeds BCRA's rules. The two sources of funds that are illegal for federal election activity under BCRA are (1) party transfers

Table 6.2 Ten State Parties with the Highest Spending on Voter Contacts in the 2000 Elections

State/ Party	Spending on Voter Contacts (per Person of Voting Age)	Percentage of Receipts from $10,000 + Donors	Percentage of Receipts from National Committees	Percentage of Receipts That Meet Levin Fund Requirements
Delaware-D	$2.12	4%	84%	12%
Delaware-R	1.02	21	46	33
Montana-R	0.99	1	86	13
Iowa-R	0.84	10	41	49
Florida-D	0.64	24	65	11
Maine-D	0.60	4	48	48
Iowa-D	0.58	17	49	34
Florida-R	0.45	49	35	16
Michigan-R	0.40	41	54	6
Maine-R	0.40	9	64	28
Party Average, All States	0.18	14	43	42

Source: Data from *State Secrets* project, provided by the Center for Public Integrity.
Note: Voter contacts include efforts to contact voters directly, including polling, direct mail, and GOTV.

and (2) contributions above $10,000 from a single source. The voter contact activities used in this analysis are rough approximations of what might be considered federal election activity under BCRA (which includes voter registration 120 days before a federal election, voter identification, GOTV, and certain kinds of generic party work).

Significantly, none of these organizations gets more that half its resources from funds that would be legal under BCRA. That is to say, all of these organizations rely heavily on resources that exceed the $10,000 federal limit or flow from party transfers now banned by BCRA. For example, the Michigan Republicans appear to spend a lot on voter mobilization—40¢ per person of voting age compared with an overall party average (Democrat and Republican) of 18¢—yet only 6 percent of their receipts come from sources that would be considered legal under the new rules. A breakdown of receipts shows they receive 41 percent of their funds through donations in excess of $10,000 and another 54 percent of their funds from national party transfers. Democratic and Republican committees in Florida will face similar difficulties, since only 11 percent and 16 percent, respectively, of the funds they collected in 2000 would be eligible to use for federal election activity under BCRA. Importantly, Florida parties appear to receive significant amounts of money from donors that give more that $10,000 (49 percent for Republicans, 24 percent for Democrats).

This static analysis of money raised and spent in 2000 cannot account for how parties will respond in a campaign environment in which they can no longer air issue ads that contain references to federal candidates. Overall, we can expect state parties to have less soft money in their accounts in 2004 precisely because portions were earmarked for the kind of issue ads that are no longer allowed under BCRA. But assuming that the 2000 figures reflect a state party's propensity to invest in voter contacts during a presidential election, it appears that parties in bigger states are hurt by BCRA more than in smaller states. These states rely far more than smaller states on contributions that exceed the Levin Amendment provisions.

Larger states will have to augment the supply of small donors if they want to take advantage of the Levin Amendment provision for federal election activity. Some parties may eventually develop the capacity to make up the difference, since they do not have to compete for nonfederal funds with national committees. For example, contributors in New York City have been a primary source of funds for the national Democrats. The state party may now benefit from having wealthy in-state donors who can no longer make large contributions to the national parties. One drawback, however, is that state and local parties must use *hard* money to *raise* Levin Amendment funds. In the past, they could use soft money to pay for costs associated with fund-raising to support federal election activities.

As state and local parties experiment with new strategies, the FEC will be confronted with difficult decisions about whether these committees are trying to evade BCRA to influence federal elections with nonfederal funds. One possible evasion scenario might involve circumventing the Levin Amendment limits. The Levin Amendment stipulates that federal election activity may be funded only with party funds raised in amounts of $10,000 or less *and* without the help of party transfers. Under the new campaign finance rules, a nonparty organization could parcel out funds to several local party committees in a state in increments of $10,000. These local committees, in turn, might choose to hire the same vendor specialist in voter contacts. Multiple checks of $10,000 would be sent from the committees to the vendor, who then would design a statewide voter contact program, emphasizing voters in crucial swing districts. Thus, by aggregating, disaggregating, and reaggregating resources, local parties may get around a provision that tries to limit the use of nonfederal money for registration and GOTV. (See chapter 5 for further discussion of vendors and consultants.)

DECENTRALIZATION

BCRA decentralizes party campaigning in two basic ways. First, it diminishes the resources controlled by central coordinating actors—the national committees. Without soft money, the national parties have fewer resources to encourage cooperation at lower levels of party, and therefore less influence in shaping the direction of campaigns in the states. Second, BCRA's broadened definition of federal election activity reduces the motivation for state and local parties to participate in federal elections, especially since they will be required to spend more hard money than previously. Instead, some state and local parties may choose to focus exclusively on state elections and leave the campaigning for federal candidates to other groups.

The Democratic "coordinated campaigns" and Republican "victory plans" were organizational mechanisms developed by the national parties to centralize past campaign operations. The national committees transferred generous amounts of hard and soft money to the state affiliates as a way to encourage them to design and implement statewide voter mobilization campaigns. Through intraparty agreements, these broad-based campaigns combined the resources of parties, candidates, and allied organizations to get targeted voters to the polls.

Coordinated campaign planning and spending is permissible under BCRA, but there is likely to be less of it because the mutual benefits of intraparty organizing are reduced considerably. To the chagrin of state party chairs, the national parties may no longer provide cash infusions of soft money to help pay for voter lists, office supplies, and other organizational costs. From the national party perspective, the state parties are no longer suitable as sponsors of soft money issue ads. While national parties may continue to transfer hard money to state organizations for party building, their generosity will be tempered by the relative scarcity of this resource. National parties will prefer to save precious hard money for candidate contributions, coordinated expenditures, and independent spending.

If state and local organizations do not want the federal law to impinge on how they raise and spend nonfederal money they must be careful to avoid federal election activity. To avoid generic party appeals that fall under the definition of federal election activity, parties may establish a "state elections mobilization program" or an association outside the formal party structure that focuses exclusively on specific state and local candidates when contacting voters. This may help them avoid having their activities "federalized" under the new law, which would compel them to spend hard money. There appears to be some ambiguity over how the FEC will interpret the new regulations in this area. BCRA sponsors hope that the FEC does not exempt voter identification and GOTV that references only state and local candidates. If this happens, then state parties may choose to distribute campaign money to local candidates for them to run their own voter identification and GOTV campaigns, as a way to avoid federal regulations.

It also appears that BCRA allows "associations of state and local candidates" to communicate freely. If this is the case, then state parties will likely help candidates establish these associations to avoid falling under federal regulations. The incentive to create separate committees exclusively for state and local candidates is especially strong in states where the parties are allowed to raise funds from sources that are prohibited under BCRA (refer back to table 6.1 to see states where the laws differ from BCRA).

Local parties may emerge stronger in particular congressional districts where there are competitive federal contests. We could even see a proliferation of local party committees in targeted areas, depending on the importance of a race. These party groups—or more specifically, the staff that run them—might migrate from one district to the next, drawn to tight congressional races like moths to fire. Thus, party activity would be less homegrown, and more like a professional "rent-a-party" with strong ties to national organizations like the Democratic State Party Organization or the Leadership Forum. The "nesting" of local committees in particular regions would allow partisans to channel as much Levin money as possible into important federal contests.

Although Senator Levin (D-Mich.) pushed for the amendment bearing his name to nurture grassroots party activity, it is unlikely that these committees will truly be grassroots organizations, because the tasks of raising and spending funds under the amendment may be too burdensome for local partisans to carry out without help from political professionals. To help strengthen local parties, BCRA raises the limit on hard money contributions to them from $5,000 to $10,000. But few local parties come close to raising even $5,000 from any single source. Raising additional hard money actually creates an administrative burden for local parties, because they must file financial reports with the FEC as soon as they collect a minimum of $5,000 in a calendar year. In the 2000 elections, only 165 local parties filed with the FEC, among many hundreds organized as Democratic or Republican committees. Since most local parties are run by volunteers, these fund-raising and administrative burdens may discourage them from taking advantage of this grassroots provision in BCRA.

The overall effect of BCRA is to distance state parties from federal candidates. Traditionally, federal elections are not the primary focus of state parties, and federal candidates tend to have weak ties to parties in the states. BCRA, however, makes it harder than ever for parties and federal candidates to cooperate. Not only are the parties barred from calling on federal candidates to help in raising nonfederal funds, these organizations must pay a hard money penalty for engaging in any kind federal election activity.

SHIFTS IN POWER AND INFLUENCE

To understand how power may shift under BCRA, I draw on another strand of organizational theory that focuses on control of resources. The core argument of "resource dependence" theorists is that organizations interact strategically to obtain resources for survival. Given scarce or limited resources in the environment, organizations must compete and cooperate with other organizations. This dynamic creates "interdependencies" among a set of organizations, and those political actors with access to critical resources will be the most powerful within the constellation of interdependent organizations (Blau 1964; Thompson 1967).

BCRA moves political actors from a regime in which national committees control most of the critical resources (money and expertise) to one in which resources are more broadly dispersed among political organizations. Now that national committees can no longer raise nonfederal funds, others may try to acquire these resources, including the state and local parties. By banning national parties from soft money activity, BCRA disperses control over campaigns, pushing a great deal of fund-raising and spending outside the national party structure. Parties in the states will have an enhanced opportunity to accumulate and invest resources in ways that extend their power relative to the national party committees. Existing and emergent interest groups will also become more prominent in the pursuit and use of nonfederal funds for campaigns.

As mentioned above, state and local parties will likely rely more heavily than in the past on partisan entrepreneurs and interest groups outside the formal party structure. Given the new limits on working together with the national committees, particularly in the realm of fund-raising, the state parties will seek closer ties with individual donors, PACs, and interest groups. The constraints on using nonfederal funds for federal election activity should also encourage state parties to develop informal ties with organizations adept at designing and implementing campaigns. These arrangements will surely include labor unions on the Democratic side. For Republicans, business and trade organizations, such as the pharmaceutical industry, appear poised to do the same (Edsall 2002a). These interest organizations are likely to gain influence in party circles relative to the many party donors in the past that provided only money.

The parties will need to enlarge their list of contributors to make up for some of the lost funds from national party transfers. This response is precisely what advocates of BCRA hope will happen, arguing that a "tough love" policy of cutting off national party funds should spur greater self-reliance and encourage state-based organizations to engage in more grassroots fund-raising than in the past (Mann 2002a). According to the testimony of party officials in *McConnell vs. FEC*, many organizations benefited from joint fund-raisers with national parties; they also used federal candidates to help raise money through appearances, letters, and phone calls to potential donors (Bowler 2002, 22; Erwin 2002, 18–21; Galloway 2002, 5). To the degree that state and local parties relied on federal candidates and national party staff to solicit funds, BCRA forces them to find new rainmakers. Under BCRA, parties can still use the drawing power of federal candidates by inviting them to appear as featured speakers. This should help parties somewhat, although some parties will miss the proactive efforts of federal officeholders who phoned donors to fill tables at Republican Lincoln Day or Democratic Jefferson-Jackson dinners. Some federal officeholders may also be reluctant to appear at fund-raisers, even if legal, since it may create the appearance of raising soft money.

State parties will need to identify "star" fund-raisers to replace federal candidates they may have relied upon in the past. Most likely, this will be the governor (for the party in power). By limiting participants who may raise nonfederal money, BCRA provides a political opportunity for a governor to extend his or her influence in the party network by becoming the fund-raiser-in-chief. Legislative leaders in the statehouse are also well positioned to assume greater responsibilities for party building. Governors, however, may become star fund-raisers for local parties and candidates in *other* states as well, now that U.S. Senators and Presidents can no longer raise and contribute soft money to curry favor with local politicians in states like New Hampshire and Iowa. This situation appears to enhance the motives for presidential aspirants to seek governorships as a launching pad to the Oval Office.

Another set of likely star fund-raisers is celebrities from the world of entertainment. Parties already pursue this strategy where they can, but they will likely intensify efforts to find movie and sports stars to headline fund-raisers. As this practice unfolds, it would be surprising not to see more entertainment figures become politically active, including some who choose to run for office. The parties will also rely on business and social elites to attract attention and resources for the organization. These "nonpolitical" elites will become increasingly prominent in party affairs, not merely as donors but as well-publicized sponsors of fund-raisers and campaign activities.

In the continuing search for resources and friendly partners, the political parties may turn to new umbrella organizations that are not part of the national party structure, but operated by experienced partisans. As I described earlier, these organizations, such as the Democratic State Party Organization and the Leadership Forum, may raise funds centrally and disburse them to local committees as donations. It is doubtful, however, that these organizations will match the fund-raising power of the national committees. Rather than amassing war chests, they will use their limited resources to coordinate the flow of political contributions to states with important electoral contests, and provide technical expertise to party operatives in the states.

Consultants at the state level could augment their influence if party leaders in the states choose *not* to take advantage of the Levin Amendment provisions to engage in federal election activity. Rather than conduct federal activity under state party auspices, state party chairs might encourage campaign professionals to set up nonparty organizations to run voter identification, registration, and GOTV exclusively for state candidates. So long as it is permitted by state laws, this strategy is one way to avoid spending hard money or Levin funds for these activities. Thus, by relying on an extended network of partisans outside the formal party organization to raise and spend nonfederal funds, states could avoid BCRA altogether. But this would come at the cost of enhancing the power of political consultants, who will influence the direction of campaigns without the direct oversight of party leaders and candidates. In this way, BCRA not only distances the national and state parties, but further decentralizes state party functions by encouraging state committees to rely more heavily than they already do on political consultants and nonparty groups.

It is also important to note that BCRA, which spurs interest group activity in federal campaigns (see chapter 1), feeds a similar dynamic at the state level. As interest groups get more involved in federal elections, state and local parties may choose to piggyback on their efforts. These parties could share campaign strategies, consultants, and voter lists with friendly groups that are trying to mobilize similar kinds of voters. In this way, an extended partisan network of allied interest groups could replace the national party committees as the primary conveners of partisan strategies. The difference, however, is that that interest groups now control relatively more of the campaign resources than in the past, and therefore have a bigger say in how they are used.

Overall, BCRA shifts power within the parties away from a Washington base of party elites toward state-based officeholders, nationally recognized celebrities, and allied interest groups. The power brokers in party circles at every level will be leaders of interest groups and political consultants who are skillful at managing independent campaigns, rather than merely wealthy organizations and individuals. Political entrepreneurs leading nonparty campaign organizations should have a greater voice in the direction of electoral strategies and issues.

Factors Attenuating a Difficult Transition to BCRA

Beyond resources, there are contextual factors that will affect the success of parties under BCRA. From a legal perspective, the winners are parties in states where few adjustments to BCRA will be required. These are the states listed in the far right column of table 6.1. Voters in these states have already chosen to regulate the political parties in ways comparable to BCRA, and the fact that most of these states have openly supported BCRA comes as no surprise. Winners also include the four states with legislative elections in the odd years (Virginia, New Jersey, Louisiana, and Mississippi). Under BCRA, federal election activity only kicks in when there are federal candidates on the ballot in that year; otherwise, the parties may use funds regulated under state rather than federal law.

From an electoral perspective, the deleterious effects of BCRA on party organizations should be attenuated in states where there is strong partisan competition. Here, we can expect parties to continue to play an important role, particularly when control of the legislature hangs in the balance. Closely contested states attract resources and generate stronger incentives to organize than weakly contested states. Party candidates and officeholders want the benefits that come with controlling the statehouse, so they are more willing to contribute resources to building a party that will help them achieve this goal. The more that office seekers need a mechanism to pursue collective goals, the more they have an incentive to support a strong party role (Aldrich 1995). The incentives to organize vigorously should be especially salient in states in the Midwest like Michigan, Illinois, and Missouri, as well as competitive states in the West, such as Washington and Oregon. To the degree that BCRA inhibits party fund-raising and spending on state elections, partisans in these states may choose to pursue electoral goals through nonparty associations.

Finally, an overlooked resource is leadership. In spite of the new challenges presented by BCRA, talented state party leaders can develop innovative strategies and attract other able individuals to the organization. Ray C. Bliss, who chaired the Ohio Republican Party and later the RNC (1965–1969), helped rebuild organizations during a period of electoral crisis for the Republican Party (Green 1994). A more recent example of effective organizational leadership is Ralph Reed, the chairman of the Georgia Republican Party. Reed organized a party operation that achieved the biggest surprises of the 2002 elections, dethroning the top three Democrats in the state—the Governor, U.S. Senator, and Speaker of the House. These examples show that energetic and capable party leaders can make a significant difference in mobilizing partisans, even under difficult circumstances.

CONCLUSION

By changing the federal campaign finance rules, BCRA should inaugurate a wave of experimentation among party committees that has not been seen since the last set of major reforms in 1974. In particular, parties in the states will be influenced by new rules on committee transfers and federal election activity that apply directly to them. It is likely that party operatives will seek innovative ways to minimize constraints these rules impose on state and local election activity. But parties will also be influenced indirectly by the behavior of groups competing at the national level in federal elections, learning new campaign strategies from Washington-based groups that are compelled by BCRA to change more fundamentally than actors in the states.

Perhaps the most lasting influence of BCRA will be its effect on intraparty relations. BCRA tries hard to make the lines more clear between money that is used in federal and state elections. The effort to do this will make it harder for parties to use nonfederal funds that help federal candidates, which means that supporters of BCRA will have achieved a chief goal of the legislation. But the bright lines will also diminish the incentives for levels of party to work together, and reduce the efforts of state and local parties on behalf of an entire party ticket. Instead, they will focus on the state elections. BCRA, therefore, should weaken the intraparty links among candidates and levels of party.

By pushing fund-raising and the spending of soft money below the level of the national committees, BCRA should trigger greater decentralization of the party structure and encourage differentiation among state and local committees. Some parties in the states may thrive in the manner reformers hoped for, by focusing on intensive grassroots efforts to win voter support. BCRA, however, will probably not spur greater party activity where parties are currently weak and may, in fact, hurt such committees, since they will no longer receive subsidies from the national committees or, in some cases, the state committee. Generally, parties in the larger states will need to adjust more under the new rules than those in the smaller states. Parties in larger states tend to rely on bigger campaign contributions—often in excess of BCRA's $10,000 limits on soft money—to pay for voter contact activities. Much of this activity will now need to be funded with hard money and Levin funds.

Instead of strong ties between national and state committees, we are likely to see more fluid and informal arrangements among committees and candidates. The restriction on raising soft money in $10,000 increments will encourage partisans to set up committees wherever there is a tight contest. We can expect more local parties in the high growth suburban areas of the country where many crucial "swing" voters reside. But these committees may come and go, depending on the importance of a federal election. Those that endure may end up having minimal ties to the state party. Instead, these local "machines" in key congressional districts may well exploit the Levin fund provisions and increased hard money contributions to conduct targeted federal election activity.

In some instances, the national committees may choose to avoid working with state organizations altogether, since they will lack soft money to influence the direction of state party activity. National party organizations may even actively discourage state and local organizations from participating in federal elections, because such activity could prevent the national committees from running independent ads. One provision in BCRA declares that the parties may pursue either coordinated or independent expenditures, but not both.

Federal candidates may also loosen their ties with state parties, because these organizations are less useful to them in their campaigns. At the same time, the state parties will have less use for federal candidates who can no longer solicit funds on behalf of the party. Some parties will continue to take advantage of the star power of federal officeholders to raise money and stay within the bounds of the law. On the other hand, the incentive to help the state party is diminished if the federal candidate is in a tough race and does not want the opposition to stir up the notion that he or she is involved in raising soft money. The cumulative effect of provisions to keep federal candidates away from nonfederal money is to diminish the ties between federal candidates and the state and local party organizations. This division elevates the importance of governors and state legislative leaders within the organization.

While BCRA reverses a trend toward party centralization, it actually accelerates some patterns we saw before the law was passed. It puts more emphasis on voter contacts and encourages greater participation in campaigns among interest groups. The irony of the latter trend is that the party and its candidates actually may end up relying even more on interest groups, although on a narrower collection that has the capacity to design and implement campaigns, usually around single issues. In subsequent elections campaign themes may appear more ideological, creating sharper distinctions between the parties on a variety of issues.

7

The Party as an Extended Network: Members Giving to Each Other and to Their Parties

Anne H. Bedlington and Michael J. Malbin

The Bipartisan Campaign Reform Act's most immediate impact is on the political parties. How one assesses the effects will depend partly on what one thinks parties are, and ought to be. Much of the early discussion about the Bipartisan Campaign Reform Act speculated about the law's likely effect on the formal national and state political party committees. The two previous chapters in this volume show, however, that these committees are not the whole party. The potential role of the not-quite-party committees makes it clear that the mission and scope of the parties are not fully encompassed by the formal committees.

In a recent study of legislative staffers in Los Angeles, J. P. Monroe argued that political parties are better understood as weblike relationships among political elites than as structured institutions (Monroe 2001). Monroe's study was about city politics, but his insight helps us understand national parties. It is helpful to think about congressional parties as a series of interwoven relationships, with the power of formal leaders and party committees depending, in the last analysis, on their ability to serve the interests of individual Members. As Robin Kolodny argued in a book about the congressional campaign committees, the Members support these committees because the committees help serve the Members' desire to be reelected, to exercise power within Congress (or "make a difference"), and to help enact good public policy (Kolodny 1998). The second of these three goals—the desire to exercise power or make a difference—covers two different concerns: collectively, the Members want to be part of a majority because of the majority party's importance for setting Congress's agenda. Individually, they would like to be leaders, either within their party or on their committees. The party's function, for incumbent Members, is to help them achieve these goals.

We are interested in this chapter in the remarkable growth over the past decade in Members' contributions to other candidates and to their parties. Why are Members giving money away instead of hoarding it? Once Member contributions were fairly limited, used primarily as vehicles for leadership candidates to purchase the favor of colleagues. The practice has since come to be a significant factor in the collective battle for majority control. With new contribution limits under the Bipartisan Campaign Reform Act of 2002 (BCRA), it may even become a significant source of replacement funds for the soft money banned by the new law.

A STORY

We'll start with a story. The Second Congressional District of West Virginia stretches in a narrow band across the middle of the state, from the Potomac to the Ohio River. Suburban sprawl from Washington, D.C., is beginning to reach the small vacation towns of the Eastern Panhandle. The district itself sprawls: 270 miles to the southwest is Charleston, the state's capital and largest city, with a population of 53,421.

For eighteen years, Bob Wise represented the district in Congress, winning reelection in 1998 with 73 percent of the vote. As long as Wise ran, it looked as if the seat would be his. But in 2000, Wise left the House to mount a successful challenge against the incumbent Republican Governor, Cecil Underwood. Most national Democrats thought the seat would be safe for their party, but Republicans saw an opportunity. In 1996, Bill Clinton earned only 49 percent of the district's vote for President, compared to 40 percent for Bob Dole and 11 percent for Ross Perot. This was significantly worse than Clinton's fifteen-point margin statewide. More importantly, it meant that the Democratic vote was not a solid majority.

Wise's decision to leave Congress attracted a strong Democratic field. Ken Hechler, the eighty-six-year-old, four-term Secretary of State, was trying to return to the institution in which he served from 1959 until 1977. State Senator Martha Walker was a respected legislator from the district's population center. The third candidate was Jim Humphreys, a former two-term state Senator who had earned a great deal of money in private law practice. He spent more than $3.5 million of it to win the primary handily, with 42 percent of the vote.

The only Republican in the race was Shelly Moore Capito, a moderate, pro-choice state legislator who had grown up in a political household as the daughter of the three-term GOP Governor, Arch Moore (1969–1977, 1985–1989). National Republicans saw this as a potentially tight race from the beginning. Capito filed her "Statement of Organization" with the Federal Election Commission in August 1999. During the remaining months of 1999, she raised $269,000. Consider that to have been seed money. Individual contributions amounted to $157,000, of which $149,000 was itemized, and $124,050 of the itemized money came from West Virginians. In other words, about half of Capito's seed money came from individual constituents. More than two-thirds of the rest came from the political action committees (PACs) of sitting Members of Congress ($40,000), or Members' principal campaign committees (PCCs) ($44,000) or from party committees ($5,000 from the National Republican Congressional Committee). This was a strong and early sign of support, signaling party leaders' belief that Capito had a good chance.

But Capito was starting behind. Shortly before the May 9 primary, the West Virginia poll showed Humphreys leading by 55 percent to 21 percent for the November election, with the rest undecided (2000). More ominously for the GOP candidate: Humphreys seemed prepared to spend whatever it would take to win. To win the May 9 primary, Humphreys began airing commercials in October 1999! (Capito's first commercials ran eleven months later, in September 2000.) During the general election, Humphreys lent his campaign another $3 million. If Capito was to have a chance, she would need help.

House Speaker J. Dennis Hastert came early and helped often. On Saturday, May 20, eleven days after the primary, the Speaker was the featured guest at a $125-a-plate fund-raiser at the Charleston Marriott. The event was not heavily attended, but it generated favorable news coverage (Tuckwiller 2000). By the end of the summer, presidential nominee George W. Bush, House Majority Leader Dick Armey, Conference Chairman J. C. Watts, Republican National Committee Chairman Jim Nicholson, and Senator John McCain had all visited the district. Senator McCain came back again in early November, as did Majority Whip Tom DeLay. (House Democratic Leader Dick Gephardt visited Humphreys' campaign in late October.) After Labor Day, the National Republican Congressional Committee (NRCC) began running the first of a series of four rounds of advertising criticizing Humphreys. Capito's own ads began at about the same time. The campaign was going well. By early October, the West Virginia poll showed the race to be essentially even.

But to win, Capito had to stay on the air. Humphreys' final two loans to his campaign, for a total of $460,000, came on October 27 and November 2. To counter this, Capito's campaign raised almost $300,000 during the final two weeks. Two-thirds came from political committees. Many were business PACs, which had finally come to see this as a race that could help determine which party controlled the 107th Congress. But during this push, $63,000 also came from Members' PACs and Members' PCCs. With the money she raised in these two weeks, Capito could put more than $200,000 into her final media campaign.

In the end, it all came together. She received 108,769 votes (48 percent) to Humphreys' 103,003 (46 percent), with 6 percent going to a Libertarian. George W. Bush's coattails may have helped: the new President carried the district by ten percentage points. But Capito needed, and got by, with help from some friends.

Two postscripts: (1) As a new Member of Congress, Capito supported the Shays-Meehan campaign finance reform bill. She was the principal sponsor of the so-called "Millionaires' Amendment" in the House, a provision that raises the contribution limits for candidates who are running against self-financed opponents (see table 1.1 and chapter 9). (2) The 2002 election was essentially a rematch. Jim Humphries once again beat Martha Walker in the primary. This time, the margin was only fifty-one to forty-nine. Former Senator Walker, now a Public Service Commissioner, was supported by EMILY's List, which ran a televised issue ad criticizing Humphreys for having made late income tax payments totaling $38,000. Ironically, the charge was the same as one the NRCC had used to advantage four years earlier. In the general election, Capito once again had her colleagues' support, raising more than $250,000 (about 10 percent of her total) from other Members' campaign committees or PACs, and another $80,000 in hard money from the party. Humphreys spent $8.1 million in 2002, $7.8 million of which came from himself. After two elections, his campaign committee owed him more than $14 million. The loan did not help politically. In the rematch, Capito won reelection by a sixty-to-forty margin.

MORE STORIES

Capito's story is dramatic but by no means unique. Six challengers defeated incumbent House Members in 2000, and another four were successful in 2002. In almost all of these races, Members' PACs, Members' PCCs, and party money were important to one or both of the candidates. For example, Michael Ross, a Democrat, defeated four-term Republican incumbent Jay Dickey in southern Arkansas' Fourth District in 2000, 51 percent to 49 percent. Dickey had voted to impeach President Clinton. According to *The Almanac of American Politics*, Clinton returned the favor by campaigning heavily for Ross, raising more than $300,000 in his behalf (Barone and Cohen 2001). (The district includes Hope, the former President's hometown.) Dickey, who refused to accept PAC contributions, raised $1.7 million from individuals. He also received more than a quarter of a million dollars in hard money help from party-related sources (we are not including soft money in any of these races): $113,000 in various party committee contributions, $66,000 in party coordinated expenditures, $12,116 from Members' PACs, and another $71,619 from PCCs. Ross also raised $1.7 million—about the same as the incumbent. He was able to do this because—unlike many other Democrats—his money from the party and from Members fully matched his rival's: Ross raised almost $50,000 from various party committees and benefited from $66,150 in party coordinated expenditures. He also raised $103,641 from Members' PACs and another $46,000 from Members' PCCs. The mixture was different, but the bottom line from all four kinds of party-related sources was equal to Dickey's.

The other three successful Democratic challengers in 2000, all from California, each received important help from Members' PACs and PCCs: Jane Harman received a combined amount of about $130,000; Susan Davis, about $130,000; and Adam Schiff, about $170,000. In each case, however, the defeated Republican incumbent received even more: $200,000 for Brian Bilbray's race against Davis; $240,000 for Steven Kuykendall against Jane Harman, and $240,000 for James Rogan against Schiff. In contrast, the two successful GOP challengers (Bob Simmons, who defeated Sam Gejdensen in Connecticut, and Mark Kennedy, who beat David Minge in Minnesota) won races in which Members' PACs and PCCs were less engaged on either side of the race.

The Members' PACs and PCCs were very important in close races without an incumbent running. Nine of the open seat contests in 2000, including Capito's, were decided by a two-candidate margin of 53 to 47 percent or less. Six of the nine were 51 to 49 percent or closer. On average, the nine Republicans in these races received $186,000 from Members' PACs and PCCs. The nine Democrats received an average of $125,000, or two-thirds as much. The Republicans won eight of these nine races. We have already seen that much of this money comes in at the end of the campaign, when it can be crucial. Since the Republicans managed to hold on to a majority in the House with only six votes to spare in 2000, every GOP Representative might well want to ask whether the party owes its control of the chamber to the effort the leaders put into stimulating Members to contribute in races where it would do the most good. The situation was less one-sided in 2002, when ten open seat races were decided by margins of fifty-three to forty-seven or less. The Republicans averaged $146,000 (versus the Democrats' $121,000) in Member-to-candidate contributions in these races, winning six of the ten.

LARGER, WITH NEW PURPOSE

It seems clear that something important is happening—important not only for scholarly conceptions about party, but for the conduct of future elections under BCRA. When Ross Baker (1989) and Clyde Wilcox (1989b, 1990) wrote about Members' PACs and Member-to-Member contributions, the phenomenon was relatively new. Members' PACs first captured public attention in 1978, when Representative Henry Waxman created and used one of the first "leadership PACs" by a nonleader to give money to colleagues as part of his successful bid to become chair of the Energy and Commerce Committee's Health subcommittee. At the time, Waxman's $24,000 in contributions were portrayed as having helped influence his colleagues' decision to vote for him over the more senior, respected moderate, Richardson Preyer (Baker 1989).

The contributions from Members' PACs and PCCs grew from a total of about $500,000 in 1978 to more than $5 million in 1986 and 1988. Figure 7.1 looks at contributions from Senate and House Members' PCCs and PACs to other candidates, from 1978 through 2002. We have combined Senate and House data to let us compare our information from 1990 to 2002 to Wilcox's for 1978 to 1988. After 1988, contributions from Members' PACs and PCCs dipped for two elections and then took off. These contributions grew by 85 percent between 1992 and 1994, another 70 percent between 1994 and 1996, 23 percent between 1996 and 1998, 61 percent between 1998 and 2000, and 44 percent between 2000 and 2002. By 2002 the Members were giving ten times as much to other candidates as they had been just one decade earlier. (Note that all 2002 data in this chapter go through November 25. Full year data were not available at the time this was written, but the November reports cover the bulk of all activity.)

It will not do, however, to leave our description in so aggregate a form. Senators with PACs give less of their money as contributions than House Members, so the remainder of this paper will focus on House Members. Within the House, the two parties have come to behave in a similar manner, but this was not always so. In raw numbers, the story is fairly simple: the Democrats started out ahead in 1992, Republicans then surged forward. The growth began for both parties during the 1994 election—the first one in decades when control of the chamber

Figure 7.1   Contributions from Senate and House Members' PACs and PCCs to Senate and House Candidates, 1978–2002

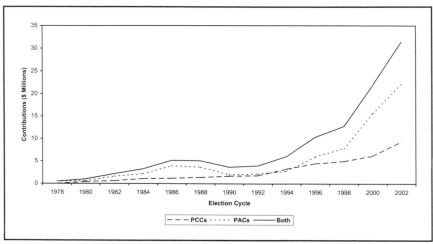

Sources: 1978–88: C. Wilcox, 1990, "Member to Member Giving"; 1990–2002: Compiled from FEC data.

was at stake. House Republicans more than tripled their giving between 1992 and 1994 and then doubled it again in 1996, when they were in the majority. Democratic giving stayed flat between 1994 and 1996. Democratic giving then grew by 20 percent between 1996 and 1998, while Republicans' levels increased by 37 percent. Then, in the 2000 election cycle, the Democrats finally started behaving the way the Republicans did, coordinating their efforts to work for a majority. Democratic Member PAC and PCC contributions to candidates more than doubled between 1998 and 2000. They now exceeded the levels Republicans had reached in the previous cycle. The Republicans continued to stay ahead, though, by increasing their own giving by 43 percent. For 2002, Democratic giving increased another 27 percent, while that of Republicans went up 45 percent. By November 30, 2002, House Democrats had given other House candidates about $2 for every $3 given by their GOP counterparts.

The growing importance of Member PAC and PCC contributions since 1994 seems to stem from the increased awareness among Members of how much is at stake for them in contested elections outside their own districts. Members of the two parties seemed to accept, and act on, that awareness at different times. Until the Republican landslide of 1994, Democrats had become complacent in their majority status, which the party had held since 1953. Most Democrats outside the formal leadership at that time saw Members' PACs and Member-to-Member contributions as relatively minor weapons in a battle that scarcely had to be joined.

Figure 7.2   Contributions from Democratic and Republican House Members' PACs and PCCs to Candidates, 1990–2002

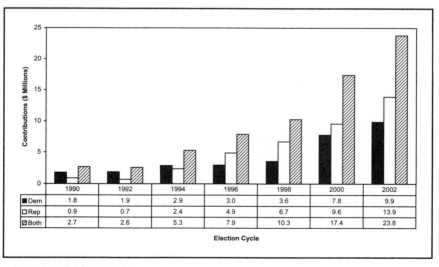

Source: Compiled from FEC data.

Republicans were split between an older faction that despaired of winning control during their legislative careers and a more activist group that believed a majority was in their reach. The young activists, led by Newt Gingrich (R-Ga.), Vin Weber (R-Minn.) and Bob Walker (R-Pa.), created the Conservative Opportunity Society (COS), outside the formal leadership, to pressure the leaders to sharpen the differences between the parties in the legislative arena, in order to help the GOP win an electoral majority. In their view, the opportunity to focus the public's attention nationally on the policy differences between Democrats and Republicans was more important than to bargain politely inside the chamber for what they thought of as the crumbs off a table they had had no role in setting.

By the late-1980s, COS's allies inside the leadership were Whip Trent Lott (R-Miss.) and Dick Cheney (R-Wyo.), the conference chairman, who had the support of both COS and the older leaders. Cheney was largely responsible for rewriting the party conference's rules to strengthen the leaders' hand in making committee appointments and selecting committee leaders. (Later party leaders used these powers to great advantage in persuading fellow Republicans to contribute their money to close races.) He also started a program to increase Member-to-candidate contributions, but with only limited success. When Cheney left Congress in 1989 to become Secretary of Defense, the program withered until Bill Paxon (R-N.Y.) replaced Guy Vander Jagt (R-Mich.) as chair of the NRCC in 1993, and was able to act with the full support of the party leadership. Looking back in a 1996 interview, Vander Jagt said that the leadership, under Bob Michel, "Wanted a Republican majority but a lot of them didn't believe it was possible. . . . [T]he House had been a comfortable place. You kind of protected one another" (*Frontline* 1996). Acting protectively meant, in part, that most Members would not give money directly to a challenger to defeat a sitting colleague. That changed under Gingrich and Paxon.

The differences in the two parties' political positions express themselves through the division of Members' contributions as well as the raw totals. In figures 7.3 and 7.4, we chart the contributions of House Democrats and Republicans in 1994–2002 to incumbent, challenger and open seat candidates.

- House Democrats in 1994 mostly pursued incumbent protection (figure 7.3); Republicans used almost all of their smaller pot of money for challengers and open seat candidates (figure 7.4).
- In 1996, the House GOP used a now larger pot of money to protect new incumbents, but it also increased its investment in open seat races. The Democratic strategy mirrored the Republicans', as the new minority looked for challenger opportunities to unseat new incumbents, increasing their Members' support for these races from $600,000 to $1.3 million.
- In 1998, the Republicans continued supporting incumbents at risk and open seat candidates, but poured all of their new money into challengers' races. Speaker Gingrich and other House GOP leaders mistakenly thought Presi-

Figure 7.3   Contributions from Democratic House Members' PACs and PCCs to Incumbent, Challenger, and Open Seat Candidates, 1990–2002

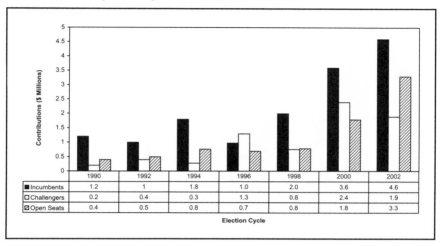

Source: Compiled from FEC data.

Figure 7.4   Contributions from Republican House Members' PACs and PCCs to Incumbent, Challenger, and Open Seat Candidates, 1990–2002

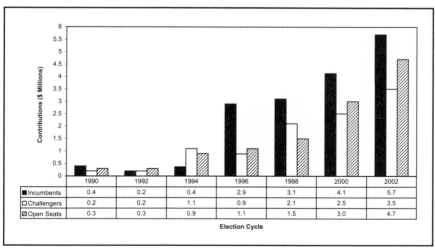

Source: Compiled from FEC data.

dent Clinton's pending impeachment would lead to major gains for their party in the midterm elections. That assumption is visible in the Members' contribution patterns. The Democrats apparently had similar thoughts, since they reduced support for challengers and open seat candidates while doubling the Members' contributions to incumbents.

- In 2000 and 2002, both parties increased their giving across all types of candidates, with one exception: the Democrats gave less money to challengers in 2002 than 2000.

For a closer look at the House Members' contributions in 2000 and 2002, we have listed the top fifty recipients of these funds for each of the two years in table 7.1 (excluding those who ran in special elections.) The table lists candidates in descending order of the combined amount received from Members' PACs and PCCs. It also gives the candidates' status (incumbent, challenger or open seat candidate) and the percentage they received of the two-party vote.

In 2000, the partisan balance in the top fifty strongly favored the Republicans, who outnumbered the Democrats two to one. In 2002, the balance was closer, with twenty-seven Republicans and twenty-three Democrats. The group of fifty in 2000 included seventeen incumbents, fifteen challengers, and eighteen open seat candidates. In 2002—a reapportionment year with several races involving two incumbents—the top fifty included twenty-seven incumbents, six challengers, and seven open seat candidate. Virtually every one of these hundred candidates was in a race that looked competitive for much of the cycle, with many staying tight until Election Day. It is also worth noting that the contributions coming into these races from House Members' PACs and PCCs meant a lot to the candidates. The median percentage for this group of candidates was 9 to 10 percent of total receipts in 2000 and 11 to 12 percent of total receipts in 2002.

The list of top givers, not surprisingly, is a sharp contrast to the list of top receivers. Table 7.2 shows the twenty-five most active contributors to other candidates in 2000 and 2002.

In 2000, the top party leaders—Dennis Hastert, Dick Armey, Tom DeLay, and Dick Gephardt—were all at or near the top of the list. Another six of the top thirty were jockeying to move up to a committee chairmanship or to a higher leadership position: Bill Thomas and Phil Crane were seeking the Ways and Means Committee chairmanship; Billy Tauzin and Mike Oxley wanted to chair the Commerce Committee; Steny Hoyer and Nancy Pelosi wanted to move up the party leadership ladder. The 2002 story is substantially similar, with leadership candidates (this time including Pelosi, Martin Frost, Hoyer, and Tom Reynolds) again prominent among the top givers.

These House Members fit the standard explanation for what motivates contributors: people who appear to have stepped up their contribution activity in part to impress colleagues. However, there are two problems with this standard explanation. First, most of the other top givers were fairly secure in their party or committee leadership positions. They appeared not to be lobbying to change

Table 7.1   Top 50 House Candidates Receiving Contributions in 2000 and 2002 from Members' PCCs and PACs

	2000				2002		
Member	Party/ Status	Election Percent	Combined PAC/PCC	Member	Party/ Status	Election Percent	Combined PAC/PCC
Fletcher, E.	R/I	60.3	240,307	Gekas, G.	R/I	48.6	256,043
Sherwood, D.	R/I	52.6	232,380	Capito, S.	R/I	60.0	250,974
Rogers, M.	R/O	50.1	232,332	Luther, B.	D/I	44.3	242,100
Nethercutt, G.	R/I	59.3	225,518	Latham, T.	R/I	55.7	240,562
Kuykendall, S.	R/I	49.1	214,688	Thurman, K.	D/I	49.1	236,503
Hart, M.	R/O	59.0	206,764	Holden, T.	D/I	51.4	225,274
Capito, S.	R/O	51.3	197,588	Rogers, M.	R/O	51.1	217,785
Rehberg, D.	R/O	52.7	195,670	Morella, C.	R/I	47.9	213,301
Rogan, J.	R/I	45.7	185,805	Shimkus, J.	R/I	54.8	209,812
Wilson, H.	R/I	50.7	177,448	Hayes, R.	R/I	54.6	208,980
Pirozzi, E.	R/C	36.8	173,043	Simmons, R.	R/I	54.1	206,960
Bilbray, B.	R/I	48.0	171,070	Pickering, C.	R/I	64.8	203,365
Hayes, R.	R/I	55.9	168,139	Phelps, D.	D/I	45.2	203,000
Holt, R.	D/I	50.1	165,988	Chocola, J.	R/O	52.5	198,615
Honda, M.	D/O	56.5	163,179	Boswell, L.	D/I	54.2	198,000
Hoeffel, J.	D/I	53.7	161,740	Maloney, J.	D/I	44.2	197,499
Tiberi, P.	R/O	54.8	157,156	Grucci, F.	R/I	49.2	192,755
Maloney, J.	D/I	54.9	150,996	Wilson, H.	R/I	54.4	191,732
Northup, A.	R/I	54.5	150,300	Swett, K.	D/C	41.8	186,274
Schiff, A.	D/C	54.3	149,073	Sullivan, J.	R/I	56.9	184,500
McDonald, D.	R/C	43.6	148,808	Hensarling, T.	R/O	59.1	172,101
Grucci, F.	R/C	58.2	148,440	Kennedy, M	R/I	62.1	172,060
Ferguson, M.	R/O	51.2	146,983	Matheson, J.	D/I	50.5	172,025
Stoker, M.	R/C	45.8	145,965	Pomeroy, E.	D/I	52.4	171,569
Evans, L.	D/I	54.9	143,930	Taff, A.	R/C	48.3	168,005
Stupak, B.	D/I	59.3	142,000	Cardoza, D.	D/O	54.8	167,478
Koster, J.	R/O	47.4	141,837	Ross, M.	D/I	60.5	165,908
Porter, J.	R/C	46.1	141,647	Shows, C.	D/C	35.2	165,500
Tancredo, T.	R/I	56.1	139,703	Toomey, P.	R/I	57.3	163,829
Byrum, D.	D/O	49.9	139,486	Thompson, J.	D/O	47.6	163,500
Kline, J.	R/C	49.2	139,337	Northup, A.	R/I	51.6	162,528
Schrock, E.	R/O	52.0	138,430	Porter, J.	R/O	60.1	162,475
Keller, R.	R/O	50.9	137,037	Mccotter, T.	R/O	59.1	159,094
Jordan, E.	D/C	45.5	136,387	Moore, D.	D/I	51.7	157,316
Chapin, L.	D/O	49.2	136,076	Norris, J.	D/C	44.3	155,499
Graves, S.	R/O	52.1	135,778	Herrera, D.	D/O	39.9	155,156
Johnson, J.	R/O	41.9	134,505	Edwards, C.	D/I	52.2	155,000
Casey, P.	D/C	47.4	134,200	Gerlach, J.	R/O	51.3	153,717
Larsen, R.	D/O	52.3	133,562	Herseth, S.	D/O	46.0	149,000
Cunneen, J.	R/O	43.5	132,850	Kline, J.	R/C	55.8	147,456
Baca, J.	D/I	63.2	131,450	Carson, J.	D/I	54.9	145,500
Baker, M. R	R/C	45.1	130,029	Richaud, M.	D/O	52.2	143,000
Smith, D.	R/C	42.5	128,598	Bentley, H.	R/O	45.5	143,000
Zimmer, D.	R/C	49.9	125,940	Beauprez, B.	R/O	50.0	140,923
Matheson, J.	D/C	57.5	123,000	Pearce, S.	R/O	56.4	140,201
Greenleaf, S.	R/C	46.4	122,927	Clark, M.	D/O	39.8	139,800
Rodriguez, R.	R/C	46.3	122,342	Johnson, N.	R/I	55.8	138,690
Keenan, N.	D/O	47.3	122,218	Thomas, J.	D/C	46.7	137,500
Forbes, M.	D/I	n.a.	121,318	Raye, K.	R/O	47.8	136,000
Kirk, M.	R/O	51.2	120,292	Feeney, T.	R/O	61.8	135,942

Note: In Party/Status column, I = Incumbent, C = Challenger, O = Open Seat.

Table 7.2   Top 25 House Members Giving to House Candidates from Their PCCs and PACs, 2000 and 2002

House Member	Party	Given by Members' PCC ($)	Given by Members' PAC ($)	Combined PCC & PCC ($)
2000				
Gephardt, R.	D	0	1,017,500	1,017,500
Pelosi, N.	D	133,709	792,800	926,509
Delay, T.	R	41,000	844,391	885,391
Hastert, J. D.	R	35,000	752,505	787,505
Hoyer, S.	D	126,000	645,500	771,500
Armey, R.	R	0	736,584	736,584
Rangel, C.	D	174,500	399,500	574,000
Boehner, J.	R	1,996	557,432	559,428
Dreier, D.	R	5,000	511,549	516,549
Waxman, H.	D	54,000	351,000	405,000
Lewis, J.	R	89,849	260,000	349,849
McCrery, J.	R	3,000	336,500	339,500
Tauzin, W.	R	26,060	291,055	317,115
Oxley, M.	R	56,100	234,500	290,600
Menendez, R.	D	29,000	245,713	274,713
Doolittle, J.	R	101,000	156,000	257,000
Crane, P.	R	56,000	197,000	253,000
Hobson, D.	R	44,500	186,303	230,803
Thomas, W.	R	44,000	182,000	226,000
Weller, G.	R	3,000	210,500	213,500
Blunt, R.	R	4,000	202,429	206,429
Bonior, D.	D	0	197,720	197,720
Watts, J. C.	R	2,000	186,156	188,156
Delauro, R.	D	169,500	0	169,500
Blumenauer, E.	D	2,250	153,500	155,750
2002				
Pelosi, N.	D	9,000	1,025,000	1,094,000
Delay, T.	R	2,000	984,855	986,855
Hastert, J. D.	R	87,000	786,000	873,000
Hoyer, S.	D	104,975	634,000	738,975
Menendez, R.	D	1,000	701,955	702,955
Rangel, C.	D	120,500	545,500	666,000
Boehner, J.	R	0	639,497	639,497
Blunt, R.	R	31,000	597,722	628,722
Sununu, J.	R	608,445	0	608,445
Oxley, M.	R	12,325	544,000	556,325
Frost, M.	D	49,000	486,408	535,408
McCrery, J.	R	8,896	520,000	528,896
Reynolds, T.	R	0	509,487	509,487
Pryce, D.	R	28,000	458,000	486,000
Lewis, J.	R	100,000	353,000	453,000
Graham, L.	R	452,044	0	452,044
Tauzin, W.	R	1,000	433,470	432,470
Clement, B.	D	425,289	0	425,289
Bryant, E.	R	413,150	0	413,150
Ganske, J.	R	384,584	0	384,584
Thomas, W.	R	30,000	352,500	382,500
Waxman, H.	D	46,000	332,000	378,000
Gephardt, R.	D	0	360,000	360,000
Dreier, D.	R	28,000	309,500	337,500
Davis, T.	R	68,200	250,500	318,700

their relative positions *within* the party, but fighting to be part of the majority—to be a committee or subcommittee chair, and not a ranking minority Member. The second problem with the theory is that it does not match the way most aspirants for committee chairmanship were behaving. Thomas, Crane, Tauzin, and Oxley were conspicuous givers. But 2000 was a year in which virtually all of the committee chairs changed, because of a three-term limit that the Republicans adopted at the end of 1994. Of the twenty-two Republicans who were identified in press reports as serious candidates for chairmanships in December 2000, only six had contributed unusually large amounts of money to other candidates. The other sixteen were much further down in the rank order.

THE PARTY COMMITTEES

Our last finding was the most surprising to us, and potentially the most important. Most accounts separate their treatment of Member PACs and PCCs from discussions of the national party committees. This separation can no longer be sustained. Figure 7.5 shows that an increasing proportion of the contributions from House Members' PCCs are going to the parties, rather than to other candidates. Figure 7.6 shows, in dollars, the amount of contributions from House Members' PACs and PCCs to the campaign committees. Figure 7.7 shows the importance of these contributions as a percentage of the campaign committees' total hard money receipts.

Figure 7.5   Contributions from House PCCs to Parties as a Percentage of Their Total Contributions, 1990–2002

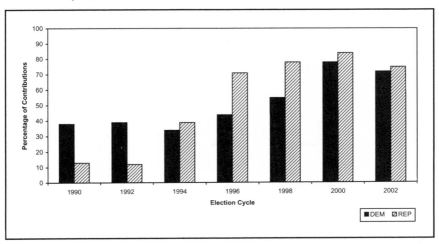

Source: Compiled from FEC data.

Figure 7.6   Contributions from House Members' PACs and PCCs to the Congressional Campaign Committees, 1990–2002

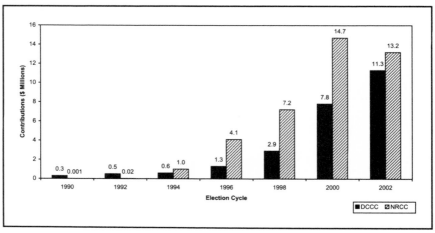

Source: Compiled from FEC data.

Figure 7.7   Contributions from House Members' PACs and PCCs as a Percentage of Congressional Campaign Committees' Hard Money Receipts, 1990–2002

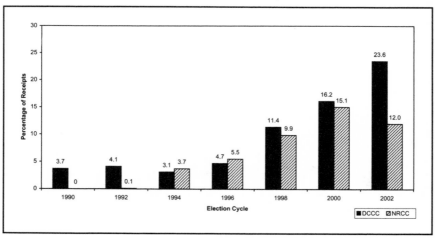

Source: Compiled from FEC data.

Table 7.3   **Top 25 House Members Giving to Party Committees from Their PCCs and PACs, 2000 and 2002**

House Member	Party	Given by Members' PCC ($)	Given by Members' PAC ($)	Combined PCC & PCC ($)
2000				
McIntosh, D.	R	925,000	0	925,000
Cox, C.	R	752,000	0	752,000
Dreier, D.	R	725,000	16,000	741,000
Armey, R.	R	602,500	15,000	617,500
Hastert, J. D.	R	480,623	20,000	500,623
Lewis, J.	R	490,000	0	490,000
Rangel, C.	D	408,500	15,000	423,500
Delay, T.	R	260,100	125,000	385,100
Matsui, R.	D	320,000	0	320,000
Lewis, J.	D	304,000	0	304,000
Kennedy, P.	D	285,000	11,075	296,075
Deutsch, P.	D	150,000	130,000	280,000
Tauzin, W.	R	270,000	400	270,400
Davis, T.	R	270,000	0	270,000
Oberstar, J.	D	269,450	0	269,450
Pryce, D.	R	255,000	10,000	265,000
Forbes, M.	D	260,000	0	260,000
Thomas, W.	R	252,500	0	252,500
Menendez, R.	D	235,000	16,787	251,787
Danner, P.	D	250,000	0	250,000
Markey, E.	D	233,000	0	233,000
Hinojosa, R.	D	216,000	0	216,000
Pelosi, N.	D	146,500	60,000	206,500
Hutchinson, A.	R	202,000	0	202,000
Herger, W.	R	201,240	0	201,240
2002				
Blagojevich, R.	D	642,000	0	642,000
Lowey, N.	D	600,500	0	600,500
Rangel, C.	D	514,500	6,500	521,000
Thomas, W.	R	505,000	0	505,000
Lantos, T.	D	492,900	0	492,900
Tauzin, W.	R	325,350	15,000	340,350
Hastert, J. D.	R	338,500	0	338,500
Dreier, D.	R	325,000	0	325,000
Oberstar, J.	D	316,800	0	316,800
Menendez, R.	D	285,000	25,901	310,901
Cunningham, R.	R	300,000	0	300,000
Delay, T.	R	260,000	40,000	300,000
Cox, C.	R	281,400	0	281,400
Granger, K.	R	278,750	0	278,750
Markey, E.	D	275,000	0	275,000
Pryce, D.	R	250,000	15,000	265,000
Davis, T.	R	250,000	0	250,000
Portman, R.	R	226,500	20,000	246,500
Matsui, R.	D	237,033	0	237,033
Hoyer, S.	D	227,750	0	227,750
Oxley, M.	R	211,300	15,000	226,300
Young, C. W.	R	210,000	15,000	225,000
Bonior, D.	D	202,000	20,000	222,000
Pelosi, N.	D	155,250	65,000	220,250
Lewis, J.	R	215,000	0	215,000

As these figures show, Democrats gave $11.3 million in 2002 to the DCCC and Republicans gave $13.2 million to the NRCC. This accounted for about 12 percent of the NRCC's hard money and an amazing 24 percent of the DCCC's. The growth in these numbers has been stunning. For some time, political scientists have described the national party committees as if they were relatively disembodied sets of professionals, working together with professional campaign consultants who perhaps had once been employed by the committees, responsible for little more than providing money and campaign services—"economies of scale"—for their otherwise independent candidates. The picture in recent elections is more complicated, and more interesting.

Anyone who follows elections was made aware during the campaign season of programs House Republican and Democratic party leaders used to set formal guidelines for Members' contributions (Rice 1999; Van Dongen 2000; Allen 2000; Bresnahan 2000; Heberlig 2001; Cillizza 2002). Our numbers show that the effort was remarkably successful. (Table 7.3 lists the top givers to the party committees.)

This table shows that most of the massive increase came from Members' PCCs and not from their PACs. That was the simplest vehicle for an increase, because the Federal Election Campaign Act explicitly allows unlimited transfers from PCCs to party committees. Members' PACs may give only $15,000 to the national parties and $5,000 to any other political committee, including a state or local party committee, so the Members tend to use their PACs to give money to candidates.

CONCLUSION

The activity registered in the last figures and table show that the party committees are not by any means disembodied. The Members are heavily involved in supplying money to candidates and to the parties, while the party committees provide candidates with the resources for coordinated message themes. The picture is not that of a party as a single committee or set of relationships. Rather, we are seeing the congressional party as a complex set of interwoven networks that weave their way in and out of the institution.

These kinds of relationships no doubt will become even more important once BCRA takes effect. The parties can no longer raise soft money, but individual contributions to Members can double from $1,000 to $2,000. This change could produce more hard money—perhaps substantially more—for the Members to give to their parties and to their potential colleagues. This effect might be counterbalanced somewhat, but not completely, if the Federal Election Commission adopts regulations—under consideration at this writing—that would force Members to merge their PACs with their PCCs. However, even such a regulation would not change the basic thrust of what has occurred: Members' money has become increasingly important for the congressional parties and is likely to become more so under BCRA.

The new importance of Members' money to the congressional campaign committees should cause us to rethink some of our paradigms about parties. In a classic 1917 book, *The History of Legislative Procedures Before 1825*, Ralph V. Harlow described parties as organizations that originated within legislatures; the electoral function came second (Harlow 1917). While it would be too pat to return to Harlow, the importance of what is happening should not be missed. The electoral parties are changing, and the impetus for one important set of these changes is coming from inside what was once quaintly referred to as the "party in government." As long as party control remains in doubt, the Members of the party in government have a major personal stake in the collective fate of the party in the election. While that situation persists, we expect the Members to continue helping their parties and candidates. Indeed, we expect them to discover new methods under BCRA—metaphorically, to spin new strands in the party web—to help them in their fight for majority control.

IV

CAMPAIGNS AND ELECTIONS

8

The Stagnation of Congressional Elections

James E. Campbell

For the overwhelming majority of districts in 2002, there was never any real question that the election would leave the status quo intact. With a week to go, *Congressional Quarterly* rated only thirteen congressional districts as having no clear favorite (about 3 percent of the 435 districts). A total of 359 districts, about five out of every six districts, were rated as "safe," with no real uncertainty as to who would win. The results a week later confirmed that very few House races were competitive. The election produced a net change of only five seats, and 98 percent of incumbents were reelected. This was not unusual.

Congressional elections are stagnant. Because of the near invincibility of House incumbents, only a handful of districts are truly competitive, and elections shift very few seats from one party to the other. Perhaps the most important reason why incumbents are nearly unbeatable is that they normally have much better financed campaigns than their opponents. Though campaign finance reformers had as their principal goal reducing the potentially corrupting impact of large contributions, they also made claims that the reforms would diminish the financial advantage that incumbents had and that this would help restore competition and revitalize elections. Opponents of reform made the opposite claim, claiming that BCRA was an "incumbent protection act" that would further smother competition. This chapter examines how House elections have become stagnant and what the likely effects of BCRA will be for competition and change in House elections.

ELECTORAL STAGNATION

Competition in House elections has been on the decline for several decades. Nearly thirty years ago David Mayhew wrote of the "vanishing marginals," the decreasing number of congressional districts that were won by close vote margins and that could be considered competitive (Mayhew 1974b). In the typical election year between 1956 and 1964, about ninety-four districts were decided by a margin of fewer than 10 percentage points (55 percent to 45 percent of the vote or closer). From 1966 to 1972, the number of marginal districts dropped to about fifty-nine. Since Mayhew's observation, competition has eroded further and is now in very short supply (Campbell and Jurek 2003, forthcoming).

One important indicator of competition is the partisan turnover of districts— the number of districts won by candidates of different parties in consecutive election years. Turnover is not essential for competition, but one would expect serious competition to result in a substantial amount of turnover. While some elections produced a great deal of turnover and others next to none, in general the amount of turnover in elections declined in the second half of the twentieth century and especially in the last few decades. As the first column in table 8.1 indicates, elections in recent years have switched fewer and fewer districts from one party to the other. The typical election in the first half of the century resulted in a shift of about 55 seats between the parties. That declined to about 38 seats between 1952 and 1974 and to only 23 seats from 1976 to 2000. Competitiveness, at least as measured by the likelihood of an election changing the partisan outcome in a district, is now less than half of what it was throughout much of the twentieth century.

The decline in competition also affected the amount of change produced by elections. Elections as instruments of popular control of the government should permit citizens to redirect the government in significant ways, but this is becom-

Table 8.1   Median Seat Turnover and Absolute Seat Swings for Elections in the Twentieth Century

Elections	Median Seat Turnover (Gross Change)	Median Absolute Seat Swing (Net Change)
1900–1924	53.9	31.6
1926–1950	56.1	31.0
1952–1974	38.3	20.0
1976–2000	23.1	7.5

Note: "Gross change" indicates the total number of seats electing a representative from different parties in consecutive elections (D to R or R to D). The net change is the net seat shift toward either the Democrats or the Republicans. The data have been adjusted to a constant House size of 435. Third-party seats are halved for the major parties. Because of reapportionment, the gross amount of partisan seat turnover could not be calculated for years ending in 2.

ing less the case for House elections (Campbell 2003). Elections used to shift large numbers of seats from one party to the other, signaling that voters wanted government set on a different course and providing the parties with enough support in Congress to have some real chance of moving government in a new direction. It was not uncommon in the first half of the twentieth century for the Democrats or the Republicans to register net seat swings of fifty seats or more. The parties gained or lost fifty seats or more in over a third of the twenty-five national elections for the House from 1902 to 1950 (nine of twenty-five). In stark contrast, setting aside the 1994 realigning election for the Republicans, neither party has gained or lost more than ten seats since 1984. As the right-hand column in table 8.1 indicates, the typical election in the first half of the century produced a shift of about thirty-one seats to a party. In the third quarter of the century the typical seat swing dropped to twenty seats, and in the last quarter it declined even further to only seven or eight seats. Seat changes are now only about a quarter of what they were. With fewer seats changing hands either way in our competition-poor electoral system, elections produce little change. The system is stagnant.

This is important. Competition is the lifeblood of elections. Without competition, elections become meaningless rituals. If few elections are truly competitive, and if elections overall produce little change in the composition of Congress, it is only natural that a large number of citizens would come to regard the process as unresponsive and crooked, grow cynical, and stay home on Election Day.

THE INCREASED INCUMBENCY ADVANTAGE

The immediate cause of the stagnation in House elections is the increased electoral advantage that accrues to an incumbent by virtue of incumbency (as opposed, for example, to the advantage that comes from being a representative of the majority party in the district). There is no doubt that running as an incumbent rather than as a challenger or in an open seat race typically attracts some number of votes to a candidate. Over the years a number of different methods have been used to assess how many votes incumbency is worth. While estimates have varied, there is a broad consensus that incumbency per se did not make much of a difference prior to the mid-1960s. Most studies indicate that incumbency added perhaps only a couple of percentage points of the vote to the incumbent's column (Erikson 1971; Cover and Mayhew 1981; Payne 1980; Alford and Brady 1993; Jacobson 2000b; Gelman and King 1990; Levitt and Wolfram 1997).

After the mid-1960s, the incumbency advantage became a larger factor. Again, while various methodologies produced different estimates, there is a consensus that the incumbency advantage grew significantly. Most estimates indicate that incumbency in recent decades has been worth between about 7 and 10 percentage points of the vote (Erikson 1971; Cover and Mayhew 1981; Payne 1980; Alford and Brady 1993; Jacobson 2000b; Gelman and King 1990; Levitt and Wolfram 1997). My own estimates, based on an examination of a causal model of the district vote in elections from 1994 to 2000, are consistent with these. I estimate that incumbency was typically worth 7.9 percent of the vote in 1994 elections, 6.9 percent in 1996, 7.6 percent in 1998, and 10.0 percent in 2000 (Campbell 2002).

The impact of incumbency quadrupled at the same time as competition and seat changes were plummeting. Districts were somehow made safer (less competitive) for incumbents and this buffered these districts from national political tides. The question is why this happened. What is the root cause of the increased incumbency advantage, the decline in district competition, and the constriction of seat swings?

THE CAUSE OF ELECTORAL STAGNATION

Several potential explanations for the increase in the incumbency advantage (and therefore electoral stagnation) have been proposed over the years. First, some have speculated that incumbents have increased their hold on their districts by manipulating the redistricting process to their advantage (Tufte 1973). In redrawing district lines after every census, there are choices to be made regarding the areas to be included or excluded from districts, and incumbents naturally attempt to have friendly areas added to their districts and areas inclined to the opposition appended to adjoining districts. Other scholars have speculated that the weakening of party identification, or party dealignment, caused voters to rely more on incumbency as a voting cue. Presumably, voters who lacked much information about the congressional candidates, their records, and their issue positions had relied on party identification to help them reach their vote choice. With their partisanship weakened, these voters gave greater weight to the low information cue of incumbency in reaching their vote decision (Burnham 1975; Cover 1977; Nelson 1978). Still others have suggested that incumbents have won by larger margins because their challengers are weaker, less appealing candidates (Levitt and Wolfram. 1997; Cox and Katz 1996). Finally, the electoral advantage of incumbency may have grown because incumbents are doing a better job in serving their constituencies, in creating a "personal vote" (Cain, Ferejohn, and Fiorina 1987). Whether through casework, or position taking on issues important to the district, or bringing home "pork" for the district, or adapting their "home style" to their constituents' sensibilities, incumbents may have used their job to secure their job (Mayhew 1974a; Fiorina 1977; Mann 1978; Campbell 1983; Herrera and Yawn 1999).

In general these explanations have fallen short of accounting for the increased incumbency advantage. There is little evidence, for example, that redistricting has strongly increased the advantage of incumbency (Ferejohn 1977). While some incumbents have had success in having district lines drawn to their liking, others have had just the opposite experience, and some incumbents are thrown into districts to run against each other. In general, given that they were all elected in the preredistricted districts, most incumbents would probably regard redistricting as more upsetting to their reelection chances than beneficial. Moreover, it is difficult to see why redistricting would have helped incumbents after the mid-1960s and not before.

The other explanations also fail to explain the increased incumbency advantage. Although partisanship weakened slightly in the 1970s, it did not weaken very much, and it rebounded in the mid-1980s (Keith et al. 1992; Bartels 2000; Campbell 2000). If dealignment had been the basis for the growth of the incumbency advantage, the effects of incumbency should have declined after the 1980s, as partisanship rebounded, but they did not. The timing of the increase in the incumbency advantage also undercuts the challenger and constituent service explanations. It is difficult to imagine that the quality of challengers should have inexplicably dropped off in the mid-1960s or that incumbents should have become much more proficient at doing their job at that time.

A THEORY OF ELECTORAL STAGNATION

If not redistricting, dealignment, weaker challengers, or improved constituency service, what accounts for the increase in the incumbency advantage and the decline in district competitiveness and changeability?

The answer is campaign spending (Abramowitz 1991; Erikson and Palfrey 1998; Campbell 2000, 2002). Figure 8.1 depicts the effects of the campaign financing system in increasing the incumbency advantage and bringing about electoral stagnation. Starting on the left, the model claims that the laws that have governed the financing of congressional campaigns have permitted huge campaign finance disparities between candidates. The laws are not the prime moving cause of these campaign finance disparities, but they allow the supply of contributions from those served by the incumbent to meet the incumbents' demand for these resources to pay for expensive campaign technologies. Together the laws and the contributions that they permit constitute a system in which incumbents have had many times the resources of their challengers. The campaign spending advantages of incumbents have funded first-rate campaigns using all of the available modern (and expensive) campaign techniques and technologies, from mass media to mass mailings to polling to whatever the candidate and his or her advisors think will help highlight the incumbent's record and appeal to the district. This spending has typically paid off in votes and generated a substantial electoral advantage for incumbents. This, in turn, depresses competition at the district level and insulates these seats from the national political forces that had pre-

Figure 8.1   A Causal Model of Electoral Stagnation

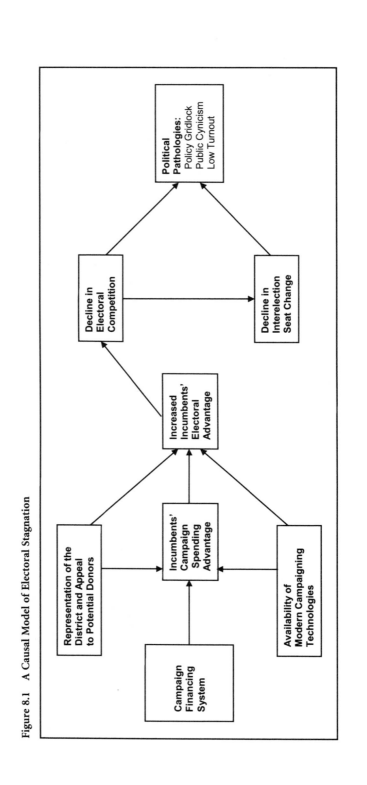

viously generated substantial seat swings. Whether it is a good year for the Democrats or a good year for the Republicans, the party balance is pretty much what it was before the election. Combined with institutional arrangements that favor the status quo, electoral stagnation fosters gridlock and the public's reactions of cynicism, apathy, and low turnout rates.

THE CAMPAIGN SPENDING
ADVANTAGE OF INCUMBENTS

There is substantial evidence for this theory of electoral stagnation. Much of the model has already been addressed. The national political pathologies of low turnout and political cynicism have been well documented elsewhere, and we have discussed the rise of the incumbency advantage and its accompanying decline in competition and electoral change. There is also no doubt that representatives do what they can to please their constituents and their potential donors outside the district and that expensive modern campaign technologies, from polling to mass media advertising, began to come into widespread use by candidates in the 1960s. The two links that remain to be established are the campaign financing advantage of incumbents over challengers (to pay for the technologies to communicate their district service to constituents) and the extent to which the incumbents' spending advantage affects their share of the district vote.

The typical incumbent is able to spend many times what his or her opponent is able to spend. Table 8.2 presents the disparity in campaign spending between incumbents and their challengers in contested House elections from 1992 to 2000. (A contested election is one with both a Democrat and a Republican candidate in the general election.) One might think that incumbents would have a significant advantage if they spent 50 percent more than their challengers, and that they would have a huge advantage if they spent twice what their challengers spent. However, in reality, the typical incumbent in every year examined spent more than five times what the challenger spent. In 1998, the typical incumbent

Table 8.2   Campaign Spending Disparities, Incumbents and Challengers in Contested House Elections, 1992–2000

House Candidates	1992	1994	1996	1998	2000
Incumbent	86%	84%	83%	90%	93%
Challenger	14	16	17	10	7
Ratio	6.2 : 1	5.3 : 1	4.9 : 1	8.6 : 1	12.8 : 1

Note: The number of contested House elections with incumbents running was 316 in 1992, 330 in 1994, 358 in 1996, 303 in 1998, and 336 in 2000. The percentages are for the median contested district in the election.

spent more than eight times what the challenger spent, and in 2000, almost thirteen times more.

Another way to see what incumbency means to campaign spending is to examine what a party's candidate spent before and then after he or she became an incumbent (a "sophomore surge" in campaign spending) and also what the party's candidate was able to spend in his or her last race before retiring, compared to what the party's candidate in the next election (a nonincumbent) was able to spend (a "retirement slump" in campaign spending) (Ansolabehere and Snyder 2000, 76). The immediate (though not total) effect of gaining (or losing) incumbency should be evident in a "before" and "after" comparison. Partisan and district conditions are effectively held constant in this sort of comparison.

Table 8.3 presents the sophomore surges and the retirement slumps in campaign spending for the four pairs of elections from 1992 to 2000. As the table indicates, while candidates who became incumbents generally outspent their opponents in their first victory (about 63 percent of spending), they raised their percentage of spending in their first reelection bid by an average of more than 12 percentage points (to about 76 percent of spending). Similarly, a party's retiring incumbent was able to spend substantially more than his or her party's successor in the next election. Retiring candidates spent about 79 percent of spending in their last race, compared to their party's successor candidates, who typically spent about 60 percent of spending in the open seat election.

Does the huge spending advantage of incumbents translate into votes? Absolutely. The impact of the spending advantage of incumbents on their share of the vote was estimated based on a statistical analysis of the vote for the incumbent in contested districts from 1994 to 2000. The estimated impact of incumbent spending on the vote is plotted in figure 8.2. The figure is a plot of the expected vote percentage for the incumbent (the vertical axis) at different levels of incumbent spending in the district's race (the horizontal axis). Incumbent spending is measured as the incumbent's percentage of total campaign spending by both major party candidates in the race. The relationship between spending and the vote was examined separately for all contested House elections in 1994, 1996, 1998, and 2000, and this is reflected in the four separate lines. The analysis statistically controlled for a number of other factors that might influence the incumbent's vote percentage. These included the presidential vote in the district (a measure of the district's partisanship), the incumbent's district vote in the previous election, and whether the challenger had previously held elective office (a rough measure of the challenger's quality as a candidate). (For the full analysis see Campbell 2002. See also Campbell 1996 and Jacobson 1993.)

The results for the four election years examined are remarkably similar. As the percentage of spending by the incumbent increases, so does the incumbent's vote percentage. The figure indicates that the incumbent could be expected to gain about 1 percent of the vote for every additional 4 or 5 percent of spending in the district. Since this is a plot of the expected or average effects of campaign spend-

Table 8.3 The Sophomore Surge and Retirement Slump in Campaign Spending, 1994–2000

| | Mean Percentage of Campaign Spending by a Party's Candidate | | | | | |
| | Effect of Gaining Incumbency | | | Effect of Losing Incumbency | | |
Elections	Nonincumbent Winners at Election 1	Incumbent at Election 2	Sophomore Surge in Spending	Departing Incumbent at Election 1	Nonincumbent of Same Party at Election 2	Retirement Slump in Spending
1998–2000	68.8	78.7	+ 9.9	85.0	64.0	−21.0
1996–1998	63.9	76.3	+12.4	76.7	61.8	−14.9
1994–1996	56.8	70.8	+14.0	76.7	60.8	−15.9
1992–1994	64.5	77.6	+13.1	78.4	53.7	−24.7

Note: The percentages are of spending by either major party in the district. Only districts contested by both major parties in both election years are included. To avoid party effects, the surges and slumps were computed for each party and then averaged between the two parties.

Figure 8.2   The Effect of Campaign Spending on the Vote for the House Incumbent in Contested Districts, 1994–2000

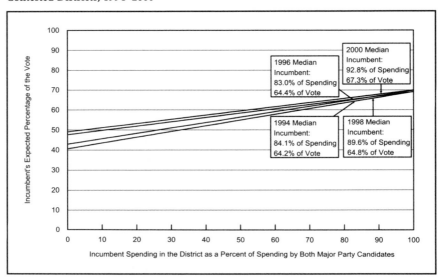

Note: The lowest regression line at the left vertical axis is for the 1994 election. The next three, reading upward, are for 1996, 1998, and 2000. The estimated effects of campaign spending were calculated from regressions of the incumbent's percentage of the two-party vote in all contested districts with an incumbent running (N = 330 for 1994, 358 for 1996, 303 for 1998, and 336 for 2000). Incumbent vote percentage was regressed on four independent variables: the percentage of campaign spending in the district by the incumbent; the two-party vote percentage in the district for the presidential candidate of the incumbent's party in the current or most recent election; the two-party vote percentage for the incumbent in the previous election (with an adjustment if the incumbent was uncontested); and a candidate quality measurement for the challenger. The simulated effects in this figure are based on substituting the median values for the other independent variables in the equation and reducing the equation to the effects of campaign spending alone. Each slope is significant at p <.01. For further details, see Campbell 2002.

ing, we should keep in mind that some incumbents would do better than this and others would do a bit worse. Nevertheless, as the figure indicates, most incumbents are at the upper end of the spending-vote distribution. That is, campaign spending by the typical incumbent in a contested election in the 1990s amounted to anywhere from 83 to 93 percent of what was spent by the two major party candidates in the district, and these incumbents typically captured about 64 to 67 percent of the two-party district vote.

To emphasize, this was the *typical* situation. Half of incumbents dominated spending in these elections to an even greater extent. If anything, the analysis may understate how much incumbent campaign spending predetermines the election outcome. The analysis examines only contested elections. There were thirty uncontested seats in 1992, fifty-two in 1994, twenty-one in 1996, ninety-four in 1998, and sixty-four in 2000. Virtually all of the uncontested elections are cases of incumbents without challengers. These are elections in which the situation for challengers is so hopeless that the opposition party does not mount even a nominal challenge to the incumbent.

With the expected effects of incumbent spending plotted, we can make an informed guess about how elections would turn out if incumbents and challengers spent equal amounts on their elections. Tracing the lines in figure 8.2 to where incumbents spent 50 percent of campaign spending in the district indicates that the typical incumbent would receive about 55 to 59 percent of the vote, a drop of 8 or 9 points from their percentage of the vote with their current spending advantage.

The impact of the incumbent's campaign spending advantage on the election is also evident in the win-loss records of incumbents in contested elections from 1992 to 2000. In the rare cases in which challengers outspent incumbents (about 5 percent of contested elections in the 1990s), incumbents won about 61 percent of the time. When incumbents outspent their challengers by less than two-to-one—and only about 15 percent of contested elections fit this description—they won about 84 percent of the time. By far the most common situation was one in which the incumbent spent more than twice what his or her challenger spent. Four out of five contested races with an incumbent running in the 1990s involved this lopsided incumbent spending advantage. Incumbents won 98.5 percent of these elections. With a three-to-one spending advantage (which characterized about two-thirds of the elections), reelection is just about an absolute "lock."

The impact of the campaign spending advantage on the electoral fortunes of incumbents can perhaps be most graphically demonstrated by an "exception that proves the rule" case. Between 1992 and 2000 there were 1,643 contested House elections in which one of the candidates was an incumbent. In 905 of these (55 percent), the incumbent spent 84 percent or more of the total spending by the two major party candidates. These elections resulted in 904 incumbent victories and only one loss. The single exception, the exception that proves the rule, was the defeat of Democratic incumbent Dan Rostenkowski in the Fifth Congressional District of Illinois. Rostenkowski, serving in his eighteenth term, spent close to $2.5 million on the election to a mere $133,000 spent by his Republican opponent. The spending advantage of better than twenty-two to one for the incumbent was, however, not enough to save him from the fallout of a seventeen-count federal indictment on charges of "misuse of personal and congressional funds, extortion of gifts and cash, and obstruction of justice" (Duncan, Lawrence, and Staff 1995, 406). This only goes to show that a lopsided campaign spending advantage does not buy an election, if you are under a seventeen-count federal indictment!

While some claim that money does not buy elections (Smith 2001), there can be no doubt that at some point it does (at least if the incumbent is not on his or her way to federal prison). The typical election to the House is not one in which the incumbent spends twice or even three times what his or her opponent spends. It could not even be compared to an arms race in which both sides ratchet up spending to astronomical levels, though this happens in the few remaining competitive districts. In the typical election to the House in recent years the incumbent spends six to twelve times what the challenger spends. This is no arms race. This is the Powell Doctrine applied to campaigns: massive and overwhelming force to crush the opposition. Incumbents are able to, and routinely do, drown out the opposition. The results are safe incumbents, very few competitive elections, very little electoral change in the composition of the House—in short, electoral stagnation. (Some might argue that this reverses causes and effects, that the candidates who raise more money are better candidates, and that money has little independent effect. This is known technically as an argument about "endogeneity." It is addressed and answered in Erikson and Palfrey 1998 and Campbell 2002, and by the sophomore surge analysis in table 8.3.)

THE IMPACT OF CAMPAIGN FINANCE REFORM

BCRA was enacted with the promise that it would break the stranglehold of money on the political process, that it would make money less important and reduce or eliminate the corrupting influence (real or perceived) of money that has tainted the democratic process. Will it live up to this billing with respect to opening up competition to incumbents and allowing for voters, when they feel the need, to register a real vote for change?

From one standpoint, one might expect that any reform would be an improvement on the current system. Competition in House elections has so seriously eroded that it would seem that there is no place to go but up. However, from another standpoint, it would be surprising if the campaign reform that was enacted had any beneficial effect in restoring competition. After all, the reforms were written with the intention of inhibiting the corrupting effects of big contributions and were not explicitly designed to make elections more competitive. Also, campaign finance reform was intended to eliminate soft money contributions to the political parties and restrict the impact of issue advocacy shadow campaigns funded by the independent expenditures of interest groups. The problems of an enlarged incumbency advantage and electoral stagnation are the results of a severe imbalance in *hard money* contributions to the candidates and not a consequence of either the huge influx of soft money into campaigns or the intrusion of issue advocacy ads funded by the independent expenditures of interest groups. Given the tremendous imbalance between incumbents and challengers in hard money, any other source of money in elections (including soft money and independent expenditures) would be welcomed as potentially helping challengers and increasing competition. It follows that any impediment to these alternative sources (such as BCRA) might not be helpful in revitalizing the process.

Whether intended to affect competition or not, four provisions of BCRA might have an impact on competitiveness: the elimination of soft money contributions to the political parties, the restrictions on issue advocacy ads in the weeks leading up to the election, the triggered increase in individual contribution limits for candidates facing high-spending, self-financed opponents (the "Millionaires' Amendment"), and the increased limits on hard money contributions by individuals to the candidates from $1,000 per election to $2,000 per election campaign.

Soft Money and Electioneering

While there is no doubt that political party soft money and nonparty expenditures on issue advocacy have grown enormously in recent election cycles, this "outside money" does not seem to have made much difference to competition levels. As we have seen, the district vote for a candidate can be quite fully explained without knowing how much soft money or independent expenditures were spent either for or against the candidate. Further, the rise in the incumbency advantage, the decline in competition, and the compression of seat change occurred well before the explosion in outside money. While it seems odd that the soft money and independent expenditure surges would not have had an effect on congressional competition (just because of their sheer magnitude), the distribution of the outside money spending may explain the absence of an effect. Both forms of outside money spending have been concentrated in the few remaining districts that are competitive rather than spread around to a larger set of races to make them competitive. This has the effect of producing a distorted and highly intense competition in a few districts (see Dwyre and Kolodny, chapter 5). As David Magelby noted in examining soft money and independent expenditures in 1998, "outside money approximately equals candidate spending in competitive districts" (Magleby 2002b, 225). However, in most districts hard money disparities secure seats for incumbents and soft money spending apparently makes little difference. Thus, since the presence of party soft money and nonparty electioneering have had little to do with the rise of the incumbency advantage or the decline in competition, there is little reason to think that the elimination of soft money and restrictions on issue advocacy campaigning would appreciably reduce the advantage of incumbency or increase competition levels.

If anything, the elimination of soft money and the restrictions on electioneering might further solidify the incumbency advantage and maintain competition at anemic levels. We know that incumbents have a huge hard money advantage. Anything that might compete with this advantage would help competition. The worst-case scenario is that soft money and issue ads reinforce the incumbency advantage. Since incumbents as a group have such a commanding control of hard money contributions, this worst-case scenario is not much different from current circumstances. The best-case scenario would be that soft money and issue ads are spent largely in behalf of challengers and would thus partially offset the incumbents' hard money advantage. Although the data on this are limited, La Raja's analysis of soft money spending (transfers from the national to state parties) in 2000 suggests that soft money is spent much more evenly between incumbents and challengers than hard money and may even be tilted slightly in favor of challengers (La Raja 2002). There is also some evidence that a significant portion of independent expenditures fund negative issue ads (Biersack and Haskell 1999, 169; Dwyre 1999, 196) and that much of this may be directed at incumbents that have in some way displeased the interest groups financing the ads. Based on this limited evidence, we might expect that the elimination of soft money and the restrictions imposed on issue advocacy would have only slight effects on competition; but, to the extent that these reforms have any impact at all, they might further *diminish* electoral competition, not enhance it.

Self-Financing Provisions

Another component of BCRA that might affect competition is the provision allowing for increased contribution limits once a self-financed candidate's spending exceeds a specified threshold. This part of the law is examined in detail by Jennifer Steen in the next chapter. However, it should be noted here that self-financing works more to the advantage of challengers than incumbents. Incumbents are so well funded by others that they do not need to finance their own campaigns. Self-financing is thus an alternative source of campaign funds for some challengers that may offset the huge campaign financing advantage that incumbents otherwise enjoy. Any obstacle to self-financing or the effects of self-financing, such as those included in BCRA, would be to the detriment of competition in those few districts in which the challenger can afford to finance a viable campaign.

Raising Contribution Limits

The final provision of BCRA that might influence electoral competition is the increase in the limits on hard money contributions to candidates by individuals. This change could work to the challengers' advantage (and restore some competition) if those taking advantage of the liberalized limit are more evenly balanced in their contributions than the other sources of hard campaign monies (smaller contributors and PACs). On the other hand, this aspect of the reform would solidify the considerable advantage of incumbents if the big contributors are as biased in favor of incumbents as other contributors. To get an insight into the likely impact of the liberalization of the hard money contribution limits we can examine the extent to which incumbents and challengers have benefited in the past from individuals who contributed the maximum allowable under the old law (though, as Wilcox et al. discuss in chapter 4, only a fraction of those who "maxed out" under the old limits say that they will do the same under the new limits).

Have incumbents or challengers generally benefited more from the contributions of those who have given the maximum in the past? The figures are presented in table 8.4 and are based on data provided to the Campaign Finance Institute by the Center for Responsive Politics. In examining individual contributions made in the 2000 election, it is clear that incumbents more than challengers have benefited from those who have made the maximum individual contribution. For our purposes, any contributor who gave a candidate at least $1,000 in the 2000 House elections is considered to have made the maximum contribution. In the 336 contested districts involving an incumbent in 2000, a total of 81,165 individuals gave at least $1,000 to a major party House candidate. Three-quarters of the candidates receiving these maxed-out contributions were incumbents (60,456 of the 81,165). The incumbent had more contributions from maxed-out contributors than the challenger in 304 (90.5 percent) of the 336 contested districts with an incumbent running.

This, in itself, is not surprising. Incumbents tend to receive more money from everyone. Even so, they fare particularly well among the big contributors. The median incumbent (in a contested election) received nearly $170,000 from contributors who had maxed out, while the median challenger received $6,500—a ratio of almost twenty-six to one. From a different perspective, 22.5 percent of contributions to the typical incumbent were from these $1,000 plus contributors, while 12.8 percent of the typical challenger's contributions (a much lower base) were from these maximum contributors. Thus, with the big contributors allowed to give even more than in the past, incumbents should be the main beneficiaries.

While liberalizing the hard money contribution limits may generally favor incumbents, there are two silver linings (of sorts) to this cloud. The first is that the increased limits cannot give incumbents much more of an advantage than they already had under the old law. In 2000, under the prereformed law, the median incumbent (in a contested race) spent 92.8 percent of what the major party candidates spent in the district. If the maxed-out contributors doubled their contributions as allowed under the new limits, the median incumbent's proportion would only increase by three-tenths of a percentage point. Of course, most challengers are unlikely to greet this news warmly, since incumbents would continue to outspend them by almost thirteen to one. Second, there are a number of districts in which the incumbent's percentage of spending would have dropped a bit under the higher limits. For the most part, these are districts in which the incumbent does well among the maxed-out contributors, only not quite as well as he or she does with other contributors. In the few districts that were competitive, the incumbent's big-contributor advantage over challengers was not as lopsided. If maxed-out contributors doubled their contributions, as

Table 8.4 House Incumbents' and Challengers' Receipts from Contributors of at Least $1,000 in the 2000 Election

Type of Candidates	Median in All Contested Elections (N = 336)		Median in Marginal Elections (N = 74)	
	Total from $1,000 + Contributors	Percent of Total Receipts from $1,000 + Contributors	Total from $1,000 + Contributors	Percent of Total Receipts from $1,000 + Contributors
Incumbents	$168,229	22.5	$340,013	25.7
Challengers	6,500	12.8	188,962	25.2

Note: Marginal elections are defined as those having two-party vote percentages within the 40 to 60 range.

allowable under the liberalized limits, the incumbents' share of district spending would rise in about 47 percent of contested districts, stay the same in about a fifth of districts, and decline in a third of districts, though usually by no more than a percentage point or two. In effect, the new limits might offer a bit of help to a stray challenger here or there.

While this analysis has focused on the percentage of district spending by the incumbent and challenger (which is what my analysis indicates is important to the vote), Gary Jacobson (1980, 1990) claims that the absolute amount of spending by the challenger is what is important. If he is correct, even though the liberalized limits provide disproportionately more resources to incumbents, the addition of resources to the challenger is more important to that campaign. Although this view offers more hope that the liberalized hard money limits will improve competition, an examination of the numbers suggests that the effect of the reform on challenger spending (and thus, competition) in most cases will be minimal. If the maximum contributors in 2000 doubled their contributions under the new limits, the median challenger would add only $6,500 more to the $41,000 he or she spent under the old rules. However, a small number of challengers would receive a significant boost in resources. About one in eight (39 of 336) challengers would add more than $200,000 to his or her campaign treasury (though the incumbent opponent would add nearly half a million to his or her campaign; see the marginal contests in table 8.4). Although my analysis indicates that the *proportion* of spending is what is important to the vote—and that the *absolute* amount of spending by the challenger does not have a significant independent effect—if it did have an effect, the liberalized contribution limits would again help only a handful of challengers.

The bottom line assessment of the liberalized hard money contributions for individuals is that they will do virtually nothing to restore electoral competition in the overwhelming majority of districts. The most likely effect of liberalizing individual hard money contribution limits, instead, would be to entrench incumbents further by adding to their already considerable spending advantage.

CONCLUSION

At a November 7, 2002, meeting of the Commonwealth Club of California, in responding to a question about BCRA, campaign finance reform champion Senator John McCain said that "our reform threatens the political life of the incumbents" (McCain 2002). Although the focus of the reform was clearly directed at the issue of corruption rather than competition, McCain had made similar statements in the national media, prior to the law's passage, about BCRA being a threat to incumbency (Cable News Network 2001; Holland 2001; Abraham et al. 2001). This analysis indicates that Senator McCain's contention that BCRA poses a threat to incumbency is wrong. BCRA will probably leave incumbents unscathed and, if anything, will further reinforce their hold on their seats. Soft money and independent expenditures that might from time to time be used to counter the hard money advantage of incumbents will be eliminated or weakened as tools. Although there are doubts about whether it will be effectual at all, to the extent that it is, the Millionaires' Amendment provision also further insulates incumbents from competition. Liberalized hard money contributions to candidates may allow challengers to collect a few more dollars, but incumbents will add many times more than that to their war chests. In short, BCRA will not solve electoral stagnation and may very well turn a bad situation worse. At the very best, it will disappoint those hopeful that reform would reduce the impact of money in our political system.

Other defenders of BCRA admit that it is unlikely to restore competition, because it was never intended to have that effect. The purpose of campaign finance reform was only to reduce the corrupting impact, real or imagined, of contributions on the process—especially large contributions. It is too early to say how successful the reform will be in keeping large contributions out of the process, though it is quite likely that much of this money will find its way to the aid of its intended beneficiaries through one route or another.

It is not too early to say, however, that the promise of campaign finance reform to reduce the corrupting impact of money in the system will not be kept. It was a crucial mistake to see concerns about the corrupting influence of the campaign finance system and the anticompetitive effects of the campaign finance system as somehow separable. The issues are joined at the heart. Campaign contributions are potentially corrupting to the political process *because* campaign spending is so important to incumbents. Campaign spending is so important to incumbents because it allows incumbents effectively to buy their elections by outspending their opponents by huge margins. If money could not secure the election's result, it would lose much of its leverage over incumbents. Moreover, competitive elections are the linchpin in a defense against corruption. The real threat of a vengeful electorate is a valuable counterweight to the temptations of corruption. The corruption issue of campaign finance is intrinsically intertwined with the competition issue. Since BCRA would appear to have failed or to have neglected the latter issue, it also risks failing on the former.

9

The "Millionaires' Amendment"

Jennifer A. Steen

The Bipartisan Campaign Reform Act of 2002 (BCRA) includes a "Millionaires' Amendment" intended to reduce the electoral advantage of those wealthy candidates who spend lavishly on their own campaigns. Many candidates, at all levels of American government, provide substantial amounts of personal money to their own campaigns. In the 2000 election cycle, candidates for the U.S. House and Senate loaned and contributed more than $175 million in campaign funds (17 percent of all receipts) to their own campaigns, and forty-one candidates self-financed more than $500,000. The most famous of the self-financers of 2000 was Jon Corzine (D-N.J.), who self-financed more than $60 million in his successful Senate campaign. Corzine's victory notwithstanding, self-financed candidates have posted a spectacularly unimpressive track record on Election Day. In 2000, self-financers' best season since 1992, less than a quarter of the $500,000 candidates (ten of the forty-one) won seats in Congress. Despite their losing tendencies, self-financed candidates have been labeled a scourge of democracy by editorial writers, political commentators, and, naturally, the candidates who have faced them.

The Millionaires' Amendment to BCRA attacks the "rich candidate problem" (as *Washington Post* editorial writers once dubbed it) on two fronts, making it easier for self-financers' opponents to raise money and harder for self-financers to recoup their campaign investments after an election. The law establishes "trigger" amounts of self-financing; if those amounts are exceeded, a self-financer's opponent (or opponents) can raise three or six times the normal limit from individuals, depending on the circumstances. In some cases, self-financing also enables unlimited coordinated expenditures by the opposing party. The Millionaires' Amendment also prohibits self-financers from repaying more than $250,000 in campaign self-loans after the date of an election.

This chapter considers the potential impact of the Millionaires' Amendment—how the provisions of the Millionaires' Amendment might have altered the dynamics of certain elections, had they been in effect in the 2000 election cycle. (I analyze the 2000 elections because the raw data for 2002 were not available at this writing.) I begin with a brief review of the political issues surrounding self-financing and legislative history. I then evaluate the new law's restrictions on the repayment of self-loans. Using the Federal Election Commission's data on individual candidates' campaign finance activity, I identify the self-financers who appear most and least likely to be deterred by the limit on self-repayment. Turning to the potential impact of increased contribution limits, the analysis proceeds with three basic steps: (1) identifying candidates whose "opposition personal funds" exceeded the trigger amounts, (2) counting those candidates' "maxed-out" contributors (individuals who contributed the maximum allowable amount), and (3) calculating revised fund-raising totals. This calculation suggests the extent to which the Millionaires' Amendment might restore parity to those lopsided contests in which a self-financer vastly outspends his opponent or opponents, assuming that all other factors remained the same. Finally, I consider potential "ripple effects," the Millionaires' Amendment's likely effect on strategic decisions like whether to run and how much to self-finance.

There is no way to know exactly how the Millionaires' Amendment would have changed the course of the 2000 elections, given the number of strategic decisions that would likely have been affected and our uncertainty about how any one of them would have been decided. Even tallying the amounts of increased contributions and party expenditures is no straightforward task. Under certain conditions, limits on party expenditures are eliminated entirely—how is an observer to divine the amount parties would spend in the absence of legal limits? Similarly, how does one know how much more maxed-out contributors would donate under increased limits? Some might have donated the maximum amount because that was exactly how much they preferred to give, regardless of legal limits, while others might be delighted to give the increased amount allowed under the loosened rules. Because of these uncertainties, this chapter is necessarily exploratory. I avoid making precise assertions; rather, I suggest a range of plausible alternatives. Still, the analysis strongly suggests that the Millionaires' Amendment would not have significantly altered the political landscape in the 2000 congressional elections.

THE POLITICS OF SELF-FINANCING

The central issue raised by critics of self-financing is political equality. If personal wealth confers a political advantage, citizens who cannot bankroll their campaigns do not have an equal opportunity to serve in representative government, regardless of their qualifications or political views. Without limits on personal spending, Senator John Pastore (D-R.I.) warned during hearings on the original Federal Election Campaign Act, "only the wealthy or those who are able to obtain large contributions from limited sources will be able to seek elective office. Neither situation is desirable and both are inimicable [*sic*] to the American system" (U.S. Senate Committee on Commerce 1971, 152).

To level the campaign finance playing field, the Federal Election Campaign Act Amendments of 1974 (Public Law 93–443) capped self-contributions at $25,000 for House candidates, $35,000 for Senate candidates, and $50,000 for presidential candidates. However, the self-financing limits were invalidated in 1976 by the Supreme Court in *Buckley v. Valeo*. The per curiam opinion held:

> The ceiling on personal expenditures by candidates on their own behalf . . . imposes a substantial restraint on the ability of persons to engage in protected First Amendment expression. . . . [The governmental] interest in equalizing the relative financial resources of candidates competing for elective office . . . is clearly not sufficient to justify the provision's infringement of fundamental First Amendment rights (424 U.S. 1 at 51, 54 [1976]).

Twenty-six years later, Congress devised the Millionaires' Amendment (Public Law 107–155, sections 304 and 319) as a creative way to undermine the advantage to self-financing without running afoul of the First Amendment and *Buckley*. The law defines "opposition personal funds," an opponent's expenditures from personal funds (including self-contributions and self-loans) less a candidate's own expenditures from personal funds (in House races this amount is offset by 50 percent of the difference between the candidates' "war chests," or off-year receipts), and establishes threshold self-financing levels that, when crossed, trigger increased contribution limits for individuals. If opposition personal funds exceed the single threshold for House elections or the highest of three triggers in Senate elections, limits on coordinated expenditure by parties are eliminated. These provisions enable self-financers' opponents to be more competitive without restricting a wealthy candidate's ability to self-finance political expression.

The other component of the Millionaires' Amendment, a $250,000 limit on repayment of self-loans after an election, discourages the most popular form of self-financing without hard limits. This provision was not challenged by the plaintiffs in *McConnell v. FEC*. The loan-repayment restriction may have been inspired by a California state law, adopted in 2000, that limited candidate self-loans to $100,000 but left self-contributions unregulated. The loan provisions in both laws make self-financing less attractive to wealthy candidates: if a candidate can lend his campaign $1 million and possibly repay himself after he gets elected, he should be more willing to self-finance $1 million than he would be if all sales were final.

With its twin provisions the Millionaires' Amendment seeks to lift the fortunes of self-financers' *opponents* without placing any explicit limits on wealthy candidates' ability to self-finance political expression. In the abstract, this seems like a "win-win" situation: advocates of political equality *and* free speech should be pleased. But political equality may in some ways be *undermined* by the Millionaires' Amendment. As Senator Carl Levin (D-Mich.) noted in floor debate, "In the effort to level the playing field in one area, we are making the playing field less level in another area" (*Congressional Record* 2001). Many beneficiaries of the Millionaires' Amendment will be incumbents, who can hardly be labeled "disadvantaged" in elections. Indeed, during the floor debate on the Millionaires' Amendment several Members of Congress (whose reelection rates typically exceed 90 percent) spoke of their personal experiences facing wealthy opponents using terms like "unfair" and "level playing field." Senator Chris Dodd (D-Conn.) noted the extreme irony in "the idea that somehow we [incumbents] are sort of impoverished candidates." As Dodd reminded his colleagues,

> [W]e are talking about incumbents who have treasuries of significant amounts and the power of the office which allows us to be in the press every day, if we want. We can send franked mail to our constituents at no cost to us. . . . We do radio and television shows. We can go back to our States with subsidized airfares. . . . I find it somewhat ironic that we are here deeply worried about the capital that can be raised and the candidate who is going to spend a million dollars of his own money to level the playing field. (*Congressional Record* 2001)

The silver lining of candidate self-financing is that it can level the playing field for challengers seeking to overcome the considerable advantages enjoyed by incumbent House Members and Senators. As one political consultant has commented, "[A] challenger who cannot jump-start his own campaign might as well forget it" (Van Biema 1994). Consider, for example, that only three incumbents were defeated in the 1998 Senate elections, two of whom lost to self-financers. In 2000, two of the six successful Senate challengers were heavily self-financed. Of course, this is no silver lining at all to incumbents and bolsters criticism that the Millionaires' Amendment is an incumbent-protection measure.

THE DIRECT IMPACT OF THE MILLIONAIRES' AMENDMENT

Self-Lending

Under the terms of BCRA, no more than $250,000 in candidate loans can be repaid after the date of an election. Would self-financed candidates have been more reluctant to invest in their own campaigns, given the restrictions on loan repayment?

Candidates' financial self-help can take two forms, contributions from personal funds and loans made or guaranteed by the candidate personally. There is only one substantive difference between self-loans and self-contributions: a self-loan can be repaid, but a self-contribution cannot be refunded to the candidate. The Federal Election Commission has suggested that a refund of candidate self-contribution would constitute a "conver[sion of] excess campaign funds to the personal use of the candidate," prohibited under the Federal Election Campaign Act (Federal Election Commission 1998). The distinction has allowed candidates to use their wealth as political leverage—candidates can spend personal funds to help their campaigns, then later solicit contributions to repay themselves.

Indeed, most self-financing candidates exercise this option. Candidates who self-finance almost always do so with personal loans instead of contributions (Jacobson 1997; Steen 2000; Wilcox 1988). In 2000, House and Senate candidates (leaving Jon Corzine aside) loaned their campaigns $87.3 million and contributed about one-quarter as much, $22.9 million. (The $22.9 million does not include $1.8 million in candidate contributions that were used to forgive previous self-loans.) House self-financers elected from 1992 through 1996 had repaid $8.1 million of $15.4 million loaned, or 53 percent, by the end of 1998 (Steen 2000).

To evaluate the potential impact of the limitation on self-repayment, I begin by identifying candidates who had more than $250,000 in outstanding loans to their campaigns on Election Day. In the 2000 congressional elections they numbered fifty-six. In House primaries, twenty-one campaign committees owed more than $250,000 to the candidate after the election, $17.5 million of which exceeded $250,000 per candidate. In Senate primaries there were eight candidates who would have forfeited some self-loans under BCRA; the total amount forfeited would have equaled $6.6 million. In general elections, twenty House candidates and seven Senate candidates were owed more than $250,000 by their campaigns, with the excess totaling $23.1 million and $67.8 million, respectively. It is important to note that 89 percent of the Senate total was owed to a single candidate, Jon Corzine. Because Corzine's activity dwarfs all other candidates' combined, I will treat him separately in the remaining analysis and exclude him from aggregate figures reported in the text.

Which of the fifty-six candidates with loans exceeding $250,000 would have been discouraged from self-lending by the Millionaires' Amendment? Of course one cannot know for sure, but there are important clues one can use to make reasonable distinctions among the candidates. Surely some candidates did not intend to seek repayment of self-loans and, therefore, would not have been deterred by the repayment restriction. Consider, as an illustration, the population of twenty-nine candidates who won elections (or reelections) in 1992 through 1998 and who reported new self-loans of at least $250,000 outstanding after the election. In this group of twenty-nine winners, fifteen subsequently repaid part or all of their self-loans, while fourteen did not. The winners who *did* seek repayment were quite successful, recouping $8.3 million of $15.7 million in self-loans. House winners reclaimed a slightly larger proportion of self-loans (57 percent) than did Senate winners (47 percent).

Fund-raising, as Hubert Humphrey once said, is a "disgusting, demeaning and degrading experience" (Adamany and Agree 1975). That candidates undertook the unpleasant task of raising contributions to repay self-debt indicates that they put a high value on reclaiming their personal funds. Under BCRA's repayment limit they would have recouped only $2.9 million, forfeiting 65 percent of loan amounts *actually* repaid. One can thus infer that the restrictions of the Millionaires' Amendment would have made these candidates reconsider the magnitude of their self-loans. In contrast, their colleagues who did *not* seek repayment would not have been affected by the repayment limits, so would likely *not* have been deterred from self-lending.

For election losers it is impractical to use actual repayment as an indicator of the desire for repayment because attracting campaign contributions is an extremely challenging task for someone who is neither a candidate for nor a holder of public office. However, there is, significantly, variation among losers in the continuing maintenance of campaign committees. I assume that losing candidates who walked away, folding their campaign committees by the end of the election year, were not terribly concerned with recouping self-loans. If they had been, they could have kept their committees alive into the 2001–2002 cycle. Losing candidates who *did* maintain their committees are deemed "repayment seeking," although some of them had other debts that required a continuing committee and thus may not have truly sought self-repayment.

In the 2000 congressional elections, only two-thirds of the candidates with funds "at risk" of forfeiture under BCRA appear to be repayment seekers. Among the fifty-six candidates with self-loans exceeding $250,000, thirty-three sought repayment and sixteen did not. An additional seven candidates maintained committees in 2002 but were repeat candidates in that cycle, so the extension of campaign activity cannot be attributed to loan retirement. (At this writing it is too early to tell whether any of them will maintain their committees into the 2004 cycle.) As expected, the losing repayment-seekers were not very successful at reclaiming their personal investments, reporting only $596,147 in loan repayments against $37.9 million in outstanding loans. Nevertheless, maintaining their campaign committees indicates that they preferred *not* to forfeit their self-loans and would have been more reluctant to self-finance in the face of BCRA's restriction on loan-repayment.

To be clear, I am not suggesting that the repayment-seeking candidates would have been totally unwilling to risk losing their money, that is, that they would *not* have self-lended had the Millionaires' Amendment governed their campaigns. Clearly, some *were* willing to assume some risk—they ran despite long odds of winning and had to realize that losing would seriously proscribe their ability to reclaim self-loans. But under BCRA they would have had more to lose, as the repayment possibilities would have been sharply curtailed.

One should remember that discouraging self-loans is not the final goal of the Millionaires' Amendment but a means to an end. Its purpose is to help non-wealthy candidates compete with self-financers. As such, the impact of the Millionaires' Amendment is not particularly relevant to elections in which (a) the self-financer is the weaker candidate, or (b) the self-financer's opponent would be weak against *any* competitor. In such elections even if the Millionaires' Amendment *did* deter self-lending, the election outcome would not likely change. One should thus concentrate on dissuadable self-lenders (i.e., repayment seekers) who won in close elections. There are but a handful of them. Among the repayment-seeking self-lenders, only two won primaries with margins of less than 10 percent of the vote, Tim Johnson in Illinois-15 and John Kelly in New Mexico-1, and two were in close general elections, Johnson again and Maria Cantwell in the Washington Senate race. This makes a grand total of *three* self-financers in 2000 who would likely have been deterred from self-lending and who might then have lost an election. This is a very limited impact by anyone's standards (except, of course, the opponents of these three candidates).

Increased Individual Contribution Limits

The Millionaires' Amendment establishes "threshold amounts" of self-financing. Once a candidate exceeds the threshold in a given election, his or her opponent enjoys increased contribution limits. If this provision had taken effect in the 2000 election, how much would self-financers' opponents have raised from their maxed-out contributors? As suggested earlier, one cannot simply assume that any contributor who gave the initial maximum would triple (or sextuple) his or her contribution if so allowed. Some donors contribute $1,000 not because it is the most they are permitted to give, but because it is the most they *want* to give. It is therefore impossible to calculate a precise estimate of the additional fund-raising for each candidate in the 2000 election cycle that would have resulted from the Millionaires' Amendment triggers. One can, however, approximate the upper bound of marginal fund-raising by counting the number of maxed-out contributors, since no contributor would have been able to give more than the increased limits. One can then consider the limiting case, in which a candidate raises this maximum, and whether it seems likely that the election outcome would have been affected.

In the 2000 cycle there were thirty-five elections—fifteen primaries and twenty general elections—in which contribution limits would have been lifted for at least one major-party candidate had the Millionaires' Amendment been operating. The general election candidates are listed in table 9.1 and the elections are grouped into four categories. In the first category, a self-financer won the election, but it is conceivable that increased fund-raising under the Millionaires' Amendment could have changed the outcome. This group includes three Senate elections and three House elections, all general election match-ups. In each case the loser's receipts would have increased by as much as 25 percent, and the loser's party would have been allowed to make unlimited coordinated expenditures. In five of the six the margin of victory was less than 5 percent, and in one election (the Fifteenth District of Illinois) the margin was under 7 percent.

Two of these elections are especially notable, one for the closeness of the margin and the other for the loser's significant base of maxed-out contributors. In Washington State, Democratic challenger Maria Cantwell self-financed $10.3 million against incumbent Senator Slade Gorton. Under the Millionaires' Amendment, Gorton would have been eligible to resolicit 601 of his contributors, potentially adding $3 million to his total receipts of $6.4 million. The Republican party, which made the maximum allowable coordinated expenditures for Gorton, would have been released from coordinated spending limits. Given the razor-thin margin in this election (one-tenth of 1 percent), the boost Gorton would have enjoyed under the Millionaires' Amendment could very well have put him over the top.

In the open Senate election in New Jersey, Democrat Jon Corzine self-financed $60 million, an amount that would have increased the individual contribution limit for his opponent, Republican Congressman Bob Franks, by a factor of six and freed the Republican party from limits on coordinated expenditures. Franks enjoyed the maximum contribution from 1,825 supporters in the general election, and had he resolicited them his own receipts could have increased by as much as 140 percent, from $6.5 million to $15.5 million. One cannot know whether such an increase would have enabled Franks to overcome the four-point deficit in the vote tally, but it is certainly possible.

The second group of elections are contests in which a self-financer won and the opponent's vote tally and/or base of maxed-out contributors was very small. This category includes the Democratic Senate primaries in Minnesota, New Jersey and Washington; House primaries in California-48 (Republican), Georgia-7 (Democratic), Tennessee-4 (Democratic), and West Virginia-2 (Democratic); the general election for Senate in Wisconsin; and the general elections for House in Alabama-2, California-48, Idaho-1 and Indiana-2. (The primary elections are not depicted in table 9.1.) In all twelve of these elections the self-financer's margin of victory exceeded 10 percent and in ten of them it exceeded 15 percent. The opponents were so comparatively weak that any boost they would have received from increased fund-raising under the Millionaires' Amendment would not likely have made a substantial difference.

In the third group the self-financer lost the election, so the likely impact of the Millionaires' Amendment would have been to roll up the margin for the winner. The fifteen elections in this category include the Democratic primary for Senator from Pennsylvania; House primaries in California-15 (Democratic), Illinois-10 (Republican), Oklahoma-2 (Republican), Texas-7 (Republican), and Virginia-1 (Republican); the general election for Senate in Nevada; and general elections for

House in Indiana-3, Maryland-8, North Carolina-3, New Hampshire-1, Tennessee-4, Texas-25, Utah-2, and West Virginia-2.

The fourth category, not listed in table 9.1, includes only the Republican primary in Pennsylvania's Nineteenth District, in which the self-financer did not win, but the Millionaires' Amendment still might have changed the outcome. Candidate Richard Stewart self-financed $425,000, which would have triggered increased contribution limits for his four opponents. Stewart placed third in the balloting behind Todd Platts (33 percent of the vote) and Alfred Masland (29 percent). Platts only had 44 maxed-out contributors to resolicit, while Masland had 152. Masland therefore could have enjoyed a much bigger boost from the increased limits than Platts, potentially adding nearly four times as much to his fund-raising total. It is thus conceivable that, under the Millionaires' Amendment, Stewart's self-financing could have cost Platts the nomination.

The Democratic primary for Senator from Pennsylvania illustrates a related possibility, although I classified it as an election in which the Millionaires' Amendment would not likely have changed the outcome. Bob Rovner received only 4 percent of the vote but self-financed enough to trigger tripled limits for the other candidates, including Congressman Ron Klink and State Senator Allyson Schwartz. Klink had more individual maxed-out contributors (596) than Schwartz (375), so he would have had more funds available in a resolicitation. However, because there are diminishing marginal returns to campaign spending, it is possible that Schwartz's increased fund-raising, although less than Klink's, could have helped her more than Klink's helped him. Klink was already a well-known congressman, so his rate of return on spending likely started off much lower than Schwartz's.

Self-Financing and Incumbents

Although self-financing is often criticized for undermining political equality, it can, as I noted at the beginning of this chapter, actually enhance political equality by giving challengers the means to combat strong, well-funded incumbents. For this reason, the Millionaires' Amendment has been viewed in some quarters as something of a wolf in sheep's clothing—an incumbent-protection measure in the guise of an equalizer. Table 9.1 reveals that there is some foundation to this notion: the Millionaires' Amendment would have benefited an incumbent Member of Congress in 40 percent of all general elections in which it was relevant in the 2000 elections.

Eleven of the elections listed involved incumbents seeking reelection. Three of the incumbents, Senator Herb Kohl (D-Wisc.), Representative Don Sherwood (R-Penn.), and Representative Terry Everett (R-Ala.), self-financed enough to have triggered increased contribution limits for their challengers. The other incumbents all stood to benefit from the Millionaires' Amendment, especially Senators Rod Grams (R-Minn.) and Slade Gorton (R-Wash.), both of whom

Table 9.1 House and Senate Races That Would Have Triggered the Millionaires' Amendment in 2000

Candidate	Status	State/District	Result	Amount Self-Financed	Maximum Amount of Additional Fund-Raising (# of Maxed-Out Contributors)		Candidate Receipts
Self-Financer Might Have Been Defeated							
Dayton, Mark (D)	C	Minn.-Sen	W (48%)	$11,772,067			$12,040,466
Grams, Rodney Dwight (R)	I		L (43%)	0	$1,555,000	(311)	5,902,543
Corzine, Jon Stevens (D)	O	N.J.-Sen	W (50%)	60,200,967			63,253,520
Franks, Robert D (R)	O		L (46%)	5,000	9,125,000	(1,825)	6,428,214
Cantwell, Maria (D)	C	Wash.-Sen	W (48%)	10,295,415			11,538,665
Gorton, Slade (R)	I		L (48%)	0	3,005,000	(601)	6,384,256
Kelleher, F. Michael Jr. (D)	O	Ill.-15	L (46%)	1,442			958,618
Johnson, Timothy V. (R)	O		W (53%)	480,000	298,000	(149)	1,926,919
Connelly, Maryanne (D)	O	N.J.-7	L (47%)	277,673			1,984,266
Ferguson, Mike (R)	O		W (49%)	878,000	600,327	(306)	2,398,279
Casey, Patrick Raymond (D)	C	Pa.-10	L (47%)	0			1,615,787
Sherwood, Donald L. (R)	I		W (52%)	490,553	490,553	(246)	2,648,057
Self-Financer Was Defeated							
Bernstein, Ed (D)	O	Nev.-Sen	L (40%)	988,000			2,483,512
Ensign, John Eric (R)	O		W (56%)	0	1,086,800	(700)	4,878,526
Roemer, Tim (D)	I	Ind.-3	W (51%)	0			679,009
Chocola, Joseph Christopher (R)	C		L (47%)	515,000	90,000	(45)	1,127,274
Lierman, Terry L. (D)	C	Md.-8	L (45%)	1,465,000			2,226,442
Morella, Constance A. (R)	I		W (51%)	3,000	328,000	(164)	1,101,894
McNairy, Leigh Harvey (D)	C	N.C.-3	L (38%)	641,000			1,178,387
Jones, Walter Beaman Jr. (R)	I		W (60%)	0		*	1,199,430

Clark, Martha Fuller (D)	C	N.H.-1	L (44%)	$ 705,500	$ 92,000	(46)	$1,151,998
Sununu, John E. (R)	I		W (53%)	0			544,265
Dunaway, David H. (D)	C	Tenn.-4	L (33%)	700,000	664,500	(737)	1,009,951
Hilleary, William V. (R)	I		W (65%)	35,500			1,415,020
Bentsen, Kenneth E. Jr. (D)	I	Tex.-25	W (59%)	0	466,000	(233)	1,325,707
Sudan, Philip P. Jr. (R)	C		L (38%)	3,075,000			3,216,793
Matheson, James David (D)	O	Utah-2	W (55%)	753	338,000	(169)	1,366,631
Smith, Derek W. (R)	O		L (41%)	1,198,674			1,692,241
Humphreys, James F. (D)	O	W.Va.-2	L (46%)	6,110,000	480,000	(240)	6,982,393
Capito, Shelley Moore (R)	O		W (47%)	51,000			1,367,504

Self-Financer Had a Large Margin; Opponent Had a Small Resolicitation Base

Kohl, Herb (D)	I	Wis.-Sen	W (61%)	4,830,800	485,000	(97)	4,986,165
Gillespie, John (R)	C		L (37%)	7,000			584,877
Woods, Charles (D)	C	Ala.-2	L (29%)	0	0	(0)	0
Everett, Terry (R)	I		W (68%)	699,373			1,242,951
Kouvelis, Peter (D)	O	Calif.-48	L (28%)	3,450	2,000	(1)	21,685
Issa, Darrell E. (R)	O		W (60%)	3,141,413			3,612,764
Pall, Linda Louise Blackwelder (D)	O	Ida.-1	L (31%)	0	4,000	(2)	72,266
Otter, Clement Leroy (R)	O		W (65%)	407,000			1,212,820
Rock, Robert W. (D)	O	Ind.-2	L (38%)	5,015	84,000	(42)	369,095
Pence, Michael Richard (R)	O		W (50%)	27,886			1,109,916

Notes: "Maximum amount of additional fund-raising" equals the lesser of (1) opposition personal funds times 110 percent (Senate candidates) or 100 percent (House candidates), or (2) "number of maxed-out contributors" times the marginal increase in the contribution limit.

In the "Status" column: I = Incumbent, C = Challenger, O = Open Seat Candidate.

*The author was unable to ascertain the number of maxed-out contributors to Walter Jones. Although the FEC summary files indicate that he received individual contributions totaling $602,416, they are not itemized in FEC data files, and Mr. Jones's FEC filings are not listed in the FEC's database of electronic images.

were defeated by lavish self-financers. Six more incumbents held off challenges, two (Representative Connie Morella, R-Md., and Representative Tim Roemer, D-Ind.) by somewhat close margins.

THE RIPPLES: STRATEGIC DECISIONS

My analysis of the Millionaires' Amendment's direct effects assumes a static context. In other words, the only changes considered are increased fund-raising, as a consequence of enhanced contribution limits, and decreased self-financing, resulting from the loan-repayment restrictions. In reality, myriad contextual factors will likely respond to the Millionaires' Amendment. Some self-financers might deliberately avoid spending enough to trigger increased contribution limits for their opponents. Wealthy candidates might self-finance even more to counteract their opponents' increased fund-raising. Strategic campaign contributors (such as PAC directors) might see the self-financers' opponents as better bets, given their enhanced fund-raising capacity, and increase their own financial support. Some potential candidates might be emboldened to run only if they expect to be able to tap some contributors for three or six times the regular contribution limit. Rich candidates might wait until the eleventh hour to commit personal funds in their campaigns, when it might be too late for their opponents to capitalize on increased contribution limits.

It is impossible to imagine the full range of possible scenarios—let alone point to one as the most likely—that could arise if we could turn back the clock and run the 2000 election again, this time with the Millionaires' Amendment in effect. Nonetheless, I would like to explore the potential implications for strategic decisions concerning candidate emergence and avoiding (or compensating for) the self-financing trigger amounts.

Candidate Emergence

Under the Millionaires' Amendment, would the field in each election have been the same, or would some candidates who sat out the 2000 cycle have joined the race? Consider, for example, the 2000 U.S. Senate election in New Jersey. When U.S. Representative Frank Pallone opted out of the Democratic primary, he attributed his decision to the "huge financial advantage of Jon S. Corzine, a political neophyte whose wealth has made him a formidable challenger" (Gray 1999). On the day he withdrew from the Senate campaign, Pallone already had 116 thousand-dollar contributors; would the knowledge that he could return to each of these strong supporters for more help have brought him to the same conclusion about running for Senate?

Self-financing has had a chilling effect on candidate emergence in congressional elections (Steen 2000). Potential candidates are strategic actors who weigh the costs and benefits of running for Congress (Stone et al. 1998), and the costs can be significantly higher when one faces a wealthy self-financer. This may be partly due to self-financers' ability to use personal funds as seed money in the critical early stages of a campaign, when campaign funds are maximally effective (Biersack, Herrnson, and Wilcox 1993). As one political consultant reports, "We tell our clients to put their own money in, and put it in as soon as possible, *to scare other candidates*" (quoted in Milligan 1999, emphasis added).

The fact that potential candidates *are* deterred by self-financing suggests that they do perform some kind of strategic calculation. Therefore, one should expect them to factor the Millionaires' Amendment into their decisions. To borrow the consultant's language, $1 million in opposition personal funds is a lot less "scary" when it comes with increased contribution limits than when it does not. The chilling effect should thus be muted by the increased contribution limits allowed by the Millionaires' Amendment.

Avoiding or Compensating for the Trigger

Would each candidate have self-financed the same amount, or would some self-financers have kept under the trigger amounts while others self-financed even more to counter the increased fund-raising ability of their opponents? Prior to the Millionaires' Amendment, the marginal expected "return" on a self-financed dollar—that is to say, the net amount by which self-financing increases a candidate's position in the final vote tally—was determined largely by the campaign activity for which personal funds were used. Under the provisions of the Millionaires' Amendment, the net return is potentially undermined by the triggered contribution limit increases.

Consider, for example, a candidate whose personal expenditures are one dollar below a trigger amount. If that candidate self-finances an additional $100,000, he will certainly be able to pay for an additional $100,000 in campaign activity, but he will also enable his opponent to raise additional sums from the opponent's strongest supporters. Triggering the higher contribution limits for an opponent may be too high a price to pay for the extra $100,000 in campaign spending. The Millionaires' Amendment thus creates pressure on certain candidates—those planning to self-finance more than the trigger, but not much more—either to stay below the trigger or to exceed it by a substantial amount.

In the population of actual self-financers in 2000 congressional elections, there appear to be few candidates who self-financed in the sensitive range, above the trigger but not by much. Rather, when candidates exceeded the trigger amounts they usually did so by a wide margin. In Senate primaries, there were ten candidates who would have been eligible for increased contribution limits. For none of them were "opposition personal funds," as defined under BCRA, within 15 percent of a trigger amount. In general elections for U.S. Senate five major-party candidates would have been eligible for increased contributions, but *all* of their opponents exceeded the triggers by more than 15 percent. In House primaries, there were thirty-two candidates who would have qualified for increased limits, and in only one case did opposition funds fall less than 15 percent above the $350,000 trigger. There were fourteen candidates in House general elections who would have been eligible for increased fund-raising; opposition funds were within 15 percent of the trigger for only two of them.

The pattern of self-financing in 2000 elections indicates that the vast majority of self-financers who *do* exceed trigger amounts do so by such a wide margin that they would seem unlikely to scale back personal funding enough to avoid increased contribution limits for their opponents. Rather, they seem more likely to respond to the Millionaires' Amendment by spending even more, to counteract their opponents' increased fund-raising.

CONCLUSION

The preceding analysis has illustrated that the Millionaires' Amendment would have had a limited impact on the 2000 election cycle, assuming that the basic parameters of elections (candidates in the race, amounts self-financed, contributions from sources other than maxed-out individuals) remained constant. The most notable aspect of this study is that it suggests that the Millionaires' Amendment would have influenced a very small number of elections.

The prohibition on loan repayments can only deter self-financing by candidates who seek loan repayment. In 2000, only twenty self-lenders with loans exceeding $250,000 sought to recoup their personal loans, suggesting that the deterrent effect of the Millionaires' Amendment will be quite limited. Even where the Millionaires' Amendment would constrain self-lending, it is unlikely to affect many election outcomes, as only three of the repayment-seeking candidates were involved in close elections.

Similarly, increased contribution limits triggered by self-financing do not promise to affect many races. Of the thirty-five elections in which one candidate's self-financing would have tripped a trigger, only six could plausibly have been swayed by increased fund-raising. However, those six elections included the three most extreme examples of self-financing in the 2000 cycle (the Senate races in Minnesota, New Jersey, and Washington), which are exactly the kinds of races the Millionaires' Amendment was intended to target. In every other election increased fund-raising would not have changed the outcome, either because it would have rolled up a winner's margin or because it would not likely have made up enough ground to overcome a self-financer's overwhelming vote tally.

As I noted previously, the assumption of a static context is a shaky one, as the new rules of the game are likely to affect a number of strategic decisions. The biggest question remaining is whether the Millionaires' Amendment will have a significant effect on candidate emergence. I have suggested that it should have *some* effect, but it is impossible to forecast the magnitude with any precision. But this is an important question—the contours of the candidate field are one of the most significant determinants of election outcomes (Jacobson and Kernell 1983). Consider again the Democratic primary for U.S. Senate in New Jersey, in which Jon Corzine self-financed $60 million to defeat former Governor Jim Florio, while Congressman Frank Pallone sat on the sidelines. If Pallone had decided to brave Corzine's millions, he may very well have been the Gray Davis of 2000. In 1998, Davis was in a sense the last man standing after self-financers Al Checchi and Jane Harman savaged each other in California's Democratic gubernatorial primary.

Different patterns of candidate emergence could also enhance the potency of the "equalizing" provision of the Millionaires' Amendment. As noted above, more than one-third of the elections in which increased contribution limits would have been triggered were uncompetitive contests, with the self-financer either winning by a wide margin or defeating a candidate who did not have many maxed-out supporters. High-quality candidates who are enticed into contests against self-financers by the promise of increased limits will be better equipped to convert increased limits into increased contributions.

In some sense, the effect of the Millionaires' Amendment on strategic decisions of potential candidates may be of greater consequence than the direct impact on fund-raising or self-lending. Of course, at this juncture I offer this as an educated guess. Observers, myself included, will be able to evaluate my propositions more rigorously after the 2004 election has run its course and provided the first set of data in the post-BCRA era.

10

The Impact of BCRA on Presidential Campaign Finance

John C. Green and Anthony Corrado

The debate surrounding the impact of the Bipartisan Campaign Reform Act of 2002 (BCRA) has focused largely on congressional campaigns, and the role of soft money and issue advocacy in them. It has largely (and to some extent deliberately) ignored presidential campaigns. Ironically, BCRA's most immediate impact may be on presidential politics, beginning with the 2004 election cycle.

Four aspects of BCRA are directly relevant to the presidential finance system, and these are unlikely to be affected by the initial court challenges (Sandler and Reiff 2002). First, BCRA increases the maximum amount an individual may contribute per election from $1,000 to $2,000, and indexes this limit for inflation. This change will make it easier for presidential candidates to raise hard dollars for their campaigns. (Individual contribution limits to parties and the aggregate limit of individual contributions are also increased; see table 1.1.)

Second, BCRA places new restrictions on the ability of party committees to spend money in support of their presidential nominees. The centerpiece of BCRA, the ban on soft money, will likely have the largest effect, since national parties will no longer be able to use soft money to finance activities that directly benefit presidential candidates before and during the general election. The use of soft money by state parties will also be restricted, with these committees allowed to spend soft money only on certain limited activities related to federal elections. The new law will thus prohibit state committees from using soft money on many of the activities that benefit presidential hopefuls, including broadcast advertisements that feature a candidate.

Third, an additional provision requires party committees to choose between independent and coordinated expenditures on behalf of a presidential candidate once nominated; this change will influence how the parties allocate federally regulated (hard money) funds in connection with the race for the White House.

The fourth relevant aspect of BCRA is a set of lacunae in the law. While the new statute increases the individual contribution limit, it does not correspondingly increase or index the $250 ceiling for public matching funds during the presidential primaries. This means that the value of matching funds will decline relative to the maximum private contributions in the primary, falling from one-quarter ($250 of $1,000) to one-eighth ($250 of $2,000). A related problem is that BCRA does not expand the expenditure limits that are tied to public financing in the primaries or general election. This raises the prospect of a primary candidate reaching the allowable spending ceiling more quickly than in the past, thus reducing the amount of public funds the candidate will receive.

Taken together, these provisions are likely to exacerbate the existing problems with the presidential system, including stronger incentives for presidential candidates to forgo public financing in the primaries (but probably not in the general election). This strategy is especially relevant to President George W. Bush, who opted out of the public financing system in the 2000 primary campaign; it may also appeal to at least one Democratic candidate in the crowded 2004 primary field. In the longer term, BCRA may alter the dynamics of presidential primaries in several ways: by generating two tiers of candidates, one privately and one publicly financed, and by making the "invisible primary" of early fund-raising even more important to candidate success. All such prospects reflect ongoing problems with the public financing system. Thus, a brief review of its structure is in order as a prelude to assessing the impact of BCRA.

THE STRUCTURE OF THE PRESIDENTIAL
PUBLIC FINANCE SYSTEM

The creation of public financing for presidential elections was the most innovative aspect of the federal campaign finance reforms of the 1970s (Corrado et al. 1997). The reforms began with the 1974 amendment to the Federal Election Campaign Act of 1971 (FECA), which was quickly reviewed in federal courts, resulting in the landmark U.S. Supreme Court decision, *Buckley v. Valeo* (424 U.S. 1 [1976]) This decision motivated subsequent amendments to FECA in 1976 and 1979. These laws, plus a series of narrower federal court rulings and regulations from the Federal Election Commission (FEC), produced the basic structure of the presidential financing system that operated between 1980 and 2000. This structure will be substantially intact in 2004.

This system has three basic elements. First, presidential candidates must abide by the same limits on contributions from individuals, political parties, and interest group political action committees (PACs) that apply to all federal candidates.

These rules also regulate the activities of parties and PACs that expressly advocate the election or defeat of a presidential candidate, including coordinated and independent expenditures made by a party committee or PAC on behalf of a candidate. BCRA makes modest changes in this basic regulatory framework, principally in the form of higher individual contribution limits.

Second, eligible presidential candidates can receive public financing in the primary and general election campaigns if they voluntarily agree to abide by a set of regulations, including spending limits. Third, this legal structure creates a three-part calendar for major party presidential contests: a "preprimary season" in the year prior to the election (when eligible candidates can qualify for public funds and raise funds that can be matched with public money); a "primary season" beginning January 1 of the election year (when eligible candidates receive matching money and states hold presidential nomination contests); and a "general election season" after the candidates are nominated, which typically begins after the national party nominating conventions in July or August and extends through to the general election in November (during which period publicly funded candidates receive a general election grant and are prohibited from raising additional monies, except for funds used to comply with the law). Minor party and independent candidates follow a similar calendar, but with different rules. BCRA does not change the public financing rules or the presidential calendar assumed within campaign finance law.

Preprimary and Primary Rules

Candidates who wish to receive public financing for their campaigns must abide by the following rules (Corrado 1993; 2000, chapter 5).

Eligibility

In the prenomination period, candidates can become eligible for public matching funds by raising at least $5,000 in contributions of $250 or less in at least twenty states (for a total of $100,000).

Matching Funds and Fund-Raising

Once a candidate is eligible, the first $250 contributed by an individual donor is matched with public funds on a dollar-per-dollar basis. In raising such funds, candidates must abide by overall contribution limits ($2,000 maximum under BCRA, up from $1,000 under FECA; candidates may accept up to $5,000 from party committees and PACs, but these funds do not qualify for the match). In addition, candidates must agree to contribute no more than $50,000 of their personal funds to their own campaign.

Individual donations raised in the preprimary season qualify for matching funds. The first payments of matching funds to candidates are made at the beginning of the primary season (January 1 of the election year). The law states that a candidate who ceases to campaign actively, or who fails to receive 10 percent of the vote in two consecutive primaries in which the candidate participated, is no longer eligible to receive matching funds after thirty days; a candidate may requalify by winning at least 20 percent of the vote in a subsequent primary (26 U.S.C. §9033[c]). The maximum amount of matching funds a candidate may receive is one-half of the overall primary spending limit.

Spending Limits

Candidates who accept public funding in the primary season must agree to abide by an aggregate spending limit as well as state-by-state spending limits. The aggregate spending limit has two parts: a base campaign expenditure ceiling and exempt expenditures. The base campaign expenditure ceiling was set in 1974 at $10 million, with a quadrennial adjustment for inflation using the Consumer Price Index (CPI). A fund-raising exemption permitted additional spending of up to 20 percent of the base ceiling to cover the costs of raising money. Under the original provisions of FECA, each candidate was also allowed to raise unlimited additional funds exempt from the spending ceilings to pay the legal and accounting costs incurred to comply with the law. However, in the 2000 election cycle, the FEC adopted regulations providing a "compliance" exemption of 15 percent of the overall ceiling while a campaign is active. Once the campaign is over and is winding down, all salary and overhead is considered exempt compliance spending and does not count against any spending limit (Federal Election Commission 2000b).

In 1976, the first election conducted with public funding, the base limit was $10.9 million, plus $2.2 million for fund-raising costs, for a total cap of $13.1 million. The maximum public subsidy was $5.5 million. By 2000, the base limit had reached $33.8 million, and with fund-raising costs of $6.7 million and compliance costs of $5.1 million included, the overall cap totaled $45.6 million (Federal Election Commission 2000b). The maximum public subsidy was $16.9 million. By 2004, assuming a 2 percent annual rate of inflation, the overall spending limit will rise to $36.6 million, the fund-raising costs to $7.3 million, and the compliance costs to $5.5 million, for a total cap of $49.4 million. Under these assumptions, the maximum public subsidy will be $18.3 million.

In addition to the aggregate spending limit, participating candidates must abide by state-by-state spending limits. The amount a candidate may spend in each state is based on a formula established in 1974 that allows 16¢ times a state's voting-age population, plus adjustments for inflation, with a minimum limit per state of $200,000 in 1974 dollars, adjusted for inflation. In 2000, these state limits ranged from $675,600 in a low-population state such as New Hampshire to $13.1 million in California (Federal Election Commission 2000b). However, the FEC has regularly expanded the types of expenditures that are not subject to state limits, and in 1991 liberalized its rules for allocating expenses to state limits, making these caps increasingly porous and less meaningful to campaigns (Federal Election Commission 1993). Since at least the 1988 election cycle, the state-by-state limits have been more of a nuisance or an accounting issue for candidates than a meaningful limitation on spending.

Outside Spending

Individuals, PACs, and parties are allowed to spend their own funds independently for or against candidates in the preprimary and primary seasons, and organizations are allowed to spend on internal communications with their members for or against a candidate. Such expenditures must be disclosed to the FEC. However, the disclosure regulations do not include much of the traditional grassroots campaigning by interest groups or the recent innovation of candidate-specific "issue advocacy" advertising (Potter 1997). BCRA will restrict broadcast, candidate-specific advertising by corporations and unions in a state or media market thirty days before that state's primary election.

Parties have rarely contributed to presidential primary candidates, who are, after all, competing for the party's nomination. However, since 1996, the Republican and Democratic National Committees have spent soft money to assist the presumptive nominee during the emerging "interregnum," the period of time between the effective end of the primary season and the national convention, the beginning of the general election season. Although technically within the primary season, these expenditures are actually directed at the general election. Under BCRA, spending soft money for this purpose will not be possible.

General Election Rules

Candidates who wish to receive public financing in the general election campaign must abide by the following rules (Corrado 1993; 2000, chapter 5).

Eligibility

A major party nominee (defined in the law as a nominee of a party that received at least 25 percent of the vote in the previous election) is eligible to receive a public grant for the general elections.

Public Grant, Fund-Raising, and Spending Limits

The amount of the general election public funds grant is 100 percent of the spending limit. The limit was set in 1974 at $20 million, with adjustments for inflation using the CPI. By 2000, this subsidy had grown to $67.6 million per candidate. Assuming a 2 percent annual rate of inflation, it will equal $73 million in 2004.

As a condition of receiving this subsidy, a candidate must agree not to raise or spend additional private funds through his or her campaign committee. There is one exception to this prohibition: candidates may raise money to finance general election legal, accounting, and compliance costs (known as GELAC funds). The magnitude of these funds is unrestricted, but they must be raised from donations subject to federal contribution limits. In 2000, the Democratic and Republican general election candidates raised about $15 million in GELAC funds (Corrado 2001).

Outside Spending

As in the primary season, individuals, PACs, and parties are allowed to spend their own funds independently for or against candidates in the general election, and nonparty organizations are also allowed to spend on internal communications with their members for or against candidates. In addition, the national party committees are allowed a limited amount of coordinated expenditures, which are adjusted for inflation, on behalf of their nominees. In 2000, the Democratic and Republican National Committees (DNC and RNC, respectively) were each allowed to spend $13.7 million in coordinated expenditures on behalf of a presidential ticket (Federal Election Commission 2000a); assuming a 2 percent inflation rate, by 2004 the amount will be $14.8 million.

Under BCRA, the national parties may make coordinated expenditures (hard dollars subject to the above limitation) *or* independent expenditures (hard dollars not subject to limitation) for their presidential candidates—but not both. The initial interpretation of this provision of BCRA by the FEC found that this provision would not apply before a candidate was nominated, which does not take place until the convention has cast a formal vote approving a candidate as the party's presidential nominee. Prior to BCRA, party committees could engage in both independent and coordinated expenditures on behalf of a presumptive nominee.

Party soft money and issue advocacy expenditures, financed by soft money, have become an important element of general election presidential spending in recent times, much more so than in the primaries. Prior to BCRA, these expenditures were not subject to any limitations. BCRA largely bans soft money and sets some limits on issue advocacy by corporations and unions within sixty days of the general election.

THE PRESIDENTIAL SYSTEM'S PROBLEMS

The public financing system was enacted just as the contemporary presidential primary system was developing. Indeed, the first presidential election held under FECA, 1976, was only the second election after reforms in the Democratic Party made primaries the dominant mechanism for determining the major party presidential nominees (Hagen and Mayer 2000). The initial parameters of FECA fit the presidential process of the early 1970s fairly well. However, as the nomination process evolved, the public financing rules became increasingly problematic, providing candidates, their parties, and interest group allies with strong incentives to press the boundaries of the finance system.

Front-Loading the Primary Schedule

Unlike the presidential finance rules, which were established by federal law, the dates and other details of the primaries are matters of state law. Although the national parties have imposed some order on the schedule, they have not prevented state governments from moving their contests forward in the primary season, closer to its traditional beginning with the Iowa caucuses and the New Hampshire primary (Busch and Mayer 2002).

The results of such front-loading are quite dramatic. For example, in 1976 both major parties had not chosen 50 percent of the convention delegates by May 4, some four months after the primary season officially began. By contrast, in 2000 the Democrats had picked 50 percent of the convention delegates by March 11 and the Republicans by March 10—a little more than one month after the Iowa caucus and New Hampshire primary. The politics of front-loading is complex, but at bottom the goal is to increase a state's influence by voting early in the process. Ironically, front-loading has increased the probability that the nomination will be settled early. What was a slow-starting and long-lasting process in 1976 (a "marathon") has evolved into a quick-starting and sudden-ending campaign by 2000 (a "sprint"). Although the 2004 primary schedule has not been set at this writing, actions by the DNC suggest that the front-loading trend is likely to continue (Busch and Mayer 2002).

The financial consequences of front-loading have been threefold. First, front-loading has made the preprimary season crucial for fund-raising. Candidates have strong incentives to raise funds before the primary season begins, because there is little time to raise funds once the closely packed contests are underway. Second, front-loading has concentrated campaign spending in the early primaries, so candidates risk reaching the aggregate spending limit quickly. Third, front-loading has modified the election calendar by creating an interregnum between the effective end of the primary season and the national conventions, the beginning of the general election campaign (Ceaser and Busch 2001, chapter 4). In 1976, the interregnum was about two months long, but by 2000 it had grown to five months. The expanded interregnum requires additional campaign funds, a problem that has been most serious for a candidate emerging from a competitive primary to face a popular incumbent president who does not face a battle for renomination.

Other Financial Problems

Front-loading might have created financial difficulties in any event, but other problems with the presidential system have exacerbated the situation. One serious difficulty is that individual contribution limits have not been adjusted for inflation (that is, until BCRA). The maximum individual contribution of $1,000, enacted in 1974, had lost substantial value by 2000, falling to approximately $380 in real purchasing power (measured by the CPI). The same erosion of purchasing power occurred with the $250 matching threshold, which had been reduced to about $95 in real terms by 2000. Although contribution limits were not adjusted for inflation, the aggregate and state-by-state spending limits were adjusted every four years using the CPI. Thus, in real terms, candidates were forced to raise the same sum of money in smaller and smaller amounts.

Although adjusted for inflation, the aggregate spending limit has not been adjusted to reflect the real costs of campaigning, which have increased much faster than the CPI. The escalation of costs has resulted in part from the increased use of modern communications technology, and in part from the need to wage campaigns in many states simultaneously. Also, the state-by-state spending limits failed to reflect the strategic importance of particular states. For example, New Hampshire is clearly the most important primary, and yet the spending limit was $675,600 in 2000—about 2 percent of the overall campaign ceiling of $33.8 million.

One final financial problem requires a brief mention. Over time, the federal income tax check-off that provides funding for the presidential system has failed to generate sufficient money to cover the matching funds obligations at the time they are due, particularly in the case of the initial payments owed to candidates on January 1 of the election year. This situation has arisen in part from the declining participation of eligible taxpayers, and in part because a decline in the number taxpayers eligible to participate (because changes in the tax code have reduced the number of individuals with a federal tax liability, a prerequisite for using the check-off). In addition, the law requires the government to set aside the funds for the general election grants and the national nominating conventions before it covers the primary matching funds (Corrado 1993). As a result, the FEC has been unable in recent elections to honor the full matching requests at the time they are made. So far these obligations have been covered within the calendar year as additional revenues become available. However, if present trends continue, the public funds may not be able to cover the primary matching funds within an appropriate time frame, which could affect the candidates.

Assessing the Impact of the System's Problems

These financial problems have interacted with the effects of front-loading in a pernicious fashion, making the primary campaigns increasingly onerous. First, candidates who do not have access to large donations or a large number of donors have increasingly fallen victim to the invisible primary in the preprimary season (Green and Bigelow 2002). Indeed, it is widely believed that candidates must raise a minimum of $20 million in the preprimary season to be competitive. Table 10.1 illustrates this trend by comparing the percentage of funds raised by the top two candidates in each major party in 1980 and 2000. In 1980, all of the candidates raised less than two-fifths of their total funds in the preprimary period. By 2000, three of the four raised more than one-half of their total funds before the primary season. John McCain is the exception that proves the rule in 2000: he raised less than one-third of his total receipts in the preelection year. His success in New Hampshire gave him a boost to raise additional money in February to run a credible contest until March, when he lost a series of important primaries.

Table 10.1 also presents data on another facet of this problem: candidates increasingly have turned to large contributions to fund their campaigns. For example, in 1980, Ronald Reagan raised less than one-fifth of his funds in contributions of $750 or more (which includes the maximum donation of $1,000). But in 2000, George W. Bush raised nearly three-quarters of his funds in such large donations, and the dependence on large contributions holds for the other candidates as well. McCain raised more than one-quarter of his funds in such large amounts as opposed to about one-sixth for George H. W. Bush in 1980. Such increases also occurred for the Democratic candidates between 1980 and 2000.

Second, the high cost of competing in the early contests means that competi-

Table 10.1   Early Fund-Raising and Large Contributions, 1980 and 2000

	1980	*2000*
Republicans		
Winner	*(Reagan)*	*(G. W. Bush)*
Percent of all individual funds before Jan 1	42%	72%
Percent of all individual donations over $750	19	74
Strongest Opponent	*(Bush)*	*(McCain)*
Percent of all individual funds before Jan 1	56	45
Percent of all individual donations over $750	16	27
Democrats		
Winner	*(Carter)*	*(Gore)*
Percent of all individual funds before Jan 1	47	82
Percent of all individual donations over $750	35	48
Strongest Opponent	*(Kennedy)*	*(Bradley)*
Percent of all individual funds before Jan 1	43	90
Percent of all individual donations over $750	20	51

tive candidates reach the overall spending limit quickly, making it difficult to continue their campaigns. Figures 10.1 and 10.2 compare the spending over the primary season of the major contenders in 1980 and 2000. In both years, candidate spending nears the aggregate spending limit by the end of the season. But in 1980, the candidates were well below the limit at the date when 50 percent of the delegates had been chosen. In 2000, this date occurred much earlier than

Figure 10.1   1980 Presidential Nomination Campaign Spending (as Percent of Spending Limit)

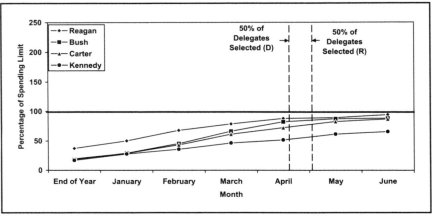

Figure 10.2   2000 Presidential Nomination Campaign Spending (as Percent of Spending Limit)

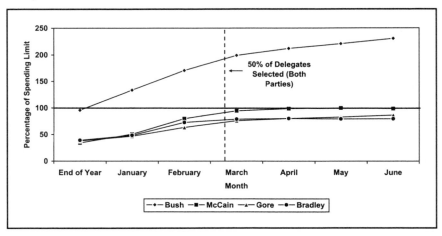

Figure 10.3   Democratic Presidential Nomination, 1980–2000
Cumulative Candidate Expenditures through March (as Percent of Limit), and Delegates
Selected through March 15 (as Percent of Total)

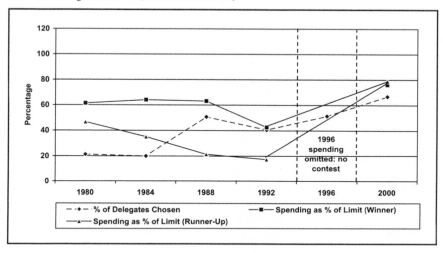

Figure 10.4   Republican Presidential Nomination, 1980–2000
Cumulative Candidate Expenditures through March (as Percent of Limit), and Delegates
Selected through March 15 (as Percent of Total)

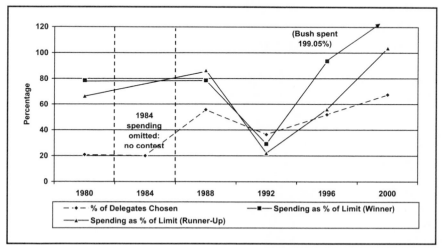

1980 (due to front-loading). John McCain had essentially reached the aggregate spending limit before the end of March. This meant that, even if McCain had won the early March primaries, he could not have continued to campaign. Because Bush opted out of the system, he was not restrained by the spending limits.

The same figures show a similar pattern for the Democrats. In 1980, both Jimmy Carter and Edward Kennedy were still below the aggregate spending limit at the 50 percent delegate mark, but in 2000 Al Gore and Bill Bradley had reached the campaign ceiling and were headed toward the aggregate limit at this point in the campaign (which, of course, occurred much earlier in the primary calendar).

An additional problem arises from the combination of the spending limits and high level of expenditures early in the primary season. As primaries occur earlier, candidates spend more of their allowed funds early. (See figures 10.3 and 10.4.) As a result, the presumptive nominee may lack sufficient funds to campaign during the interregnum. For example, in 1996, Bob Dole emerged from a tough primary contest only about $10 million short of the primary spending limit, while President Clinton had about $25 million left to spend. This severely limited Dole's ability to campaign in the five months leading up to the national convention, while Clinton could campaign vigorously (Corrado 1997; 1999). The shoe was on the other foot in 2000. Al Gore emerged from the primaries with about $11 million left in spending authority. George Bush, who faced no such restrictions, eventually raised and spent $27 million before the convention. In fact, one reason Bush opted out of the public financing system was to avoid Bob Dole's fate (Green and Bigelow 2002).

THE CANDIDATES RESPOND

Presidential candidates have responded to these problems in a number of ways. As the problems have become more serious, the scope of the response has expanded. One early response was to violate the system's rules. For example, some candidates deliberately exceeded the state-by-state spending limits and were forced to repay public funds to the treasury (Corrado 1993). Others have created separate "delegate" committees to engage in additional spending (Alexander and Haggerty 1987). At least one aspirant, Republican Pat Robertson, acquired mailing lists and other financial resources that were later ruled illegal (Babcock 1987). Such tactics gave campaigns tactical flexibility at the cost of legal sanctions and poor publicity. These kinds of responses threaten the legal integrity of the public financing system.

Other responses operated within the legal framework of FECA, albeit in a fashion contrary to the spirit of the public financing system. For example, some candidates have formed "leadership PACs" to develop fund-raising lists and pay for campaign activities prior to the official beginning of a campaign (Corrado 1992). This tactic allows candidates to expend funds not subject to the spending limits.

Yet another response has been to rely on outside money (Corrado 2001; Green and Bigelow 2002). Such funds include independent public, and internal, communications costs from allied PACs (which are sanctioned by FECA), and in recent times, issue advocacy spending during the preprimary and primary seasons (which pushes the boundaries of FECA). This strategy has been even more common—and more controversial—in the interregnum. An important example is national party soft money spending during the interregnum to rescue a presumptive nominee who had reached the aggregate spending limit. In 1996, the RNC announced a $20 million issue ad campaign in support of Bob Dole using soft money (Republican National Committee 1996). Similarly, in 2000, both major parties began spending substantial sums of money in June on issue advocacy advertisements designed to support their respective nominees, spending that was probably more important for Al Gore, the Democratic nominee, who was close to the aggregate spending limit.

Outside money has also become important in general elections (Corrado 2002). The major party nominees have increasingly relied on party operations to supplement their campaign spending. In every recent election, the national party committees have essentially spent the maximum permissible amount in coordinated expenditures to supplement the public funding given to their respective nominees. They have also taken advantage of the opportunity to raise and spend soft money on voter registration and mobilization efforts, spending tens of millions of dollars in support of their respective presidential nominees. Moreover, these efforts have allowed candidates to reduce their voter registration and turnout budgets, freeing public funds for advertising or other campaign expenses. Interest groups have also engaged in issue advocacy spending for and against presidential candidates, adding substantial spending (Magleby 2002a).

Outside money allows campaigns to expand their financial resources. For example, outside spending is estimated to have totaled some $22 million in the 2000 Democratic and Republican primaries (Green and Bigelow 2002). In the general election, Republicans, Democrats, and their interest group allies spent nearly $50 million more on each side in the presidential campaign than was specified by the public funds grant (Corrado 2002). Outside money thus threatens the structure of the public financing system—which is one principal reason that BCRA tries to restrict it.

A final response to the system's problems is for candidates to forgo public financing altogether. This tactic allows candidates a maximum of flexibility: they can raise and spend money early to cope with front-loading, without worrying about spending limits. Then, if they win, they can raise more money for the interregnum. Because the public financing system is voluntary, this option is legal, but were it to become widespread it would render the public financing system less relevant to presidential politics.

There are also some costs to opting out from a candidate's perspective. A candidate would be likely to forgo public funds in the primaries or general election if three conditions were met: (1) the candidate could replace the forgone public funds with private monies (or could finance a campaign from personal resources); (2) the candidate could substantially increase his or her funds above the aggregate spending limit; and (3) the candidate could opt out without engendering substantial adverse publicity.

These conditions have rarely been met, and thus few candidates have chosen to forgo public funds. From 1976 to 2000 just 7 percent of the major party candidates that were eligible for matching funds opted out (six of eighty-six). All these candidates were Republicans, and all but one case occurred between 1996 and 2000, reflecting the increasing problems with the system. Among the six, three were serious contenders for the GOP nomination, one running twice. Publisher Steve Forbes opted against public financing in 1996 and 2000 largely so he could spend more than $50,000 of his personal fortune. He came close to meeting the first condition above, but not the second—he raised $41.6 million in 1996 (when the aggregate spending limit was $37.7 million) and $48.1 million in 2000 (when the spending limit was $45.6 million). To the surprise of some observers, Forbes also met the third condition: criticism for forgoing public funds apparently did not harm his campaigns.

The two other serious candidates, both former governors of Texas, decided to forgo public financing largely to avoid spending limits: John Connally in 1980 and George W. Bush in 2000. Connally raised $12.7 million, less than the maximum spending limit of $17.7 million. Thus, he failed to meet the first and second conditions above and may have failed to meet the third condition as well (Pomper 1981). Rightly or wrongly, Connally's experience helped deter other viable candidates from forgoing public funds until 1996.

In 2000, George W. Bush raised $94.5 million, a little more than twice the aggregate primary spending limit of $45.6 million (Green and Bigelow 2002). In fact, his total in the prenomination period *alone* was larger than the *combined* maximum public funds available to a candidate of $84.5 million ($16.9 million in the primary and $67.6 million in the general election). Bush met all three of the above conditions handily: he more than replaced the amount he might have received in public matching funds; he raised additional funds beyond what was needed in the primaries; and he suffered no serious consequences from adverse publicity.

Bush's 2000 primary fund-raising effort was extraordinary by any standard, surprising his campaign officials and outside observers alike. This feat may have resulted from Bush's unique circumstances: he was simultaneously the sitting governor of Texas, the son of a former President and heir to his father's immense fund-raising network, and the consensus choice of the GOP establishment desperate to win back the White House. It is possible that Vice President Al Gore could have performed a similar feat within the context of the Democratic primaries. However, given the liberalism of Democratic primary voters, adverse publicity might have harmed Gore in his contest against Bill Bradley.

In any event, Bush was the first candidate to forgo public financing and win his party's nomination. Moreover, his large war chest proved helpful in the interregnum campaign. But like every major party nominee since 1976, Bush accepted public funds for the general election. One reason for this decision was that Bush had spent more than $67 million securing the Republican nomination; also, raising another $67 million in contributions of $1,000 or less in five months was a daunting task. Finally, this effort would have taken hard dollars from other Republican Party causes, funds that were needed to effectively spend the prodigious amounts of soft money available to the RNC.

THE IMPACT OF BCRA IN 2004

In this context, how will the provisions of BCRA influence presidential campaigns? Simply put, BCRA is likely to exacerbate the problems of the presidential system by offering stronger incentives for candidates to opt out of the public financing system. We can assess the magnitude of this impact by using the 2000 campaign as a baseline and estimating the changes in candidate finances that might have occurred if BCRA had been in effect. We will also note how such changes may alter the dynamics of presidential primaries in the longer term.

Prospects for the Primaries

Estimates of Change

Table 10.2 presents estimates of fund-raising in 2004 dollars under four scenarios for the principal major party candidates in 2000: Bush and McCain for the GOP, Gore and Bradley for the Democrats. These estimates are, of course, speculation, and so it is worth carefully reviewing the various assumptions behind them.

All the estimates in table 10.2 take the funds raised in the 2000 campaign and the four candidates as illustrations of some of the main types of viable presidential candidates. Scenario 1, "2000 Replay" lists the private funds raised by these 2000 candidates in 2004 dollars (assuming inflation at 2 percent per annum). This scenario also presents the matching funds received by the 2000 candidates, also adjusted for inflation (in italics). In this regard, one figure must be kept in mind, and that is the maximum matching funds in 2004, estimated to be $18.3 million (listed at the bottom of the table).

The next three rows in table 10.2 report estimates of the funds that would be raised by each candidate under varying assumptions. The first scenarios assume that the candidates have the same number of contributors in 2004 as in 2000,

Table 10.2   What If the 2000 Primaries Had Been Run under BCRA?
(All estimates in millions of 2004 dollars)

	Republicans		Democrats	
Estimates	*Bush*	*McCain*	*Gore*	*Bradley*
Scenario 1: 2000 Replay				
Assume no change in donors, and assume size of donations increases only for inflation. No additional impact because of BCRA.				
Funds Raised	102.3	33.0	36.7	32.2
Matching Funds	0.0	15.7	16.6	13.4
Scenario 2: The Survey				
Assume no change in donors. Assume doubled contributions from a percentage of each group of givers that equals the percentage who told the major donor survey that they would give more if the limits went up. Assume halved contributions from a percentage equal to those who said they would give less.				
Funds raised (private funds)	125.6	35.9	43.7	38.9
Scenario 3: Double $1,000 Donors,				
Again assume no change in the donor pool, but double the contributions from half of the $1,000 donors reported in Federal Election Commission data. This assumes more people would give more than said they would in the donor survey.				
Funds raised	135.6	39.1	47.1	42.5
Scenario 4: New Donors				
Add twice as many donors at all levels (except for Bush) and double the contributions from half of the $1,000 contributors, old and new.				
Funds raised	—	73.7	97.1	88.8

Note: Estimated 2004 maximum matching funds: $18.3 million.
Source: 2000 Presidential Donor Survey. See chapter 4.

but are able to raise more money because of the increased individual contribution limits under BCRA. Scenario 2, "The Survey Scenario" uses two sources of data: a very accurate count of the number of donors of $200 to each campaign[1] (to which all the assumptions are applied), and the 2000 presidential donor survey (see chapter 4 for details about this survey).

In the 2000 presidential donor survey, respondents were asked to predict their own behavior if the contribution limits were raised. Overall, 22 percent of the donors of $200 or more predicted that they would give more if allowed to do so by law (76 percent predicted their giving would not change and 2 percent claimed they would give less). Donors of under $200 were less likely to predict an increase: just 4 percent did so (and 8 percent predicted a decline). These figures are best thought of as a *minimum* estimate of how donors will respond to increased limits, since they were asked to predict their giving in the abstract, before the passage of BCRA and in the absence of a real campaign.

The Survey Scenario estimate applies the survey responses of people who identified themselves as Bush, McCain, Gore, and Bradley donors. It takes the percentage of respondents who said they would give more, and applies it to the pool of actual 2000 donors of $1,000, $200 to $999, and under $200. It further assumes that donors who predicted increased giving would double their 2000 gifts, and that the donors who said they would give less would cut their gifts in half. For example, 33 percent of Bush's $1,000 donors predicted they would give more, and so Bush's 2000 funds were increased by taking one-third of his $1,000 donors and assuming they would give $2,000. The same procedure was used for the other sizes of donations. Interestingly, a similar percentage of the $1,000 donors for Gore (32.5 percent) and Bradley (31.1 percent) said they would increase their giving, but only 18 percent of McCain's $1,000 donors made the same claim, so the higher limits would have helped him less, under these assumptions.[2]

Scenario 3, "Double $1,000 Donors" is the same as the Survey Scenario, with one exception: it assumes that for each candidate one-half of the $1,000 donors would double their gifts to $2,000 (instead of what the survey predicted). All such assumptions are in some sense arbitrary, but campaign professionals believe that the 50 percent figure is a reasonable upper figure for 2004.[3] It is tempting, of course, to assume that all of the $1,000 donors will double their donations in 2004, but there is no evidence this would actually happen.

Scenario 4, "New Donors" moves beyond the existing donors in 2000. The secret of Bush's extraordinary fund-raising in 2000 was expanding the number of donors to his campaign. For example, his 59,279 $1,000 donors were almost four times Bob Dole's 14,875 $1,000 donors in 1996 (and more than twice the 26,246 $1,000 donors to all the other Republican candidates in 2000). The increased contribution limits in BCRA will make it easier for future candidates to repeat Bush's feat. For instance, a $2,000 limit would have allowed Bush to raise the same amount of money with a little over 29,000 maximum donors— only twice as many as Dole had in 1996. The new Donor Scenario assumes that each candidate would add twice as many donors of all types as he did in the 2000 campaign. (Because Bush already made this move in 2000, we did not calculate such an estimate for him. If Bush could expand his base once again, perhaps by mobilizing the donors to his 2000 primary rivals, he could substantially increase his total. Such a possibility would once again break precedent.)

Thus, scenarios 2, 3 and 4 in table 10.2 provide, respectively: a low estimate based on donors' predictions of their own behavior in the abstract; a high estimate based on the first estimate plus the wisdom of campaign professionals on the likely increase in $1,000 donors; and another high estimate, adding to the second estimate a doubling of the number of donors in the 2000 campaign.

The Impact of the Change: Bush and McCain

The logical place to begin discussing these estimates is with George W. Bush, the only one of the 2000 candidates who is likely to run again in 2004 (Associated Press 2003). If Bush simply replicated his 2000 fund-raising (row 1), his primary war chest would total $102.3 million in 2004 dollars. If all of Bush's donors who predicted an increase doubled their gifts (The Survey Scenario), then Bush would raise $125.6 million. If, however, the Double $1,000 Donors Scenario prevailed, Bush would have $135.6 million. These figures are impressive, but less than the $200 million some political observers have said they expect the Bush campaign will generate in 2004 (Edsall 2003).

These estimates strongly suggest that Bush will once again forgo public financing in the 2004 primaries. After all, the lowest prediction of the funds he will raise is nearly seven times greater than the maximum matching funds in 2004 ($18.3 million), and is roughly one-third greater than the combination of matching funds and the general election grant ($91.3 million). If Bush is unopposed in the primaries (as often happens with an incumbent president), his campaign could use the bulk of these funds for the interregnum and general election campaign (see below). Of course, a large war chest is one way to ward off potential primary challengers.

How would the new law affect a challenger to an establishment candidate, such as John McCain in 2000? If the McCain campaign is any guide, then the impact of BCRA is likely to be quite different than for an establishment candidate like Bush. In the 2000 Replay Scenario, McCain raised $33 million, and he gains relatively little in the Survey Scenario ($35.9 million) and Double $1,000 Donor Scenario ($39.1 million). These gains are far less that the matching funds he would be eligible for in 2004. The reasons for these low figures are straightforward. First, relatively few of McCain's donors said they would give more (just 18 percent of his $1,000 donors). Given McCain's focus on campaign finance reform (which eventually resulted in the passage of BCRA), this reluctance to give more by his donors makes some intuitive sense. Second, McCain had relatively few $1,000 donors (just 10,040), having financed his campaign with a large proportion of smaller donations (Green and Bigelow 2002). McCain has much larger gains under the New Donors Scenario, with the assumption of doubling the number of donors to the campaign. However, a challenger may not be able to attract this kind of donor support, even in Republican circles.

It is likely, then, that candidates such as McCain will continue to accept public financing under BCRA. Some of the new rules may well be beneficial: the large contribution limits will make it easier to raise a large war chest in the preprimary season. Other aspects of the new rules would be less advantageous, such as the fact that the matching threshold of $250 is just one-eighth of the maximum donation of $2,000 (instead of one-fourth of the previous $1,000), and each $2,000 would count toward the spending limit. And such a campaign would still suffer from the system's other problems, including front-loading and spending limits. Indeed, McCain's apparent inability to raise a large amount of extra money would have been of little consequence in 2000, since he would have reached the aggregate spending limit in March in any event (Green and Bigelow 2002).

Taken as a whole, this analysis suggests that BCRA may encourage two tiers of primary candidates: privately financed establishment candidates (and self-financed millionaires) versus publicly financed challengers and insurgents. The latter will be increasing plagued by the presidential system's other problems. Thus, while such candidates might prevail in the primaries, the window of opportunity for such a victory is likely to be even narrower than in the past.

The Impact of the Change: Gore and Bradley

Table 10.2 reveals a variation on these themes for the Democrats. Al Gore's 2000 fund-raising performance equals $36.7 million under the 2000 Replay Scenario. The Survey Scenario would generate $43.7 million for Gore, and the Double $1,000 Donors Scenario produces $47.1 million. Both increases are substantial, but neither is larger than the maximum public matching funds ($18.3 million). So, by these estimates, Gore would have accepted public funds in 2004. Like McCain, he might have found it somewhat easier to raise funds due to the higher contribution limit, but would still have suffered under the system's problems.

Once again, the big gains occur in the New Donor Scenario. The resulting $97.1 million is comparable to Bush's $102.3 million (see 2000 Replay for Bush). The net gain of $60 million is three times larger than the maximum matching funds, allowing for a well-financed and flexible primary campaign, and then an adequate interregnum campaign. Under these circumstances, it would make sense for Gore to forgo public financing. And BCRA would make this strategy much easier. For example, he would have to expand the number of $1,000 donors from some 19,289 to 38,575—far less than Bush's 59,279 (and about equal to Gore's and Bradley's combined $1,000 donors of 37,634).

If Gore is an example of an establishment Democrat, then Bill Bradley represents a well-funded challenger. The estimates for the Bradley campaign closely resemble those for Gore, because Bradley's 2000 fund-raising was quite similar (for instance, Bradley had 18,345 $1,000 donors). As with the Gore campaign, the Survey and Double $1,000 Donors Scenarios estimates would allow for a more adequate campaign within the public financing system, while the New Donor Scenario would allow Bradley to forgo public financing. Indeed, Gore's and Bradley's fund-raising performances are close enough to suggest that a strong challenger might decide to run a privately financed primary campaign against an establishment candidate who accepts public funds.

It is worth stressing that opting out of the public financing system would require a substantial expansion of Gore's and Bradley's 2000 donor bases. But would it really be possible for a Democratic candidate to expand the number of donors in this fashion? Some observers are quite skeptical of this possibility, arguing that there are simply not enough donors in Democratic circles for this purpose (Edsall 2003). The evidence certainly suggests that it would be difficult for *all* the major 2004 Democratic candidates to forgo public financing simultaneously. However, this same evidence also suggests a more nuanced view of the possibility of such a strategy for at least *one* of the candidates.

To begin with, the Republicans' 1996 experience would have suggested that the 2000 Bush fund-raising effort was next to impossible: in that year the $1,000 donors to GOP candidates totaled only 41,927, far fewer than Bush's 59,279 in 2000. Few candidates may be able to duplicate Bush's spectacular 2000 effort, but due to BCRA, they have to perform only one-half as well in 2004. In addition, past Democratic primary fund-raising was premised on public funds, since no Democrat had ever opted out of the system. Indeed, some observers believe that Gore could have raised enough private funds to forgo public money in 2000 (although perhaps not the same amount of money as Bush).

Finally, the 2000 donor pool is only a small fraction of the number of people with high incomes who could make a significant contribution to a Democratic presidential candidate. For example, the 2000 Voter News Service exit polls found that 29 percent of voters with incomes of $100,000 or more were Democrats,[4] and the 2000 National Election Study found that 37 percent of respondents with household incomes of $95,000 or more identified or leaned Democratic. Such figures reflect recent social and educational changes among upper status groups (Galston and Kamark 1998). While these percentages may seem small, when applied to the 14 million households with annual incomes of $100,000 or more found in the 2000 U.S. Census (DeNarvas-Walt, Cleveland, and Roemer 2001), they produce between 4 and 5.1 million potential donors. If one were to assume that 5 percent of such donors would make a donation of over $200 to a candidate if asked (about one-half of the percentage that reported making a campaign contribution in the 2000 National Elections Study), the size of the potential donor pool is between 200,000 and 255,000. These figures are more than twice the 68,488 actual donors of $200 or more to Democratic candidates in 2000. So, there is certainly room in the income structure of American society to expand the Democratic donor pool—much as Gore and Bradley in 2000 over the 1996 Clinton effort. The trick, of course, is for a candidate actually to find and obtain donations from such people.

Several of the initial Democratic candidates for 2004 might well be able to achieve this feat (Edsall 2002b). Among the establishment figures are former House Minority Leader Richard Gephardt (D-Mo.), who may be able to draw on a large pool of donors from his years in Congress, and the 2000 Democratic Vice Presidential nominee, Senator Joseph Lieberman (D-Conn.), who may find a strong base of support in the Jewish community. Potentially well-funded challengers include Senators John Edwards (D-N.C.), whose connections with trial lawyers might produce sufficient funds, and John Kerry (D-Mass.), who may be able to rally progressive activists. One factor militating against such a strategy is the possibility that forgoing public funds could become a campaign issue, given the reform orientation of many Democratic activists and primary voters. Indeed, at least one candidate, Howard Dean (D-Vt.), has promised to pursue this issue vigorously should any candidate opt out of the public financing system.

If even one Democratic candidate successfully opted out of the public financing system, the invisible primary could become draconian. One candidate's early fund-raising success could drive many rival candidates from the race for lack of funds. And if one adds to this prospect the absence of spending limits and the ability to finance an interregnum campaign, then opting out of the system could be very attractive. The fact that Bush may be especially well funded in 2004 may add additional pressure on less competitive Democratic candidates to drop out early so as to maximize the total funds available to the front-runner—as happened with the Republican candidates in 2000. And the absence of soft money for the national party committees may persuade Democratic leaders and activists that getting behind the most likely nominee will be necessary, under the circumstances.

Prospects for General Election Funding

Will BCRA provide incentives for candidates to forgo public funds in the general election? Here our assessment must be even more speculative than for the primaries, because no major party nominee has ever refused the general election grant. As before, Bush presents the most relevant case. In order to forgo the general election grant, the Bush campaign would have to raise more than $73 million (a good estimate for the size of the grant in 2004). Even if we assume that the scenarios in table 10.2 could be repeated after the primary and interregnum campaigns have ended—a highly unlikely assumption—the new funds would fall short of the amount needed. For example, the Double $1,000 Scenario produces just $33 million over the Replay 2000 Scenario, and it is highly unrealistic to expect the large Bush donors to double their gifts *twice* in a single election year.

In addition, the Bush campaign will face other incentives to accept the general election grant. First, by accepting the general election grant (and not seeking additional private funds), the Bush campaign would not interfere with the Republican efforts to maximize hard-dollar fund-raising in the absence of soft money. Second, Bush could be actively involved in such fund-raising for the party and its candidates, and probably could raise more funds in aggregate. Finally, any funds left over from the primary and interregnum campaigns could be transferred to Republican Party committees, which could use them for coordinated spending or other election activities. All such efforts would strengthen both the Republican Party and Bush's position within it. Finally, if Bush has strong incentives to accept the general election grant, then surely the Democratic nominee will do so as well.

CONCLUSION

The estimates presented above strongly suggest that President Bush will once again forgo public matching funds for the primaries in 2004. It is also possible that at least one Democratic presidential contender in 2004 will forgo matching funds in the primaries, but this will require a dramatic expansion of the number of donors as well as an increase in the size of gifts from existing donors. Most Democratic candidates are likely to participate in the public financing system and face a mix of new advantages and old difficulties. Finally, it is unlikely that Bush will forgo general election public funds, and the Democratic nominee will certainly accept them.

Key provisions of BCRA are central to these assessments. The doubling of the individual contribution limit from $1,000 to $2,000 is critical; the lack of change in matching funds and the banning of soft money matter as well. In addition, the increasing problems with the presidential public finance system, such as the front-loading of the primary schedule, are important factors.

If nonparticipation in the presidential primary system becomes commonplace, especially among the prospective front-runners in each party, the public financing system will become less relevant to presidential politics. Under such circumstances, the system is unlikely to achieve the goals that motivated its enactment: enhancing competition, increasing participation, and limiting the influence of money in presidential politics.

In the longer term, BCRA may alter the dynamics of presidential primary campaigns. One can imagine a system with two tiers of candidates: privately funded establishment candidates (and self-financed millionaires) facing publicly funded challengers and insurgents. One can also imagine a more draconian invisible primary winnowing the field of potential candidates much earlier in the process, as party leaders and activists seek to maximize overall funds for the prospective nominee. In sum, BCRA is likely to exacerbate the existing problems in the public financing system.

NOTES

1. The campaign finance data come from a careful study of individual contributions of $200 or more in the 1996 and 2000 election cycles by Anthony Corrado and Heitor

Gouvêa at Colby College, removing refunds and combining multiple donations from a single individual. This work was conducted with the support of The Pew Charitable Trusts, and the views expressed here are solely those of the authors.

2. For Bush, the assumptions used in row 2 yielded a 33 percent increase for $1,000 donors, a 17.3 percent increase for donors of $200 to $999, and a 7 percent increase for donors of under $200. For McCain, the comparable figures were 18, 10.5, and 3 percent, respectively; for Gore, 32.5, 12.8, and 0 percent, respectively; and for Bradley, 31.1, 13.9, and 0 percent respectively. One might reasonably ask why donors of less than $1,000 should be included. After all, they legally could have given more in 2000 and did not do so. We include an increase in their estimated giving because of an important feature of fund-raising: many solicitations and responses are keyed to the maximum contribution limit. For instance, if the maximum is $1,000, many personal requests and "ticket" prices for events will be set at $500 or $750. Likewise, when prospective donors are asked for $1,000, many routinely give less.

3. The authors shared the 50 percent figure with a dozen consultants who have been active in past presidential campaigns, and all agreed that it would be a worthy goal.

4. The 2000 donor survey found that 28 percent of presidential donors who gave $200 or more and had incomes of $100,000 or more identified with the Democratic Party.

Postscript

Michael J. Malbin

I am writing these words months after completion of the rest of this book. When we planned this project, we had expected this chapter to contain our reactions to an anticipated Supreme Court decision in *McConnell v. FEC*, the main constitutional challenge to BCRA. That is not meant to be. As I write, the case is on its way to the Supreme Court.

BCRA contained a provision calling for expedited judicial review of the law's constitutionality. Instead of the normal three-level review—district court trial, appeal, and then a second appeal to the Supreme Court—the law called for a trial before a three-judge district court panel, followed by a direct appeal to the Supreme Court. As mentioned in chapter 1, the plaintiffs filed suit against BCRA the day after it became law on March 27, 2002. Lawyers for both sides began the process of fact-finding and discovery a month later. Oral argument was held on December 4, 2002. During the oral argument, the lawyers for both sides said they hoped for a district court decision by February, to allow for a Supreme Court decision by June 2003. But the district court's deep divisions prevented this.

On May 1, the district court panel issued an unprecedented 1,638-page mixed set of opinions, upholding some parts of BCRA while declaring others unconstitutional. The judges who heard the case were Karen L. Henderson, who sits on the U.S. Court of Appeals, and District Court Judges Colleen Kollar-Kotelly and Richard J. Leon. President George H. W. Bush appointed Judge Henderson to the Appeals Court; President Clinton appointed Judge Kollar-Kotelly; and President George W. Bush appointed Judge Leon. Judge Henderson would have declared most of BCRA unconstitutional; Judge Kollar-Kotelly would have upheld most of it. That left Judge Leon's opinion as the deciding one on most issues.

Judge Leon—and therefore the Court—said that it was permissible for Congress to limit contributions to national party committees if the money is used for election advertising to support or oppose a specific candidate, but threw out the ban on soft money for all other purposes. He reached the same conclusion with respect to the law's definition of federal election activities conducted by state and local parties. If sustained, the effect would be to gut Title I, the soft money provisions of BCRA.

The lower court's electioneering holdings were another story. Judges Leon and Kollar-Kotelly accepted that corporate and labor expenditures for candidate-specific advertising may be regulated, even if the advertising does not meet the "express advocacy" test the Supreme Court laid out in *Buckley v. Valeo* (1976). Kollar-Kotelly accepted BCRA's definitions and prohibitions. Leon started from the First Amendment principle stating that even if a law's purpose is sufficiently important to permit regulation, Congress must tailor its regulation narrowly to meet its legitimate goal. Leon then turned to evidence gathered in studies of the 1998 and 2000 elections done for the Brennan Center (Krasno and Seltz, 2000; Holman and McLaughlin, 2001). Accepting the basic factual findings in those studies about the number of electioneering and non-electioneering issue ads before and after September 1, Leon noted that among those ads that would have been considered "electioneering" under BCRA's "bright line" definition, about 15 percent of the 1998 ads, and 17 percent of the 2000 ads, were not perceived by research coders as being about election persuasion. Leon said this meant the definition was overly broad and therefore unconstitutional. However, the statute also included a "backup" definition to be used if the first were declared invalid. Leon thought half of the backup definition was unconstitutionally vague, but left the other half intact. Under this half of a backup definition, any radio or TV ad would be considered electioneering if it were to promote, support, attack, or oppose a federal candidate. Remarkably, the new definition made the restriction apply all year around. In the name of curing "overbreadth," the district court's ruling made the law reach more speech than the original, not less.

Immediately after the decision, political actors of all stripes began speculating who would gain or lose if the Supreme Court were to uphold all of the lower court's twenty distinct constitutional holdings. Democratic party professionals who were having a difficult time raising hard money in 2003 were hoping the district court decision would give them at least one more chance to raise soft money. Advocacy groups were thrown into deep uncertainty. Under BCRA as written, the electioneering rules do not have an effect until thirty days before a primary or sixty days before a general election. Except for a special election, these rules would not have been likely to affect any advertising until after the Supreme Court had a chance to decide the case. Now, several of them reported that at the last minute, they had to cancel advertisements about the pending tax bill, and about firearms legislation, because the ads criticized sitting members of Congress or the President by name.

As a result of such situations, none of the litigants was happy with the landscape the district court opinion had left behind. The law's supporters were upset at what the court had done to the soft money restrictions. The original plaintiffs could not believe the court had restricted electioneering ads even more than the original law. Most of them therefore asked the lower court to stay the effects of ruling, to spare election participants from having to conduct the 2004 election under three sets of rules—BCRA as written, the law after the district court opinion, and the law as revised yet again by the Supreme Court. On May 19, 2003, the lower court agreed with the litigants and took the unusual step of staying its own ruling, leaving the original BCRA in effect for the time being, in all of its parts. For at least a few months, therefore, the political actors will know where they stand.

This will change again. The U.S. Supreme Court has scheduled the case for a four-hour oral argument on September 8, 2003—one month earlier than its fall term would normally begin. The early date, requested by both sides, responded to the law's provision for an expedited decision. The long oral argument—four times the normal time—implicitly recognized the constitutional complexity. It is impossible at this stage to predict a Supreme Court decision. We can feel fairly certain, however, that it will not be the same, in all major parts, as the district court's ruling. We get a hint of this from some early court filings. The Solicitor General's request for an appeal asked the high court to depart from normal procedure and let the original plaintiffs and defendants continue to write their briefs as plaintiffs or defendants of the original law, rather than asking each to write as an appellee or appellant on this or that point of the lower court's decision. The Supreme Court agreed to this procedure. Some time after oral argument on September 8, 2003, we will be told the result. Until then, BCRA remains as it was written, and so do the analyses we set out in this book.

Works Cited

Abraham, Yvonne, et al. 2001. "Political Capital; Swift Looking to Person of Color as Running Mate for 2002 Election." *Boston Globe,* 24 June, sec. B, p. 4, third edition.

Abramowitz, Alan I. 1991. "Incumbency, Campaign Spending, and the Decline of Competition in House Elections." *The Journal of Politics* 53 (1): 34–56.

Adamany, David W., and George E. Agree. 1975. *Political Money: A Strategy for Campaign Financing in America.* Baltimore: Johns Hopkins University Press.

Aldrich, John. 1995. *Why Parties: The Origin and Transformation of Political Parties in America.* Chicago: University of Chicago Press.

Alexander, Herbert E. 1983. *Financing the 1980 Election.* Lexington, Mass.: D. C. Heath.

————. 1999. "Spending in the 1996 Elections." In *Financing the 1996 Election*, edited by John C. Green. Armonk, N.Y.: Sharpe.

Alexander, Herbert E., and Brian A. Haggerty. 1987. *Financing the 1984 Election.* Lexington, Mass.: D. C. Heath.

Alford, John R., and David W. Brady. 1993. "Personal and Partisan Advantage in U.S. Congressional Elections, 1846–1990." In *Congress Reconsidered*, 5th ed., edited by Lawrence C. Dodd and Bruce I. Oppenheimer. Washington, D.C.: Congressional Quarterly.

Allen, Mike. 2000. "House GOP Goes Within for Money; Fund Drive Ties Members' Success, Committee Status." *Washington Post*, 14 June.

Ansolabehere, Stephen, and James M. Snyder, Jr. 2000. "Money and Office: The Sources of the Incumbency Advantage in Congressional Campaign Finance." In *Continuity and Change in House Elections*, edited by David W. Brady, John F. Cogan, and Morris P. Fiorina. Stanford: Stanford University Press.

Associated Press. 2000. "Humphreys Leads Congressional Race, Poll Says." Associated Press State and Local Wire, 3 May.

————. 2003. "Bush Faces Choices for 2004 Fund Raising." *New York Times*, January 21, sec. A, p. 4.

Babcock, Charles R. 1987. "Charity Begins at Home . . . and Ends at the Campaign Headquarters." *Washington Post*, 16 November, p. 12–13, weekly edition.

Baker, Ross K. 1989. *The New Fat Cats: Members of Congress as Political Benefactors.* New York: Priority Press Publication.

Barone, Michael, and Richard E. Cohen. 2001. *Almanac of American Politics 2002*. Washington, D.C.: National Journal.

Bartels, Larry M. 2000. "Partisanship and Voting Behavior, 1952–1996." *American Journal of Political Science* 44 (1): 35–50.

Bauer, Robert F. 2002. *Soft Money, Hard Law: A Guide to the New Campaign Finance Law*. Washington, D.C.: Perkins Coie.

Biersack, Robert, and Melanie Haskell. 1999. "Spitting on the Umpire: Political Parties, the Federal Election Campaign Act, and the 1996 Campaigns." In *Financing the 1996 Election*, edited by John C. Green. Armonk, N.Y.: Sharpe.

Biersack, Robert, Paul S. Herrnson, and Clyde Wilcox. 1993. "Seeds for Success: Early Money in Congressional Elections." *Legislative Studies Quarterly* 18:535–51.

Blau, Peter M. 1964. *Exchange and Power in Social Life*. New York: John Wiley.

Bolen, Cheryl. 2001a. "Bush Maintains Stance on Soft Money, Other Campaign Finance Reform Issues." *BNA Money & Politics Report*, 16 March.

———. 2001b. "Possible Increase in Hard Dollar Limits Dividing Senate, Coalition for Reform Bill." *BNA Money & Politics Report*, 26 March.

Bolen, Cheryl, and Kenneth P. Doyle. 2001. "Senate Votes for Compromise Increase in Limits on 'Hard Money' Contributions." *BNA Money & Politics Report*, 29 March.

Bolen, Cheryl, and Nancy Ognanovich. 2002. "Shays-Meehan Measure Overcomes Hurdles in Floor Debate Beset by Partisan Bickering." *BNA Money & Politics Report*, 14 February.

Bowler, Kathleen. 2002. *McConnell v. FEC: Fact Witness Statement of Kathleen Bowler, Executive Director, California Democratic Party*, 14 October, at www.camlc.org/advocacy-court2-31.html.

Bresnahan, John. 2000. "Hastert Backs Off Threats over Committee Slots but Staffers Insist GOP Members Who Fail to Deliver for 'Battleground 2000' Will Face Some Heat." *Roll Call*, 15 June.

Brown, Clifford, Jr., Lynda W. Powell, and Clyde Wilcox. 1995. *Serious Money: Fundraising and Contributing in Presidential Nomination Campaigns*. New York: Cambridge University Press.

Burnham, Walter Dean. 1975. "Insulation and Responsiveness in Congressional Elections." *Political Science Quarterly* 90 (3): 411–35.

Busch, Andrew E., and William G. Mayer. 2002. *The Front-Loading Problem in Presidential Nominations*. Unpublished manuscript.

Cable News Network. 2001. "McCain-Feingold Foe Vows Court Battle If Reform Measure Becomes Law." 1 April, at www.cnn.com/2001/ALLPOLITICS/04/01/campaign.finance/.

Cain, Bruce, John Ferejohn, and Morris Fiorina. 1987. *The Personal Vote*. Cambridge: Harvard University Press.

Campaign Finance Institute. 2001. "Democratic and Republican Challengers Rely on $1,000 Contributions More than Incumbents," at www.cfinst.org/pr/062701.html.

———. 2002a. *The Campaign Finance eGuide*, at www.cfinst.org/eguide.

———. 2002b. *Soft Money eGuide: Evading Soft Money Restrictions*, at www.cfinst.org/softmoney/.

Campaign Finance Institute Task Force on Disclosure. 2001. *Issue Ad Disclosure: Recommendations for a New Approach*. Washington, D.C.: Campaign Finance Institute.

Campbell, James E. 1983. "The Return of the Incumbents: The Nature of the Incumbency Advantage." *Western Political Quarterly* 36 (3): 434–44.

———. 1996. *Cheap Seats: The Democratic Party's Advantage in U.S. House Elections.* Columbus: Ohio State University Press.

———. 2000. *The American Campaign: U.S. Presidential Campaigns and the National Vote.* College Station: Texas A&M University Press.

———. 2002. "Is the House Incumbency Advantage Mostly a Campaign Finance Advantage?" Paper presented at the annual meeting of the New England Political Science Association, Portland, Maine, May.

Campbell, James E. 2003. "The 2002 Midterm Election: A Typical or an Atypical Midterm?" *PS: Political Science and Politics* 36 (2): 203–7.

Campbell, James E., and Steve J. Jurek. 2003, forthcoming. "The Decline of Competition and Change in Congressional Elections." In *The United States Congress: A Century of Change*, edited by Sunil Ahuja and Robert Dewhirst. Columbus: Ohio State University Press.

Cantor, Joseph E. 1997. "Campaign Finance Legislation in the 105th Congress." Washington, D.C.: Library of Congress, Congressional Research Service. 26 November.

Carney, Eliza Newlin. 1996. "Reform Could Strike Out over Labor." *National Journal*, 30 November.

———. 1998. "Campaign Reform's Last Gap." *National Journal*, 14 February.

Carr, Rebecca, and Jackie Koszczuk. 1998. "Probe Reports Decry Abuses, but Overhaul Still Unlikely." *Congressional Quarterly Weekly Report*, 14 February.

Ceaser, James W., and Andrew E. Busch. 2001. *The Perfect Tie.* Lanham, Md.: Rowman & Littlefield.

Cigler, Allan J. 2002. "Interest Groups and Financing the 2000 Elections." In *Financing the 2000 Election*, edited by David B. Magleby. Washington, D.C.: Brookings Institution.

Cillizza, Chris. 2002. "Money Chase: Parties Push for Late Cash: Campaign Committees Set Fundraising Goals for Members." *Roll Call*, 27 June.

Clymer, Adam. 2001. "Black Caucus Members Find Themselves Courted Heavily in Soft Money Fight." *The New York Times*, 12 July.

Cochran, John. 2001a. "Not Victory but Vitriol for Campaign Finance Reform Bill." *Congressional Quarterly Weekly Report*, 14 July.

———. 2001b. "Rival Campaign Finance Bills' Prospects in House May Hinge on Allaying Black Caucus' Concerns." *Congressional Quarterly Weekly Report*, 23 June.

Congressional Record. 2001. 107th Cong., 1st sess., vol. 147, p. S2548, 20 March.

Corrado, Anthony. 1992. *Creative Campaigning: PACs and the Presidential Selection Process.* Boulder, Colo.: Westview.

———. 1993. *Paying for Presidents.* New York: Twentieth Century Fund.

———. 1997. "Financing the 1996 Elections." In *The Election of 1996*, edited by Gerald Pomper et al. Chatham, N.J.: Chatham House.

———. 1999. "Financing the 1996 Presidential General Election." In *Financing the 1996 Election*, edited by John C. Green. Armonk, N.Y.: Sharpe.

———. 2000. *Campaign Finance Reform.* New York: Twentieth Century Foundation.

———. 2001. "Financing the 2000 Election." In *The Election of 2000*, edited by Gerald M. Pomper. New York: Chatham House of Seven Bridges Press.

———. 2002. "Financing the 2000 Presidential General Election." In *Financing the 2000 Elections*, edited by David B. Magleby. Washington, D.C.: Brookings Institution.

Corrado, Anthony, Thomas Mann, Daniel Ortiz, and Trevor Potter. 1997. *The Campaign Finance Source Book*. Washington, D.C.: Brookings Institution.

Cover, Albert D. 1977. "One Good Term Deserves Another: The Advantage of Incumbency in Congressional Elections." *American Journal of Political Science* 21 (3): 523–41.

Cover, Albert D., and David R. Mayhew. 1981. "Congressional Dynamics and the Decline of Competitive Elections." In *Congress Reconsidered*, edited by Lawrence C. Dodd and Bruce I. Oppenheimer. Washington, D.C.: Congressional Quarterly.

Cox, Gary, and Jonathan Katz. 1996. "Why Did the Incumbency Advantage in U.S. House Elections Grow?" *American Journal of Political Science* 40 (2): 478–97.

Cyert, Richard M., and James M. March. 1963. *A Behavioral Theory of the Firm*. Englewood Cliffs, N.J.: Prentice-Hall.

DeNarvas-Walt, Carmen, Robert W. Cleveland, and Marc I. Roemer. 2001. *Money Income in the United States, 2000*. Washington, D.C.: U.S. Department of Commerce. Economic and Statistical Administration, U.S. Census Bureau.

Doherty, Carroll J. 1997a. "Death Rattle Sparks Search for Signs of Political Life." *Congressional Quarterly Weekly Report*, 11 October.

———. 1997b. "Overhaul Bill Faces Long Odds as Filibuster Threats Loom." *Congressional Quarterly Weekly Report*, 4 October.

———. 1997c. "Shift in Political Wind Detected among Howls over Dead Deal." *Congressional Quarterly Weekly Report*, September.

———. 1998. "Senators' Votes Seem Set in Stone." *Congressional Quarterly Weekly Report*, 28 February.

———. 1999. "Campaign Finance Crusaders Regroup after Latest Defeat." *Congressional Quarterly Weekly Report*, 23 October.

Doyle, Kenneth P. 2000. "McCain-Feingold Supporters Need Only One or Two More Votes to Break Filibuster." *BNA Money & Politics Report*, 21 November.

———. 2002a. "Bush Quietly Signs Reform Legislation as Suits Filed, Toner Appointment Eyed." *BNA Money & Politics Report*, 28 March.

———. 2002b. "Senate Clears Bill Overhauling Campaigns by 60–40." *BNA Money & Politics Report*, 21 March.

Doyle, Kenneth P., and Cheryl Bolen. 2000. "McCain Says He Has 60 Votes for Bill as Hagel Indicates He May Back Cloture." *BNA Money & Politics Report*, 18 December.

Duffy, Jennifer E. 2002. "One-Seat Edge, 15 Real Races." *The Cook Election Preview: A Supplement to National Journal*, 27 July.

Dunbar, John, Katy Lewis, Eric Marx, Robert Moore, and MaryJo Sylwester. 2002. *State Secrets*. Campaign finance data on state political parties during the 2000 election cycle compiled jointly by the Center for Public Integrity, the Center for Responsive Politics, and the National Institute on Money in State Politics.

Duncan, Philip D., Christine C. Lawrence, and *Congressional Quarterly*'s political staff. 1995. *Politics in America 1996: The 104th Congress*. Washington, D.C.: Congressional Quarterly.

Dwyre, Diana. 1999. "Interest Groups and Issue Advocacy in 1996." In *Financing the 1996 Election*, edited by John C. Green. Armonk, N.Y.: Sharpe.

Dwyre, Diana, and Victoria Farrar-Myers. 2001. *Legislative Labyrinth: Congress and Campaign Finance Reform*. Washington, D.C.: Congressional Quarterly.

Dwyre, Diana, and Robin Kolodny. 2002. "Throwing Out the Rule Book: Party Financing of the 2000 Election." In *Financing the 2000 Elections*, edited by David B. Magleby. Washington, D.C.: Brookings Institution.

Edsall, Thomas B. 2002a. "Drug Industry Financing Fuels Pro-GOP TV Spots." *Washington Post*, 23 October.

———. 2002b. "Privatized Primaries? Some Leading Democrats May Eschew Public Funding in '04." *Washington Post*, 10 July, sec. A.

———. 2003. "Democrats Go to Bat With Two Strikes." *Washington Post*, 12 January, sec. A, p. 4.

Eismeier, Theodore J., and Philip H. Pollock, III. 1988. *Business, Money, and the Rise of Corporate PACs in American Elections*. Westport, Conn.: Quorum Books.

Epstein, Edwin M. 1980. "Business and Labor under the Federal Election Campaign Act of 1971." In *Parties, Interest Groups, and Campaign Finance Laws*, edited by Michael J. Malbin. Washington, D.C.: American Enterprise Institute.

Erikson, Robert S. 1971. "The Advantage of Incumbency in Congressional Elections." *Polity* 3:395–405.

Erikson, Robert S., and Thomas R. Palfrey. 1998. "Campaign Spending and Incumbency: An Alternative Simultaneous Equations Approach." *The Journal of Politics* 60 (2): 355–73.

Erwin, Ryan. 2002. *McConnell v. FEC: Fact Witness Statement of Ryan Erwin, Chief Operating Officer, California Republican Party*, 4 October, at www.camlc.org/advocacy-court2–31.html.

———. 1978. *Advisory Opinion 1978–10, "Allocation of Costs for Voter Registration,"* at herndon3.sdrdc.com/ao/ao/780010.html.

———. 1993. *The Presidential Public Funding Program*. Washington, D.C.: Federal Election Commission.

———. 1998. *Advisory Opinion 1997–21*, 20 April, at herndon3.sdrdc.com/ao/ao/970021.html.

———. 2000a. "FEC Announces 2000 Party Spending Limits." Press release, 1 March.

———. 2000b. "FEC Announces 2000 Presidential Spending Limits." Press release, 1 March.

———. 2001. "FEC Reports Increase in Party Fundraising for 2000." Press release, 15 May.

———. 2002a. "Final Rules and Explanation and Justification on Coordinated and Independent Expenditures." Federal Election Commission open hearing, 5 December, at http://www.fec.gov/agenda/agendas2002/agenda20021205.html.

———. 2002b. "National Party Fundraising Strong in Pre-election Filings." Press release, 30 October.

———. 2002c. "Party Fundraising Reaches $1.1 Billion in 2002 Election Cycle." Press release, 18 December.

———. 2002d. "Public Rulemaking on Coordinated and Independent Expenditures." Transcript of testimony, 23 October, at www.fec.gov/pages/bcra/rulemakings/coordinated_independent_expenditures.ht m.

Ferejohn, John A. 1977. "On the Decline of Competition in Congressional Elections." *American Political Science Review* 71 (1): 166–76.

Fiorina, Morris P. 1977. "The Case of the Vanishing Marginals: The Bureaucracy Did It." *American Political Science Review* 71 (1): 177–81.

208   *Works Cited*

Fleisher, Richard, and Jon R. Bond. 2000. "Congress and the President in a Partisan Era." In *Polarized Politics*, edited by Richard Fleisher and Jon R. Bond. Washington, D.C.: Congressional Quarterly.

Francia, Peter L., Rachael E. Goldberg, John C. Green, Paul S. Herrnson, and Clyde Wilcox. 1999. "Individual Donors in the 1996 Elections." In *Financing the 1996 Election*, edited by John C. Green. Armonk, N.Y.: Sharpe.

Francia, Peter, John C. Green, Paul S. Herrnson, Wesley Joe, Lynda W. Powell, and Clyde Wilcox. 2000. "Donor Dissent: Congressional Contributors Rethink Giving." *Public Perspective*, July/August, 29–32.

Francia, Peter, John C. Green, Paul S. Herrnson, Lynda Powell, and Clyde Wilcox. 2003, in press. *Investors, Ideologues, and Intimates: Fundraising and Contributing in Congressional Campaigns*. New York: Columbia University Press.

Frontline. 1996. *The Long March of Newt Gingrich*. Public Broadcasting System, 16 January, at www.pbs.org/wgbh/pages/frontline/newt/newtintwshtml/vanderjagt1.html.

Galloway, Christopher. 2002. *McConnell v. FEC: Fact Witness Statement of Christoper Galloway, Executive Director, Kansas Democratic Party*, 3 October, at www.camlc.org/advocacy-court2–31.html.

Galston, William A., and Elaine C. Kamark. 1998. "Five Realities That Will Shape Twenty-first Century Politics." *Blueprint Magazine*, 1 September.

Gelman, Andrew, and Gary King. 1990. "Estimating Incumbency Advantage without Bias." *American Journal of Political Science* 34 (4): 1142–64.

Gerber, Alan S., and Donald P. Green. 2000. "The Effects of Personal Canvassing, Telephone Calls, and Direct Mail on Voter Turnout: An Experiment." *American Political Science Review* 94: 653–64.

Gray, Jerry. 1999. "Citing Foe's Money, Democrat Ends His Bid for a Senate Seat." *New York Times*, 29 June, sec. B, p. 2, final edition.

Green, John C., ed. 1994. *Politics, Professionalism, and Power: Modern Party Organization and the Legacy of Ray C. Bliss*. Lanham, Md.: University Press of America.

Green, John C., and Nathan S. Bigelow. 2002. "The 2000 Presidential Nomination: The Costs of Innovation." In *Financing the 2000 Election*, edited by David B. Magleby. Washington, D.C.: Brookings Institution.

Hagen, Michael, and William G. Mayer. 2000. "The Modern Politics of Presidential Selection: How Changing the Rules Really Did Change the Game." In *In Pursuit of the White House 2000*, edited by William G. Mayer. New York: Chatham House of Seven Bridges Press.

Handler, Edward, and John R. Mulkern. 1992. *Business in Politics: Strategies of Corporate Political Action Committees*. Lexington, Mass.: Lexington Books.

Harlow, Ralph V. 1917. *The History of Legislative Methods in the Period Before 1825*. New Haven: Yale University Press.

Heberlig, Eric. 2001. "Congressional Fundraising and Committee Ambition." Paper presented at the annual meeting of the American Political Science Association, San Francisco, Calif., 30 August–2 September.

Herrera, Richard, and Michael Yawn. 1999. "The Emergence of the Personal Vote." *The Journal of Politics* 61 (1): 136–50.

Herrnson, Paul S., and Kelly D. Patterson. 2002. "Financing the 2000 Congressional Elections." In *Financing the 2000 Election*, edited by David B. Magleby. Washington, D.C.: Brookings Institution.

Hitt, Greg, and Tom Hamburger. 2002. "Innovation Fuels Drive for Voter Turnout." *Wall Street Journal*, 2 November.

Holland, Gina. 2001. "Senators Brace for Uglier Round Two of Campaign Finance Reform." *North County Times and Associated Press*, 26 March.

Holman, Craig B., and Luke P. McLoughlin. 2001. *Buying Time 2000: Television Advertising in the 2000 Federal Elections*. New York: Brennan Center for Justice at New York University School of Law. Also available at www.brennancenter.org/programs/downloads/buyingtime2000/summary.pdf.

Jacobson, Gary C. 1980. *Money in Congressional Elections*. New Haven, Conn.: Yale University Press.

———. 1990. "The Effects of Campaign Spending in House Elections: New Evidence for Old Arguments." *American Journal of Political Science* 34 (2): 334–62.

———. 1993. "Getting the Details Right: A Comment on 'Changing Meanings of Electoral Marginality in U.S. House Elections, 1824–1978.'" *Political Research Quarterly* 46: 49–54.

———. 1997. *The Politics of Congressional Elections*. New York: Addison-Wesley.

———. 2000a. "Party Polarization in National Politics: The Electoral Connection." In *Polarized Politics*, edited by Richard Fleisher and Jon R. Bond. Washington, D.C.: Congressional Quarterly.

———. 2000b. "Reversal of Fortune: The Transformation of U.S. House Elections in the 1990s." In *Continuity and Change in House Elections*, edited by David W. Brady, John F. Cogan, and Morris P. Fiorina. Stanford, Calif.: Stanford University Press.

Jacobson, Gary C., and Samuel Kernell. 1983. *Strategy and Choice in Congressional Elections*. New Haven, Conn.: Yale University Press.

Johanson, Karin. 2002. Interview by Diana Dwyre and Robin Kolodny, chapter 5. Silver Spring, Md., 9 January.

Katz, Jeffrey L. 1998a. "Campaign Finance Gets Day in the Sun, but Senate's Shadow Is Looming." *Congressional Quarterly Weekly Report*, 8 August.

———. 1998b. "Petition Pushes House GOP Leadership to Schedule Campaign Finance Reform Debate." *Congressional Quarterly Weekly Report*, 25 April.

Keith, Bruce E., David B. Magelby, Candice J. Nelson, Elizabeth Orr, Mark C. Westlye, and Raymond E. Wolfinger. 1992. *The Myth of the Independent Voter*. Berkeley: University of California Press.

Keller, Amy. 2002a. "McCain Takes Aim at 'Shadow' Groups." *Roll Call*, 18 November.

———. 2002b. "NRSC or the NCRS?" *Roll Call*, 25 November.

Kollman, Ken. 1998. *Outside Lobbying: Public Opinion and Interest Group Strategies*. Princeton, N.J.: Princeton University Press.

Kolodny, Robin. 1998. *Pursuing Majorities: Congressional Campaign Committees in American Politics*. Norman: University of Oklahoma Press.

Kolodny, Robin, and David A. Dulio. 2003. "Political Party Adaptation in U.S. Congressional Campaigns: Why Political Parties Use Coordinated Expenditures to Hire Political Consultants." *Party Politics* 9, forthcoming.

Kolodny, Robin, and Diana Dwyre. 1998. "Party-Orchestrated Activities for Legislative Party Goals: Campaigns for Majorities in the U.S. House of Representatives in the 1990s." *Party Politics* 4.

Kosterlitz, Julie. 1996. "Laboring Uphill." *National Journal*, 2 March.

Krasno, Jonathan S., and Ken Goldstein. 2002. "The Facts about Television Advertising and the McCain-Feingold Bill." *PS: Political Science* 35:207–12.

Krasno, Jonathan S., and Daniel E. Seltz, 2000. *Buying Time: Television Advertising in the 1998 Congressional Elections.* New York: Brennan Center for Justice at New York University School of Law.

La Raja, Raymond J. 2002. "How Soft Money Was Spent in 2000." Paper presented at a meeting of the Campaign Finance Institute, Washington, D.C., January.

La Raja, Raymond J., and Elizabeth Jarvis-Shean. 2001. "Assessing the Impact of a Ban on Soft Money: Party Soft Money Spending in the 2000 Elections." Berkeley, Calif.: Institute of Governmental Studies and Citizens' Research Foundation.

Levitt, Steven, and Catherine Wolfram. 1997. "Decomposing the Sources of Incumbency Advantage in the U.S. House." *Legislative Studies Quarterly* 22:45–60.

Magleby, David B., ed. 2001. *Election Advocacy: Soft Money and Issue Advocacy in the 2000 Congressional Elections.* Salt Lake City: Center for the Study of Elections and Democracy at Brigham Young University.

———, ed. 2002a. *Getting Inside the Outside Campaign.* Salt Lake City: Center for the Study of Elections and Democracy at Brigham Young University.

———, ed. 2002b. *The Other Campaign: Soft Money and Issue Advocacy in the 2000 Congressional Elections.* Lanham, Md.: Rowman & Littlefield.

Malbin, Michael J., Clyde Wilcox, Mark J. Rozell, and Richard Skinner. 2002. *New Interest Group Strategies—A Preview of Post McCain-Feingold Politics?* Washington, D.C.: Campaign Finance Institute.

Mann, Thomas E. 1978. *Unsafe at Any Margin.* Washington, D.C.: American Enterprise Institute.

———. 2002a. "Political Parties Now Facing 'Tough Love.'" *Boston Globe,* 10 November.

———. 2002b. "Political Science and Campaign Finance Reform: Knowledge, Politics, and Policy." Paper presented at the annual meeting of the American Political Science Association, Boston, August 29–September 1.

Martinez, Gebe, and Carroll J. Doherty. 1999. "Narrower Campaign Finance Reform Bill Still a Long Shot in Senate." *Congressional Quarterly Weekly Report,* 18 September.

Mayhew, David R. 1974a. *Congress: The Electoral Connection.* New Haven, Conn.: Yale University Press.

———. 1974b. "Congressional Elections: The Case of the Vanishing Marginals." *Polity* 6:295–317.

McCain, John. 2002. "Worth the Fighting For." Speech given at the Commonwealth Club of California, San Francisco, 7 November. At www.commonwealthclub.org/archive/02/02-11mccain-intro.html.

Milligan, Susan. 1999. "Candidates with Cash Narrow Field." *The Boston Globe,* 25 October, sec. A, city edition.

Moller, Alexandra C. 2002. "Airtime Provision Stripped." *Congressional Quarterly Weekly Report,* 2 March.

Monroe, J. P. 2001. *The Political Party Matrix: The Persistence of Organization.* Albany: State University of New York Press.

Nelson, Candice J. 1978. "The Effect of Incumbency on Voting in Congressional Elections, 1964–1974." *Political Science Quarterly* 93 (4): 665–78.

Ornstein, Norman J., Thomas E. Mann, Paul Taylor, Michael J. Malbin, and Anthony

Corrado. 1997. "Five Ideas for Practical Campaign Reform." In *Campaign Finance Reform: A Sourcebook*, edited by Anthony Corrado, Thomas E. Mann, Daniel R. Ortiz, Trevor Potter, and Frank Sorauf. Washington, D.C.: Brookings Institution.

Payne, James L. 1980. "The Personal Electoral Advantage of House Incumbents, 1936–1976." *American Politics Quarterly* 8: 465–82.

Pomper, Gerald. 1981. "The Nomination Contests." In *The Election of 1980*, edited by Gerald Pomper. Chatham, N.J.: Chatham House.

Potter, Trevor. 1997. "Issue Advocacy and Express Advocacy." In *Campaign Finance Reform: A Sourcebook*, edited by Anthony Corrado et al. Washington, D.C.: Brookings Institution.

Republican National Committee. 1996. "RNC Announces $20 Million TV Advertising Campaign." Press release, 16 May.

Rice, Andrew. 1999. "House Dems Squeezed for $23 Million." *The Hill*, 17 November, p. 1.

Rosenbaum, David. 1997. "White House Guests Differ over Solicitation of Money." *New York Times*, 17 September, New England edition.

Salant, Jonathan. 1996. "Finances Take Priority in This Year's Races." *Congressional Quarterly Weekly Report*, 26 October.

Sandler, Joseph E., and Neil P. Reiff. 2002. *Bipartisan Campaign Act of 2002: Law and Explanation*. Chicago: CCH.

Schattschneider, E. E. 1960. *The Semi-Sovereign People*. New York: Holt, Rinehart and Winston.

Sinclair, Barbara D. 1997. *Unorthodox Lawmaking: New Legislative Processes in the U.S. Congress*. Washington, D.C.: Congressional Quarterly.

Smith, Bradley A. 2001. *Unfree Speech: The Folly of Campaign Finance Reform*. Princeton, N.J.: Princeton University Press.

Steen, Jennifer Anne. 2000. *Money Isn't Everything: Self-Financed Candidates in U.S. House Elections, 1992–1998*. Ph.D. diss., University of California, Berkeley.

Stone, Peter H. 2002. "New Channels for Soft Money." *National Journal*, 7 September.

Stone, Walter J., Louis Sandy Maisel, Cherie Maestas, and Sean Evans. 1998. "A New Perspective on Candidate Quality in U.S. House Elections." Paper presented at the annual meeting of the Midwest Political Science Association, Chicago, Ill., April.

Taylor, Andrew, and John Cochran. 2001. "McCain-Feingold Tradeoffs Heighten Qualms within Coalition." *Congressional Quarterly Weekly Report*, 24 March.

Taylor, Andrew, Derek Willis, and John Cochran. 2001. "McCain-Feingold Survives Hard Fight over Soft Money." *Congressional Quarterly Weekly Report*, 31 March.

Tennille, Lacye R. 2002. "Turning Your PAC into a Powerhouse!" *BIPAC Elections Insight* 30 (10): 6.

Thompson, James D. 1967. *Organizations in Action*. New York: McGraw-Hill.

Tucker, Neely. 2002. "States Back Campaign Finance Law." *Washington Post*, 7 November, sec. A.

Tuckwiller, Tara. 2000. "U.S. House Speaker Stumps for Capito in City." *The Sunday Gazette Mail*, 21 May, sec. A, p. 1.

Tufte, Edward R. 1973. "The Relationship between Seats and Votes in Two-Party Systems." *American Political Science Review* 67 (2): 549–53.

USA Today. 2002. "Fear of Enron Taint Forces Key Vote on Political Reform." Editorial, 12 February.

U.S. Senate. 1971. Committee on Commerce, Subcommittee on Communications. *Hearings on S.1, S.382, and S.956, Federal Election Campaign Act of 1971.* 92d Cong., 1st sess., serial no. 92–6.

Van Biema, David. 1994. "What Money Can Buy." *Time,* 20 June, 35.

VandeHei, Jim. 2002. "Campaign Finance's New Face." *Washington Post,* 9 July.

Van Dongen, Rachel. 2000. "NRCC Gets 3.2M Boost." *Roll Call,* 24 July.

Walter, Amy. 2002. "House Races Take Shape." *The Cook Election Preview: A Supplement to National Journal,* 27 July.

Webster, Benjamin A., Clyde Wilcox, Paul S. Herrnson, Peter L. Francia, John C. Green, and Lynda Powell. 2001. "Competing for Cash: The Individual Financiers of Congressional Elections." In *Playing Hardball: Campaigning for the U.S. Congress,* edited by Paul S. Herrnson. Upper Saddle River, N.J.: Prentice Hall.

Weisman, Jonathan. 2002. "Adopting Union Tactics, Firms Dive More Deeply into Politics." *Washington Post,* 24 October.

Weissman, Steve. 2003. "Comments of the Campaign Finance Institute, Re: Proposed IRS Form 990 Changes, Announcement 2002–87." Washington, D.C.: Campaign Finance Institute, 28 January.

Wilcox, Clyde. 1988. "I Owe It All to Me: Candidates' Investments in Their Own Campaigns." *American Politics Quarterly* 16:266–79.

———. 1989a. "Organizational Variables and the Contribution Behavior of Large PACs: A Longitudinal Analysis." *Political Behavior* 11:157–73.

———. 1989b. "Share the Wealth: Contributions by Congressional Incumbents to the Campaigns of Other Candidates." *American Politics Quarterly* 17: 386–409.

———. 1990. "Member to Member Giving." In *Money, Elections, and Democracy,* edited by Margaret Latus Nugent and John R. Johannes. San Francisco: Westview.

———. 2002. "Campaign Finance after the 2000 Elections: A New Regime?" In *Contemporary Readings in American Government,* edited by Mark J. Rozell and John C. White. Englewood Cliffs, N.J.: Prentice-Hall.

Wilcox, Clyde, Clifford Brown, and Lynda Powell. 1993. "Sex and the Political Contributor: The Gender Gap among Contributors to Presidential Candidates in 1988." *Political Research Quarterly* 46:355–76.

Wilcox, Clyde, John C. Green, Paul S. Herrnson, Peter L. Francia, Lynda W. Powell, and Benjamin A. Webster. 2002. "Raising the Limits: Campaign Finance Reform May Hold Some Surprises." *Public Perspective,* May/June, 11–15.

Wisconsin Advertising Project. 2001. *Final Report on the 2000 Election.* Madison, Wis.: Wisconsin Advertising Project.

———. 2002. *Final Report on the 2002 Election.* Madison, Wis.: Wisconsin Advertising Project.

Index

About the Authors

THE EDITOR

Michael J. Malbin, Executive Director of the Campaign Finance Institute (CFI), is also a Professor of Political Science at the State University of New York at Albany. Before SUNY, he was a reporter for the *National Journal* and resident scholar at the American Enterprise Institute, and then worked for Richard B. Cheney in Congress and at the Pentagon. His most recent coauthored books are *The Day After Reform: Sobering Campaign Finance Lessons from the American States* and *Vital Statistics on Congress, 2001–2002*.

THE CONTRIBUTORS

Anne H. Bedlington, a Senior Research Analyst at CFI, was supervisory statistician at the Federal Election Commission in the late 1970s and early 1980s. She has taught at George Washington, American, and Georgetown Universities. Bedlington's Ph.D. in Government is from Cornell University.

Robert G. Boatright, a Research Analyst at CFI, was an assistant professor of political science at Swarthmore College from 2000 to 2002. He received his Ph.D. from the University of Chicago in 1999 and served as an American Political Science Association Congressional Fellow in 1999–2000. His book, *Expressive Politics: How Congressional Challengers Confront the Incumbency Advantage*, is to be published next year by Ohio State University Press.

James E. Campbell is a Professor of Political Science at the State University of New York at Buffalo. He previously served as an American Political Science Association Congressional Fellow and a program director at the National Science

223

Foundation. He is the author of *The American Campaign, Cheap Seats*, and *The Presidential Pulse of Congressional Elections.*

Alexandra Cooper is an Assistant Professor at Lafayette College in Easton, Pennsylvania. She received her Ph.D. from the University of North Carolina at Chapel Hill. Her special interests include presidential nominations and campaign finance.

Anthony Corrado is Charles A. Dana Professor of Government at Colby College and cochair of the Campaign Finance Institute's Board of Trustees. He is the author or coauthor of numerous studies of political funding and campaign finance law, including *Campaign Finance Reform: A Sourcebook* and *Inside the Campaign Finance Battle.* He currently serves as principal investigator for a campaign finance reform project sponsored by The Pew Charitable Trusts.

Diana Dwyre is an Associate Professor of Political Science at the California State University at Chico. She served as the American Political Science Association's Steiger Congressional Fellow in 1998, and worked for Representative Sander Levin on campaign finance issues. Dwyre and Victoria Farrar-Myers coauthored *Legislative Labyrinth: Congress and Campaign Finance Reform.*

Peter Francia is a Research Fellow and Program Coordinator for the Center for American Politics and Citizenship at the University of Maryland. He is the author of *The Future of Organized Labor in American Politics* (Columbia University Press, forthcoming), as well as several book chapters and articles. He received a Ph.D. in Government and Politics from the University of Maryland in 2000.

John C. Green is a Professor of Political Science and director of the Ray C. Bliss Institute of Applied Politics at the University of Akron, a research and teaching institute dedicated to the "nuts and bolts" of practical politics. He edited the Citizens' Research Foundation's book, *Financing the 1996 Election*, and coauthored *The State of the Parties*, which is now in its third edition.

Paul S. Herrnson is the director of the Center for American Politics and Citizenship and is a Professor of Government and Politics at the University of Maryland. He is the author of several books, including *Congressional Elections: Campaigning at Home and in Washington*, and is the principal investigator of the Campaign Assessment and Candidate Outreach Project. He received his Ph.D. from the University of Wisconsin at Madison in 1986.

Robin Kolodny is an Associate Professor of Political Science at Temple University. She studies political parties, the U.S. Congress, and parties and legislatures in comparative perspective. She is also the author of *Pursuing Majorities: Congressional Campaign Committees in American Politics*, published in 1998.

Raymond J. La Raja is an Assistant Professor of Political Science at the University of Massachusetts at Amherst. His Ph.D. dissertation—written for the University of California at Berkeley—was entitled "American Political Parties in the Era of Soft Money." La Raja is the author or coauthor of more than a half dozen scholarly articles about party funding.

Lynda Powell is a Professor of Political Science at the University of Rochester. She focuses on American politics; her current research centers on state legislative elections, particularly on the impact of term limits and congressional elections, with some emphasis on campaign finance.

Jason Reifler is a doctoral student in Political Science at Duke University.

Mark J. Rozell is a Professor of Politics at The Catholic University of America. His two most recent books are *Interest Groups in American Campaigns: The New Face of Electioneering* (with Clyde Wilcox) and *Second Coming: The New Christian Right in Virginia Politics*.

Richard M. Skinner is a Visiting Instructor at Hamilton College for 2003–04. In 2002–03 he was a Visiting Lecturer at the State University of New York, College at Geneseo. In 2000–02 he was a Research Analyst at The Campaign Finance Institute. Skinner's dissertation in progress, for the University of Virginia, is entitled "Beyond the Limits: Direct Action by Interest Groups in Congressional Elections."

Jennifer A. Steen is an Assistant Professor of Political Science at Boston College. The author of several recent journal articles on electoral politics, Steen received her Ph.D. in Political Science from the University of California at Berkeley in 2000 for her dissertation on self-financed candidates.

Benjamin A. Webster is a Ph.D. candidate in American Government in the Department of Government at Georgetown University.

Clyde Wilcox is a Professor of Government at Georgetown University. His books include *Serious Money: Fundraising and Contributing in Presidential Nominating Campaigns*; *Onward Christian Soldiers: The Christian Right in American Politics*; *Interest Groups in American Campaigns*; and *The Financiers of Congressional Elections*.

Campaigning American Style

CAMPAIGNING AMERICAN STYLE

Series Editors

Daniel M. Shea, Allegheny College
F. Christopher Arterton, George Washington University

Few areas of American politics have changed as dramatically in recent times as the way in which we choose public officials. Students of politics and political communications are struggling to keep abreast of these developments—and the 2000 election only feeds the confusion and concern. *Campaigning American Style* is a new series of books devoted to both the theory and practice of American electoral politics. It offers high quality work on the conduct of new-style electioneering and how it is transforming our electoral system. Scholars, practitioners, and students of campaigns and elections need new resources to keep pace with the rapid rate of electoral change, and we are pleased to help provide them in this exciting series.

Titles in the Series

Life After Reform: When the Bipartisan Campaign Reform Act Meets Politics
Edited by Michael J. Malbin

Political Polling
by Jeffrey M. Stonecash

High-Tech Grass Roots: The Professionalization of Local Elections
by J. Cherie Strachan

Campaign Mode: Strategic Vision in Congressional Elections
by Michael John Burton and Daniel M. Shea

The Civic Web: Online Politics and Democratic Values,
edited by David M. Anderson and Michael Cornfield

Forthcoming

The Rules: Election Regulations in the American States
by Costas Panagopoulos

Negative Campaigning
by Richard R. Lau and Gerald M. Pomper